Race and the Houston Police Department, 1930–1990

Number 102
Centennial Series
of the Association of Former Students,
TEXAS A&M UNIVERSITY

Race and the Houston Police Department, 1930–1990

A CHANGE DID COME

Dwight Watson

TEXAS A&M UNIVERSITY PRESS   COLLEGE STATION

First edition

The paper used in this book
meets the minimum requirements
of the American National Standard for Permanence
of Paper for Printed Library Materials, Z39.48-1984.
Binding materials have been chosen for durability.

∞

Library of Congress Cataloging-in-Publication Data

Watson, Dwight.
Race and the Houston police department, 1930–1990 : a change did come / Dwight Watson.— 1st ed.
p. cm. — (Centennial series of the Association of Former Students, Texas A&M University ; no. 102.)
Includes bibliographical references and index.
ISBN 1-58544-437-5 (cloth : alk. paper)
1. Police—Texas—Houston. 2. Houston (Tex.)—Race relations.
I. Title. II. Series.
HV8148.H732W38 2005
363.2'3'0890097641411—dc22 2005007868

Contents

Acknowledgments

The study of the Houston Police Department (HPD) changed my life fundamentally, I hope for the better. I would like to thank my family, friends, colleagues, and the HPD. A special debt of gratitude for assistance with this project goes to the Manuscript Division of the Library of Congress, Washington, DC; the National Regional Archives–Fort Worth, Texas; the Houston Metropolitan Research Center at the Houston Public Library; the University of Houston Archives and Library; a National Endowment for the Humanities Research Grant; Cullen and Murray Miller Research Grants, University of Houston; a Junior Faculty Research Enhancement Grant from Texas State University, Office of Research and Sponsored Programs; and Dean Anne Marie Ellis, College of Liberal Arts, Texas State University–San Marcos, whose help allowed me an opportunity to refine my research data in the work's final stages.

I have benefited from the knowledge, encouragement, suggestions, and criticisms of my mentors, Joe Pratt, Gregg Andrews, Richard Blackett, Jewel Prestage, Merline Pitrie, Sue Kellogg, Marvin Delaney, Vikki Bynum, and Mack H. Jones. I am indebted to the men and women of the Houston Police Department, who talked to me, encouraged me, and criticized me in order to make this project better. Special thanks to Police Chief Sam Nuchia and Chief Clarence Bradford for welcoming me and extending to me the resources of the HPD. Thanks also to Denny Hair, HPD police museum curator and historian, for his discussions, his insights, and his complete knowledge of the Houston Police Department.

I am grateful to my colleagues in the Texas State University–San Marcos History Department for pushing me to complete the manuscript and giving me their unqualified support. I am particularly indebted to Leigh Fought, Babu Shrinivasin, Charles Frank Robinson, Paul Hart, Amilcar Shabazz, Jimmy MacWilliams, Mike Botson, Eugene Buchanan, Joy Blumenreich, and Lori Gray, who either read parts of the manuscript or gave me insightful criticism along the way.

When arthritis claimed my hands, my typists, Jerusha Vaz, Dalinda Dupree, and Rose St. Rose, stepped in and helped with final revisions. Thanks to graduate students Hugh O'Donovan, Josh Bashera, Ryan Kanstanispour, Elva Negrette, and Brad Shreve, and the Phi Alpha Theta Brown Bag Lunch series, where I hashed out ideas for this manuscript.

Family members have stood with me throughout the process, with good humor, understanding, support, and love. Thank you, Don, Ken, Rodney, Subrena, Shalonda, Kassidy, Lil Don Howard, and my mama, Mrs. Emma. My grandmother Vermel Lois Cook and my inlaws, O. B. and Lillian Mitchell, native Houstonians, all gave me invaluable insights into African American life and history in Houston. Family, I could hear all of your voices encouraging me to continue when I thought of giving up.

Finally, much love to my wife, Pam, and my daughters, Kamilah, Koran, and Kaela, for letting me finish this book. A new teddy bear to my two baby girls, whose question made me understand the importance of my work.

To my God who grants me Grace, and everyone else who believed that a change did come, I am eternally grateful.

Race and the Houston Police Department, 1930–1990

Thieves respect property: They merely wish the property to become their property that they may more perfectly respect it.

—G. K. CHESTERTON

Introduction

Recent well-publicized cases of the abuse of power by the police in Los Angeles, New York, Atlanta, and Houston have revealed how little we know about how the police function and how pervasive race is in determining police behavior. When Lee Patrick Brown was named chief of the Houston Police Department in 1982, the HPD desperately needed a makeover. Its long history of brutality, corruption, and racist practices had led to cries for reform.

This story is about the Houston Police Department and race. Yet it is more than a simple narrative of racist cops, because it examines how public institutions changed through time and how that change was rendered less significant when race was the crucial hurdle to clear. Public fear made the police the first defense against the threat of loss of property and potential loss of life. The police, in turn, have anointed themselves purveyors of justice and the guardians of moral order and decency. The problem is not that all police have been evil and racist; it is, rather, that race has historically been a barrier to social change in America, including changes in policing. The heart of the problem has been that the police possess the authority to use lethal force to maintain the status quo, which, under Jim Crow, included racial segregation in social institutions, including the police force itself.[1]

Three things shape how society sees the police and how the police view society: (1) perspective, or how one's experience influences world view; (2) social status, or how one's social or economic class governs how the police react; and (3) race and ethnicity, or how the police comport themselves among racially and culturally mixed peoples. I argue that the police have historically accepted race prejudice and custom as an essential component of their job. By using Houston as a model, this book shows how racial, social, political, and institutional change have occurred. By examining the racial history of the Houston Police Department, my work attempts to foster a greater awareness of how the police as an institution have reacted to social transformation. A constant theme is how racial tension between police and citizens has shaped Houston's multicultural society.

In the twentieth-century South, one of the major factors shaping the behavior of the police was race. Houston, Texas, as a relatively young city, offers a good overview of the process. Houston was founded in 1836, and grew faster, richer, and larger than most other southern cities. Its sustained growth over decades produced tremendous demand for the expansion and modernization of public services. But city government's response was hampered by fiscal conservatism, a Bourbon political culture, and a commitment to the preservation of Jim Crow laws and customs. To understand the development of Houston and what it tells us about the changing urban landscape in the twentieth century, we must also understand how racism impeded the delivery of police services to a large segment of society for generations.

Because Houston is a large southern city, its public services in general and its policing in particular were slower to develop and less modern than similar services offered in many northern cities. Throughout the South after the turn of the twentieth century, the most powerful force governing police conduct was Jim Crow attitudes and customs; their maintenance was deemed more important than the law. In his monumental study of the segregated South, Leon Litwack agrees, emphasizing that "as the enforcers of white supremacy, the police assumed a pivotal role."[2] The maintenance of Jim Crow segregation took shape as a strong rural tradition that influenced cultural norms in Houston and acted as a barrier to social change. Thus, change came slowly, as the police department remained tangled in an increasingly irrational system.

Houston's economic, population, and geographical growth in the twentieth century made maintaining the status quo impossible. In the 1930s, growth led business and civic leaders to push for an amelioration of harsh race-based practices in the city because they were bad for business and hurt the city's image. These pressures sometimes placed the police in the awkward position of being responsible for holding the color line while serving as unwitting keepers of the clock of social change.

As dreams of democracy spread in the 1940s, blacks increased their demands for legal, political, and economic change. However, many in the state and the city viewed these challenges as an assault on traditional culture and resorted to political repression in the form of police intimidation and, at times, the use of extreme force.

The HPD's reluctance to tolerate social change evolved as indirect legal challenges by blacks in the 1930s and the 1940s led to more direct action in the 1950s. The latter placed the police and the citizenry on a collision course that would erupt in violent episodes.

In the 1960s, black activism brought a profound sense of urgency to the demands for more equal policing. In-your-face clashes emerged at downtown businesses and lunch counters around the city. The confrontations led to a tacit agreement to integrate various businesses in controlled numbers.

Things failed to change beneath the surface, however, and tensions continued to mount. Rather than accept the logic of becoming a force for civil decency in a modernizing city, the police force under the leadership of Chief Herman Short tried to maintain racial subordination and impose its will on minority communities. A much-publicized riot at Texas Southern University (TSU) on May 16–17, 1967, brought tensions to a head. During this confrontation, police clashed with students at this historically black university, leaving one officer dead, two injured, and relations between the police and segments of the city's black community permanently strained. The incident politically invigorated the black community.

Some blacks steadfastly resisted, but the rhetoric of the Black Panther Party was singled out as an egregious assault on moral order and decency that had to be neutralized. On July 26, 1971, a heavily armed HPD assault team, acting on the orders of Mayor Louie Welch and Chief Herman Short, killed Black Panther activist Carl Bernard Hampton, the local party's twenty-year-old leader, after a forty-five-minute gun battle.

The TSU Riot, as the HPD came to call the confrontation with TSU students, and the "Dowling Street shootout," which led to Hampton's death, permanently altered the city's political and social culture, as more blacks rejected police domination and white political control. These episodes did little to foster understanding or improve relations with the police.

Interestingly, the HPD also began to act as if it were independent of the city council's political control and lashed out at the city's radicals and liberals. Most citizens supported the police and felt that challenges to the social structure and racial order should be met with increased force, but they were divided on the use of lethal force.

In the 1970s, a series of public controversies racked the HPD. The shooting of two white youths—Billie Keith Joyvies and Randall Webster—involved officer use of throw-down guns and led to embarrassing criminal and civil prosecution of several officers. In the civil trial the jury held the city and the officers liable in both Webster's and Joyvies's deaths, but the judge negated the Joyvies ruling. In May, 1977, the events surrounding the beating and drowning of a Mexican American veteran named José Campos Torres while in the custody of HPD officers prompted Vance Muse to label HPD the "the worst cops in the nation."[3] The circumstances surrounding Torres's death helped unify Houston's Mexican American community, especially after the Moody Park riot in 1978, which involved Mexican American activists who were angry about the outcome of the Torres murder trial.

Following Torres's death and the Moody Park riot, the U.S. Department of Justice accelerated local political reform by forcing the city to accept a compromise reapportionment plan called the "9-5-1 rule." The new plan created nine district-specific city council seats, five at-large seats, and a mayor elected at large. This structure fundamentally altered politics in the city by giving minorities more representation on the city council.

Any attempt to understand the complex interaction of race and reform in HPD's history must move forward in the context of the relationship between the police and society as a whole. As an integral part of the political and social order, the police are sworn to enforce the law, uphold justice, ensure domestic tranquillity, and maintain order. The policing function, however, is constantly redefined by changing social and political mores. This study begins with the assumption that there is a reciprocal relationship between the police force as an institution and these social, economic, and political systems. Accordingly, I analyze the role of the police in the transformation of the Jim Crow South and examine the evolutionary impact of social, economic, and political changes on law enforcement. In so doing, my work helps establish a new paradigm for southern urban history in which institutional change in law enforcement through time is investigated holistically. Therefore, it is crucial to understand the literature on policing and the impact of police conduct on American society. The lack of historical narratives about the impact and importance of southern police forces on the civil rights movement reflects the general dearth of historical literature about the police in America.

Some historians have waded into the void of information and produced important works on institutional policing. Roger Lane's *Policing the City* suggests that in Boston the police evolved from watchmen charged with keeping the peace and protecting the streets to enforcers of the law and morality. Further ambiguity defined their function, which changed as political forces shaped their responsibilities, which in turn depended upon the needs of the municipality. Lane's use of court records and city council minutes helped him document the institutional role of Boston's police force and its importance as the city developed. He says that "during the formative years of the nineteenth century the business of an urban police department covered so great a range of politically sensitive local affairs that its development was inextricably part of the wider history of the city."[4] He also shows how city politics affected basic police functions.

James F. Richardson's *The New York Police* traces the evolution of policing from colonial America through the nineteenth century. His work does not place the police in a broad societal perspective, however, and fails to analyze how public institutions change.

Another important work on police history is Eric Monkennen's *Police in Urban America,* which covers the period from 1860 to 1920. Monkennen moves police history into the realm of urban social history. He succinctly states that his book "is a social history of policing. It examines the function and social effects of modern uniformed police in American cities." He uses court records and detailed statistics to illustrate his argument, that "the best and most important role that they [police] can play is not clear." The reader concludes that the police were enforcers of morality who made a significant number of arrests for public offenses such as drinking and disorderly conduct, not law enforcement officers.[5]

The most significant work thus far written on nineteenth-century southern policing is Dennis Rousey's *Policing the Southern City*. Exquisitely detailed and meticulously researched, this book argues that militias and slave patrols were the origins of southern police forces. While Rousey stretches his argument farther than the facts of southern society support, he correctly observes that slave patrols were militias with emergency policing powers. But there were limits to their powers. In most places, including Houston, these patrols were ceremonial; members received no salary, and the cities assumed no official municipal responsibility for them. According to Rousey, these militias originated because of slavery and the growth of southern cities, which went on "to adopt a martial style of policing when their populations were no larger than 10,000 people." Again he errs in suggesting that the constant presence of these militias and slave patrols laid the foundation for modern police departments. If they did have such power in New Orleans, they surely did not in Houston, where militias were ceremonial, elitist clubs that performed at balls and parades. Rousey incorrectly argues that vigilance alone made southern police the precursors of modern police forces.[6] No other work has attempted to explain the policing function in the nineteenth-century South. My work will fill in some of the gaps.

Works on the history of twentieth-century policing are not as developed as those documenting the nineteenth century. A popular and readable account by Jonathan Rubinstein entitled *City Police* is an insightful and informative look at Philadelphia. He claims that his book "is a study of policemen at work" that provides "a systematic description of police work." For example, he asserts that "the call box and the pull system greatly improved the contact between headquarters and the districts and between the station and the men in the street, but it did not solve the basic problems of supervision, morale and public service."[7] Rubinstein fails to illustrate the importance of communications in improving policing and does not frame the police force and its functions within the context of the larger society. This is an important area; no historian has yet produced a broad monograph on the effects of technology on police work. My work highlights some factors that caused low morale in the HPD and illustrates how innovations in communications have improved policing in Houston and depersonalized the police force within the community.

Perhaps the most insightful works on policing have evolved out of criminal justice, political science, and sociology. Works from these fields provide us with functionalist and bureaucratic insights into the broader criminal justice system, but they fall short in fostering an in-depth understanding of how police forces fit within the broader historical shifts in society. All of these works generally attempt to rationalize police violence or place it in a local paradigm of societal uprisings spurred by allegations of institutional police misconduct.

Criminologist Louis Radelet's *The Police and the Community*, first published in 1973 and now in its seventh edition, is the best overall synthesis of law enforcement's function and its relationship to the community it serves. Radelet's work addresses "the police in the democratic community. In such a community, the police exercise power with those from whom they derive authority. Police authority is delegated, leased, so to speak, by the community served by the police . . . Law, community, justice and morality: the cornerstones of Western democracy are inextricably linked."[8] Therefore, the police and the community are linked in a mutually agreed upon marriage, in which each has responsibility to the other. Although Radelet successfully applies this promising analytical framework to contemporary issues, he fails to illustrate in detail how the police fit within the context of historical and social change.

Three important works on problems associated with institutional policing in a changing society were published in the 1970s. The best are by sociologist Jerome Skolnick, political scientist James Q. Wilson, and historian Samuel Walker, each of whom helped create a new awareness of policing with discussions of popular reactions to police misconduct. These works provide a critical view of the police and grew out of the riot commissions and federal oversight hearings of the 1960s and the 1970s. The latter produced an impressive body of literature that tried to rationalize urban decay, police aggression, and rioting and generally conclude that "white racism and police brutality were the major cause of social melee."[9]

Skolnick's *Justice without Trial* sees police as trying both to influence and to control social change. He views police responses to social change as provoking social discord, but he does not adequately place police behavior in historical perspective. Nor does he go beyond the sociological theories that justify police group behavior. His later works further address the breakdown of policing when societal stress alters traditional functions.

James Q. Wilson's *Thinking about Crime* tries to advance the understanding of police conduct beyond the characterization of law enforcement officers as simple brutes who inspire riots and offend the citizenry. Wilson feels that police departments must consist of "the properly trained and recruited officer placed in an organizational role that maximizes his chances of being able to work collaboratively with those parts of the community he serves that want and welcome his presence."[10] He argues in this book that the police fight the citizens they are supposed to serve because they misunderstand their function and remain a separate culture. He views poverty and urban decay as the chief problems affecting police and community relations. In *Bureaucracy: What Government Agencies Do and Why They Do It,* his views have shifted and become more conservative. He argues in this book that bureaucracy causes isolation of and discontent among police officers by standardizing policing, where "one part of the police job, order maintenance, was sacrificed to another part, law enforcement."[11] Although the idea of a separate police culture was contrived by police reformers who sought to define themselves, Wilson feels that the nature of police work produces the potential for conflict between police and citizens.

Works on police reform also reveal much about police work and suggest that the police accepted some changes because of federal and private demands for reform. For example, from 1930 through 1980, there were no fewer than ten major federal hearings on police conduct and reforms. Samuel Walker's *A Critical History of Police Reform* is a broad synthesis of the motivations for and impulses behind police reform in America. He says that the "book was a study of the changes that have overtaken police service in America during the past century."[12] His work is a point of departure for a more in-depth inquiry into the motives behind police reforms and their historical significance. My work builds on Walker's by examining the reform movement as it has changed from an internally controlled device to an externally guided reform movement.

Minority police officers have been treated in the literature as an anomaly. Within police departments they have been employed as pseudopolice, with their power limited by racial custom, that is, by the imposition of social restrictions on the black officers. Elliot Rudwick, the author of *Negro Police in the South: 1954–1961*, compiled reports on black police officers for the Southern Regional Council from 1954 to 1961. He concludes that "Negro neighborhoods were inadequately patrolled by whites, whose methods were often harsh and not infrequently brutal to Negroes."[13] Rudwick demonstrates the need for and problems that Negro police officers faced in the South during the period he studied.

Following Rudwick's lead, works appeared after the urban riots of the 1960s that suggest that part of the problem was the absence of minority officers on the force. Nicholas Alex's *Black in Blue: A Study of the Negro Policeman* examines the social implications of blacks as police officers in the community. Important for its insights into the pressures resulting from being a black officer and the effects of racism, the book fails, however, to provide the reader with an understanding of why Negroes would want to be police officers and how they functioned in that role.

W. Marvin Dulaney's *Black Police in America* provides the first broad synthesis of the role of black police officers. Dulaney believes that the absence of literature on black officers makes his study all the more important, because it is "the only comprehensive study of the origin, role, and accomplishments of African American police officers throughout the United States."[14] This long-overdue work addresses many forgotten or formerly unknown points about blacks as police officers in America. Black police officers faced the same limitations as other black workers during the Jim Crow era. Even blacks with stellar job performance were not promoted to the rank of sergeant in the Deep South until the 1970s. Although detailed and well documented, Dulaney's work fails to illustrate the day-to-day pressures black officers faced. He also portrays them as victims rather than as players who often negotiated their way through Jim Crow. My work departs from portrayals of black police officers as either victims or heroes; they were rational actors making difficult choices and mistakes, just like their white counterparts.

There are two studies on the Houston police. The first is a monograph by historian Louis Marchiafava entitled *The Houston Police: 1878–1948*. Marchiafava's study traces the origins of the Houston Police Department through 1948, but he fails to elaborate adequately on race and the impact of external factors on the development of the HPD. Nor does he clearly show the early development of the police force.

The second work, *The History of the Black Police Officers in the Houston Police Department, 1878–1988*, was written by African American police officer Mae Walker. Her study is a retrospective look at the police force from the standpoint of the black officer. Advised by Dulaney, Walker presents the basic history of black officers in the HPD. Her work is meant for an internal HPD audience and fails to offer a balanced serving of facts and conditions that blacks and whites face as officers in a large and rapidly changing city.

By examining in detail the history of the HPD, *A Change Did Come* demonstrates how race complicated the internal impulses for change, change that finally came as a result of external pressures on the police department. When placed within the context of broad societal change, this work builds on the strengths of its predecessors. It illustrates how traditional attitudes toward and customs concerning race limited the HPD's development. It shows how external factors such as the civil rights movement, modernization, annexations, and court-ordered political realignment forced change within all public institutions, but particularly within the Houston Police Department. Before the 1980s, the HPD was a national symbol of resistance to change. Eventually, change did come in its attitudes toward the races and its racial composition.

War forcibly alters a nation.

The economic, political, and social structure

is tested, perhaps shaken or crumbled.

—JAMES BURRAN

CHAPTER 1 "A Change Gonna Come"

Jim Crow Challenges during the Depression and World War, 1929–43

On Thursday August 1, 1929, Mayor Walter Monteith appointed Percy Heard as chief of the Houston Police Department. Heard's appointment signaled the beginning of a new era in policing for Houston. By this time, the city was unique as a southern city, with a strong emerging industrial economy and a growing population of almost 300,000. A burst in the 1920s had made it one of the largest cities in the South. Even more interestingly, had its African American population of about 63,000 been counted independently from the white population, "black Houston" would have been larger than many southern cities at the time.

The city's Jim Crow racial ethos reflected the segregationist attitudes and policies strictly enforced throughout the South by white power and custom. Jim Crow also shaped the attitudes and defined the procedures and practices of the HPD. As Houston experienced an influx of migrants, the police were called on to enforce segregation while responding to other challenges caused by urban growth (see Table 1).

Table 1. *Growth of Houston's Black Population, 1870–1980*

Year	*Total Population*	*Black Population*	*% Black*
1870	9,382	3,691	39.3
1880	16,513	6,479	39.2
1890	27,557	10,379	37.7
1900	44,633	14,608	32.7
1910	78,800	23,929	30.4
1920	138,276	33,960	24.6
1930	292,352	63,337	21.7
1940	384,514	86,302	22.4
1950	596,163	125,400	21.0
1960	938,219	215,037	22.9
1970	1,232,802	316,551	25.7
1980	1,594,086	440,257	27.6

Source: U.S. Bureau of the Census, Census of Population and Housing, 1900, 1910, 1920, 1930, 1940, 1950.

Thus, the HPD in 1929 found itself on the front lines of a battle that would shape the development of the region for the rest of the century, the battle between the Jim Crow practices inherited from rural areas and small towns and cities and the increasing demand for public services in an emerging "big city" metropolitan area.

The city's business and civic leaders embraced economic growth as the prime mover of Houston's future. Many understood the need to ameliorate the city's harsh racist image to attract investment and industry. Segregationists all, they sought an orderly, modern, "gentle" version of Jim Crow. After the June 20, 1928, lynching of Robert Powell, a black man being held in protective custody and accused of shooting police detective A. W. Davis, the city worked hard to reconstruct its image.

Following the 1928 Democratic Party convention, the Houston Police Department disbanded the mounted patrol unit, some of whom might have been involved in Powell's lynching, although there was never any evidence to corroborate the allegation. This marked the beginning of reform and reorganization of the department.

Chief Heard seemed well suited to straddle the fence between a city committed to growth and change and to Jim Crow practices more easily enforced on the courthouse square of small rural towns than in the sprawling wards of a big city. Heard seemed capable of overseeing the transformation of a small, conservative police department into a more modern entity capable of serving a major city. He was politically ambitious and well connected to Houston's political elite. He was also a family man who valued time with his four children and a white man firmly committed to the southern way of segregation. Like many other Houstonians, he was from rural Texas, but he adapted well to urban life and rose through the ranks to become a popular captain in the HPD. Politically astute, Heard had supported the correct candidate during the 1928 mayoral election and was rewarded for his support. Louis Marchiafava suggests that the attitude within the department at this time was "to the victor go the spoils," and if an officer lined up on the wrong side of the political equation, he might be demoted or arbitrarily fired.[1]

When Heard took control of the HPD, he made it clear that he would maintain department customs and reduce violent crime in the city. The force was ill-trained, poorly paid, and unprofessional at best. In 1929, population growth and crime had stretched thin its 328 officers, who had to service a city with a population of approximately 300,000. The black population exceeded 60,000, constituting 21.7 percent of the population, but in 1930, there were only seven black police officers on the force. Blacks had served in the HPD continuously since the 1870s, yet no black officer would serve in a supervisory or decision-making position until 1970.

In the late 1920s, the HPD's enforcement of Prohibition also stretched its resources. The fear of gangsterism and the accelerated pace of modernization forced the police department to spread itself thin trying to control blacks and aggressively enforce Prohibition. The Houston Police Department's Annual Report for 1931 reveals that the department had destroyed "ten thousand, seven hundred and forty-two gallons of whiskey mash, one thousand six hundred and sixty-two gallons of whiskey, two thousand one hundred and nine gallons of beer mash, thirty-six thousand four hundred and four pints of beer, one hundred ninety-five gallons of wine and ninety-three gallons of gin."[2] The enforcement of Prohibition caused a reduction in the city budget due to lost revenue from legal liquor taxes. The law also led to allegations of corruption, because many officers did not believe in the spirit of the Prohibition law and allegedly looked the other way when violations were committed. Moreover, because of their lack of professionalism and their low salaries, some officers accepted bribes, some ignored increasing violence, and still others became brutally aggressive toward citizens who demanded more equal policing and adequate police protection.

Responding to growing lawlessness and corruption in law enforcement nationwide, J. Edgar Hoover, director of the Federal Bureau of Investigation, brought together reform-minded police chiefs August Vollmer of Berkeley, California, and O. W. Wilson of Chicago, Illinois, to lead a national campaign for police reform. Their ultimate goal was to create professionally managed departments around the country. However, in Houston the strong internal impulse for police reform was hindered by an insistence on the maintenance of traditional customs and practices regarding the races; segregation at times took precedence over efficiency.

As a veteran of the force, Chief Heard vowed to clean up and modernize the Houston Police Department. His reform efforts specifically targeted fears of general lawlessness and a rise in violent crime during the Prohibition era. Heard immediately tried to reform policing with a series of administrative and organizational modifications. While changes in management and improvements in professional decorum were necessary, the HPD was ill-prepared for the pains of modernization and the social problems of a changing urban economy. His efforts eventually led to a gradual attitudinal change that helped make the police force more professional.

Houston's political and civic leaders were marginally more responsive toward the department after Heard's confirmation. Heard even had the support of most members of the city council, with the exception of Commissioner S. A. Starkey, who had a personal and political grudge against him. Commissioner Starkey opposed Heard's confirmation by voicing what he saw as the public's concern over gross police misconduct. Starkey, who had once opposed Heard in a Harris County sheriff's election (which both lost), complained that the "police department had not been functioning very well, and as Senior Captain, Heard was virtually in charge" and had done little to correct the problems.[3]

On September 1, 1930, Chief Heard responded to Commissioner Starkey's accusations by firing four officers and replacing others.[4]

These firings and replacements were clearly politically motivated. As Marchiafava points out, any efforts to bring standards and merit-based promotions to the HPD met stiff opposition within the force.[5] But the police force's resistance to new ideas in the face of an ever-changing world revealed a lot about an emerging police culture that saw itself as increasingly detached from the larger community. Marchiafava suggests that officers within the Houston Police Department tried to take on "political patronage [which] became increasingly important aspect of police service after 1920."[6]

Heard's reform efforts moved the HPD in the same direction as other police departments throughout the nation that were taking steps to protect themselves from the political machinations of elected officials. Thus, police forces were trying to abate the lethal consequences of political patronage on the rank and file. Before this trend could gain momentum, however, the economy stalled and collapsed.

The Great Depression devastated the national economy, but its bitter sting did not severely damage some sectors of Houston because of the city's phenomenal economic and industrial growth. Even in the depressed 1930s, Houston needed expanded public services, including police and fire fighting.

Between 1935 and 1945, the HPD gained some of the institutional acceptance that it had sought from the city's political and civic leaders. In the struggle for legitimacy, the rank and file stood behind the HPD's leaders as they created a quasi-professional, paramilitary-styled police force. But again, deeply entrenched traditional customs, attitudes, and practices harmed the HPD's efforts to become more professional. In the 1930s, as throughout the HPD's history, as the city's population and territory expanded, racism and brutality hampered legitimate efforts to change.

Between 1900 and 1940, Houston's population grew from 44,633 to 384,514, an increase of approximately 900 percent (see Table 1).[7] Such growth created a public-service nightmare; the lack of sound municipal fiscal policies and professional management heightened Houston's problems. Conservative fiscal policy placed tremendous economic constraints on the HPD, as the city's growth accelerated and demands for public services increased. The business elite exhibited great vision in providing capital, expertise, and effective leadership; however, it refused to provide or demand this same kind of vision for city government and public services. As Joe Feagin suggests in his study of Houston's development, the elites received much more from the development of the city than they contributed to it.[8]

Without proper direction or sufficient motivation, Houston's officials exhibited indifference and, at times, negligence in providing adequate public safety for all of the city.[9] This was evidenced by the city's refusal to increase the size of a police force that was perennially understaffed in terms of police-to-citizen ratio. For example, in 1930, the average size of the force was 265 officers, with a ratio of only one officer to each 1,000 citizens. Other cities of comparable size had 4 police officers for each 1,000 citizens. The recommended Federal Bureau of Investigation standard for the police-to-citizen ratio in urban areas that exceeded a population of 25,000 was 2.5 police officers per 1,000 population. Compounding the problem for the HPD was the city council's willingness to use special police officers for some police work rather than hiring or relying on regular officers.[10]

Neither poor funding nor a lack of trust and commitment on the part of Houston's elected officials to the department relieved the HPD of its responsibility to protect the population, however. Because of the department's limited resources, it was unable adequately to serve and protect the city.

Blacks who migrated to Houston from the rural areas of Texas and Louisiana found both opportunity and oppression in the city. During the 1930s, black migrants tried to broaden democracy, but police hardened the racial attitudes that shaped policy and guided procedures. The constant migration into the city led to more demands for bureaucratic change and organizational reforms within the police department. Police efforts to impose society's harsh system of racial subordination proved increasingly difficult to maintain in a rapidly urbanizing city.

Houston's business elite used the police to serve its own purposes, which also impeded the HPD's development and made it the pawn of politicians. Harold Platt emphasizes that municipal fiscal reforms were always linked to the economic concerns of Houston's business elite, which apparently did not feel that a large police force was necessary.[11] Thus, city officials used the police as their pliant enforcement arm to guarantee compliance from workers and to control crime as the elite pursued business development. Their blueprint even included using the police as strike breakers and brutal enforcers of order during labor disputes.[12] The business elite, however, did not trust the police and feared that a professionally trained force might not perform this vital function for them. This lack of trust, combined with fiscal conservatism, resulted in a police force that was poorly funded, poorly trained, and poorly motivated.

The lack of consistent and appropriate police training fostered paternalistic attitudes in the force. Paternalism was the prevailing attitude of the department's officers, who, for example, would paddle a wayward youth to set him on the straight and narrow. The desire for law and order and deference to authority often resulted in more violent displays of police control when adults were involved, especially if they were black. The use of fear to ensure respect for the law was an essential ingredient in police job performance and was a common practice throughout the nation, but the degree of brutality used by the HPD in the performance of its duties led to serious breaches of the public trust.[13]

A reputation for brutality, continued rumors of corruption, and a lack of professionalism ensnared the HPD in the 1930s.[14] For example, between 1934 and 1936, the HPD fired thirteen officers for brutality and gambling. Complaints of police brutality caused a strong public reaction. Common in Houston was the "third degree," a brutal method of interrogation and intimidation employed by police throughout the United States to maintain order and to instill respect for the law.[15] The tactic was so widespread that Pres. Herbert Hoover called a national conference to study the issue in 1931.

Locally, charges of brutality against the department from the 1920s through the 1930s caused an erosion of popular support and heightened suspicion of the department.[16]

National events soon forced law enforcement agencies to modernize. The new Prohibition laws led to unparalleled criminal activity while fundamentally altering society by attempting to legislate moral conduct. One of progressivism's major drawbacks was that ultraconservative Jim Crow attitudes lay at their heart, precluding progressive leaders from seeing the potentially negative results of Prohibition's moral crusade. During this time of growth, racial attitudes and social change overwhelmed law enforcement agencies that lacked the professional training and sophistication to support these reforms.

The police simply resorted to increasingly more aggressive law-and-order tactics to combat the rise in crime. Escalating violence in the 1930s became a complicated issue for HPD officers, making police work more hazardous. On September 20, 1930, shortly after Chief

Heard's appointment, for example, two motorcycle patrolmen were shot trying to apprehend a fugitive robbery suspect. That year, 1930, was a horrendous year for the HPD, as six other officers died as a result of job-related injuries. Three of the eight officers were killed in the line of duty. These deaths caused fear throughout the department and heightened the level of anxiety in the community.[17]

Chief Heard used the murder of the motorcycle patrolmen as an opportunity to demand increased appropriations for the department.[18] In response, in December, 1930, the city council furnished him with additional money to increase the HPD's armaments. Heard spent the money like a kid in a candy store. He purchased three riot guns, twelve shotguns, two Thompson submachine guns, and six grenades.[19] Ever the politician, Heard publicly displayed the new weaponry in a shooting exhibition on December 12, 1930. He told an enthusiastic crowd that "we have had no need for them yet," but "when we do we will not have to go out and buy them. We are preparing for war in a time of peace."[20] Heard's public display of the HPD's weaponry was a combination of grandstanding and a warning to lawbreakers and gangsters.

The fortification of the department was a legitimate response to fears created by increased criminal activity. Ominously, however, the weapons buildup revealed the limitations of having an untrained force and an absence of clear administrative direction in terms of the allocation of people and resources.

To his credit, Heard was the first HPD chief to exercise his full political and administrative clout to increase the department's ordnance and to begin to reorganize the HPD. His reform efforts were most probably modeled after those of police reformer August Vollmer, police commissioner of Berkeley, California. Vollmer was one of the leaders of the national crusade for police professionalization and training in the 1920s and the 1930s.[21] Heard's administrative and organizational changes were in line with national efforts to reform police departments.[22]

Another likely source for some of Heard's ideas was his affiliation with the International Association of Chiefs of Police and the Texas Police Chiefs Association. The national group stressed education, efficiency, and accountability for police departments. All these were lofty concepts for a local police force that hoped merely to maintain traditional policing practices in the city. These professional organizations were clearinghouses of ideas for law enforcement leaders, but they touched only a small group of progressive-minded police managers.

Their growth was possibly a reaction to police reform movements, such as the national Commission on Law Observance and Enforcement, or Wickersham Commission, created by President Hoover in 1931 to make recommendations for police reforms.

Some police chiefs acted quickly to abate outside interference in their departments. Thus, in many places the refinement of the police bureaucracy was a conservative reaction to change rather than a liberalizing trend in law enforcement. Police officers were essentially conservative agents who used reform as a tool for controlling the pace of change rather than accept the benefits of change. Egon Bittner emphasizes "that among the institutions of modern government the police occupy a position of special interest: it is at once the best known and the least understood." Michael Banton suggests that this is true of the police because the conservative nature of the force and its desire for law and order place police officers apart from the community they serve.[23]

Pres. Herbert Hoover's national directive for police reform did not move Houston's city council to act. The police department remained a low priority, and no organized reforms originated from the council. The development of police bureaucracy went forward, informed by a desire from within to maintain racial subordination in the city. Heard attempted to deal with this lack of administrative direction by creating three new divisions within the police department. On February 1, 1930, the Auto Theft Division was established under Capt. B. W. Payne; the Homicide Division was established on February 5, 1930, under Lt. George Peyton; and the Records Division was formed on June 1, 1930. Heard also created an In-Service School for Detectives on June 1, 1930, which was one of the HPD's most important administrative changes. The establishment of the school was an attempt to institute departmental standards for the training of detectives, but it offered no training for regular patrol officers.[24]

Heard's administrative reorganization did not immediately change the HPD into a rationally managed department. While noteworthy, the creation of the Police School revealed the administration's limitations in grasping the necessity of properly training recruits. Heard's changes were a reaction to external pressures, such as citizen complaints, to curb police corruption, brutality, and unprofessional conduct.[25] Some changes resulted from public and political criticism, not from a genuine desire to change.

Despite local and national calls for reform, a local newspaper immediately attacked Heard's modest efforts. On September 20, 1930, the day of the shooting of patrolmen Fitzgerald and Phares, the *Houston Post-Dispatch* editorialized that "we need better enforcement of existing regulations instead of new methods of doubtful value."[26] Even though the subject of the editorial was proposed changes in the HPD's Traffic Division, it exemplified the divided mind-set in Houston between a desire for expanded police protection and a fear of increased police responsibility.

The HPD placed a high priority on traffic control, assigning nearly a third of the force to traffic duty because of the potential revenue from tickets. The use of tickets to generate revenue had the unwanted effect of heightening public and governmental criticism of the department for overzealousness.[27]

As the Depression worsened, in 1932, the HPD fired eighteen officers.[28] Some of these firings appear to have been politically motivated. Siding with the wrong political regime could, and, indeed, did cost some officers their jobs.[29] In an effort to ward off any further layoffs or firings, police officers took a voluntary reduction in wages. Heard stated in a Houston Post editorial on February 19, 1932, that in order "to prevent twenty men from losing their jobs, every man earning $100 a month will work five days without salary for three months for a savings of $18,000." Heard further stated that through this action the department was "eliminating the necessity of reducing the force."[30]

Historians who have studied Houston argue that the effects of the Depression on the city were mild when Houston is compared to other southern cities. While the city suffered during the Depression, its economic woes were only temporary, because Houston's economy was bolstered by the expansion of the ship channel and increased demand for petrochemicals. According to Feagin, "between January 1932 and March 1933, the nadir of the depression, hundreds of companies opened for business in Houston, including dozens of oil-related firms."[31]

Yet as Houston's private sector rebounded from the shock of the Great Crash, most of its public institutions remained badly shaken. With almost no direct relief from the federal government, the city's conservative fiscal policies caused further reductions in necessary services. As the city council's legendary frugality and the extreme economic conditions of the Depression collided, the council questioned the necessity of expanding police protection.[32]

On July 14, 1932, Mayor Monteith and members of the city council argued feverishly through two special sessions about where to find $25,000 to maintain a city fertilizer plant. City commissioners offered several recommendations, including disbanding the Traffic Division. As the meeting progressed, commissioners and the mayor continued to clash over expenditures. Commissioner Andy Delery, who at the time was in a four-man race for Harris County sheriff in which Chief Heard was the front-runner, recommended taking money from the Police Department.[33] Delery confirmed, "The police department is not doing anything anyhow. We still have a bunch of robberies and hijackings every night."[34] Mayor Monteith angrily disagreed, requesting that the council support the police at their current level of funding. The HPD dodged the budgetary axe as the city council found the money for a fertilizer plant by making cuts in other city services, not the police.

Despite financial hardships, Heard continued to increase the HPD's firepower in an attempt to give officers a tactical edge against the more violent criminals they were encountering. While it may not have given the police an advantage, it did ease some of the fears within the department that gangsters had bigger guns than the police.[35]

Initially, however, changes in weapons and some reorganization did not alter prevailing racial attitudes or customs, nor did they affect traditional practice within the HPD.[36] Technological innovation accelerated the clash between traditionalists and those favoring modernization within the HPD. In 1932, the introduction of the mobile radio proved to be more important than more powerful guns.

Once perfected, the new technology helped transform police service. The Radio Division improved efficiency through better communications between field officers and central command. Originally, the HPD's radio patrol consisted of two one-way radio cars that could only receive calls. Moreover, the radio patrol shared a tower with KPRC radio. When the station was broadcasting, the police had to turn off their radios.[37] However inane it seemed at first, the radio was one tool of modernization that improved police performance and political relationships in the city.

Radios not only improved police efficiency and response time, but they also improved the HPD's relationship with city council members, who flocked to the department to see firsthand how the new radios worked. Many council members rode with the HPD's radio patrol. The radios even gave Chief Heard at least the tepid support of his opponents on the city council, such as Starkey and Delery. Delery stated in the Houston Press on September 12, 1932, that "he did not understand why the city had been without a radio-equipped department."[38] The lending of the equipment on a trial basis by RCA also aided the department in convincing city officials of its necessity. Additionally, the Kidd-Russ Company agreed to equip police cars with the two-way radios and defer payment until January 3, 1933.[39]

The radio also facilitated the department's efforts at modernization and helped it gain important institutional acceptance from the political elite.[40] But the introduction of the radio and the increased use of the patrol car began the gradual depersonalization of the force and its isolation from the community. While technology improved police efficiency, it also caused some to view the HPD as an external actor in the communities it served. The initial radio dispatch relayed information that officers previously had had to get from community members or the old Gamewell box system.

In spite of technological innovations, the HPD remained a poorly trained force that tried to maintain traditional racial customs and practices as the basis of most of its policy decisions. Although there were changes in the social and legal culture of race relations in Houston in the 1930s, it is important to note that any substantial changes in general police attitudes and customs lagged behind organizational and technological changes in society at large. This was especially true in the South, where the maintenance of traditional customs and attitudes was singularly important. Moreover, the conservative nature of the police at times overrode the commitment to uphold the law. The police force's perception of the changes happening around it caused it to retreat to familiar customs and practices.

Houston's police reacted with extreme force to challenges to the city's racial segregation. Houston, like most southern cities, was segregated residentially, medically, religiously, and socially, but it was not as rigidly segregated in the commercial and economic sectors. Business leaders all played the race card when appropriate, for example, but did not deny blacks complete access to merchandise in local department stores.

In the 1930s, black Houstonians began challenging segregation. Frustrated with political exclusion, underemployment, abysmal living conditions, and inadequate public services, they called for change. The population growth summarized in Table 1 suggests that increases in the black population made contact between blacks and public servants more frequent. Greater intimacy and frequency of contact seriously challenged the city's race-related customs and threatened its fragile political hegemony as new leaders arose from the black community.[41] Black leaders such as Carter Wesley, the owner and editor of Houston's premier black newspaper, the Houston Informer, represented new and formidable challenges to the city's traditional racial politics.

The movement of blacks to Houston also placed them in contact with the police, who were often the only public servants they encountered. Police service was woefully inadequate in predominantly black sections of the city. Huge disparities existed in the ratio of black police to black citizens: one police officer per seventeen thousand citizens. City officials seemed unconcerned with or unconvinced that enlarging the force was necessary; however, the *Smith v. Allwright* decision (1944), which outlawed the white primary in Texas, caused a gradual shift in the political makeup of the city.[42] Whites reacted by forming coalitions with black leaders in exchange for their support and to ensure economic relationships between merchants and blacks. Mercantile traditions were altered, but they were not completely changed, because most blacks in the city did not know about the agreement to integrate downtown stores.

Nationally, the twin phenomena of modernization and urbanization led to demands for increased police protection. Locally, these issues became intertwined with white civic leaders' need to enforce segregation and to control any movement toward desegregation. The police linked the protest movement with communism and radicalism, thereby creating an atmosphere of suspicion toward blacks and anyone else who advanced the liberal cause. Protests reflected an evolution in attitudes throughout the country. Police, though, saw these changes as a decline in respect for authority, particularly as citizens called for police professionalization and accountability. The HPD reacted like a catfish out of water—stunned—as once-quiet and compliant citizens began questioning their authority.[43]

The city's rapid growth hampered the HPD's efforts to maintain traditional race-related customs. As the city boomed, its black population grew steadily (see Table 1). As James SoRelle characterizes it, Houston was the "the darker side of heaven" for all blacks who migrated.[44] The city's economic growth coupled with rural poverty served as a tremendous pull factor for blacks, who saw moving to Houston as an opportunity for advancement. However, though employment was available, Jim Crow traditionalism made Houston a hellish nightmare for minorities in the crowded neighborhoods that made up black Houston.

The extraordinary growth of the city overwhelmed the HPD's capacity to provide adequate police protection. Moreover, its poorly trained managers caused serious internal divisions that threatened efforts to expand the force to keep pace with Houston's expansion. At the same time, allegations of gambling, graft, and corruption rocked the department and eroded the public's faith in the police. The HPD's bureaucratic expansion and efforts to build a more professional force were incompatible.

The HPD's hierarchy, long a slave of political patronage and believing the force would be a victim of political fallout, feared Oscar Holcombe's reelection.[45] Their fears were warranted, because changes in the city's charter gave the mayor the powers of a city manager, making the office one of the most powerful in the South.

The city's changing social dynamics, created by the dual processes of modernization and urbanization, thrust the police into the middle of the vortex of change. Officers proved ill-prepared or unwilling to accept racial or any other social change. In Houston's overcrowded black neighborhoods, the only consistent form of public service was the presence of the police. Due to overcrowding and neglect by real estate owners, these neighborhoods rapidly decayed. City officials did little to extend basic services or make internal improvements. Robert Bullard, in *Invisible Houston*, argues that blacks were basically roped off in decaying areas of the city and did not get the services they deserved.[46]

Houston's city council had traditionally placed a low priority on services for the politically impotent black community. Only the voting white population fully benefited from elites' control of city politics. The passage in 1923 of the White Primary Law addendum to the Terrell Election Law of 1903 had effectively negated black political power in the state and city.[47]

In conjunction with the National Association for the Advancement of Colored People (NAACP), Houston's black elite began to raise a series of legal challenges to the established order, but blacks did not fully comprehend how to use their growing economic power as a tool for their transformation. Houston's black activists placed their political struggles in the deliberate hands of the courts. However, their public safety was in the hands of the HPD, which controlled blacks and other minorities through the use of brute force.

As the HPD's growth stalled in 1933, Chief Heard's attempts to gain legitimacy for his department dramatically ended with the reelection of Oscar Holcombe.[48] As mayor from 1933 to 1937, Holcombe imposed a number of politically motivated changes on the department. He created the Department of Public Safety and abolished the independent Police and Fire Departments. He appointed George Woods as the director of public safety and abolished the position of the chief of police. Woods threatened, "If anyone calls me Chief, they had better take to their heels when they say it."[49]

Woods's flamboyant statements were an egotistical attempt to show that he had the strength to reshape alliances within the department. He created the position of superintendent of police and appointed captain of detectives and district attorney's investigator Banyon Wylie Payne to the position. Payne was an eighteen-year veteran of the police force who had worked his way up through the ranks to captain of detectives. Chief Heard and Captain of Detectives J. K. Irwin were fired, and other high-ranking officers in Heard's administration were demoted.[50] Woods emphasized that "the discharge of the department heads was made necessary by the condition of city finances."

The constant turnover of chiefs caused by political patronage, as well as Holcombe's reelection and a weak economy, dramatically hurt the HPD's reorganization. From 1933 to 1937, the HPD underwent only one significant bureaucratic change and three administrative changes. On November 15, 1934, it created the Missing Persons Division; the Matrons Division was renamed Women's Division; and the women officers were called "police-women" instead of "matrons." In 1935, the Identification Division became a twenty-four-hour operation, and the Record Division followed suit later in the year.[51]

An upturn in the local economy in the mid-1930s spurred growth in appropriations for the HPD from 1934 to 1940, and a gradual increase in staff began.[52] The economic boost was primarily due to growth and expansion of the ship channel and industries along the channel. The rapid growth of petrochemical production ameliorated the effects of the Depression on both the city and the region. The Port of Houston and industries along the ship channel recovered with a high bounce, encouraging recovery for the city. From 1933 to 1939, tonnage in the port moved at a near record pace.[53] The jobs created by the city's increase in manufacturing attracted additional migration into Houston. The city did not disappoint most who came there fleeing the stinging effects of rural poverty.

Houston's business development plans were attributed largely to bold and dynamic leaders like Jesse Jones, who continued to press for the city's development, despite the nation's worsening economic crisis. Later, as chairman of the Reconstruction Finance Corporation, Jones was instrumental in improving development along and expanding the Houston ship channel. The federal government also made a commitment to assist Houston with its effort to build and maintain the ship channel by allocating millions of dollars to assist local authorities in the development of the city's waterways. The growth of Houston's economy helped the municipal sector pull out of its slump by 1939.[54]

The efforts of Jones and other civic leaders paid off. By 1941, New York was the largest port in the United States, followed by Philadelphia, with the Port of Houston surging into third place. In the process, it had surpassed New Orleans. The oil, gas, and petrochemical industry made Houston an important player in the nation's defense.[55] The growth of these industries attracted thousands to the area, but despite the city's economic promise, racist attitudes limited the prosperity of blacks who came for wartime jobs in defense-related industries.

Houston's maritime contribution to the war effort was shipbuilding and ship repair. The vulnerability of the Atlantic and the Pacific fleets after the bombing of Pearl Harbor made Houston ideal for the placement of defense-related industries. Marilyn Sibley stresses that "these and other defense-related installations made the Ship Channel an important arsenal of democracy during the war."[56] The location of Houston's relatively secure harbor helped facilitate the growth of shipbuilding and repair along the ship channel during the war.[57] Additionally, other new industries were attracted to the ship channel, thus helping fuel Houston's phenomenal growth. Industrial and economic development eased the Depression in the city, but public services lagged and experienced only moderate increases in appropriations.

While the city's economy stabilized, the HPD remained racked with political infighting and administrative shake-ups. In 1939, another change in the position of police chief brought a new wave of promotions and demotions. On January 22, 1939, new chief L. C. Brown demoted twenty-six officers, forced seven to retire, and fired three. He closed three police substations and promoted many of the officers who, when Holcombe was reelected, had been demoted earlier to their former positions. The most notable promotion was that of traffic captain James Henry Tatum, who had been instrumental in creating most of Houston's early traffic rules by expanding and training the traffic squad.[58] Tatum's expertise helped him survive repeated demotions and promotions as HPD's chief changed time and time again. Tatum also exemplified the internal desire for the professionalization of HPD officers.

In the fall of 1939, the first police school for training recruits opened, and the HPD introduced the systematic method of recruitment and screening of prospective applicants used by the military. Of the 362 applicants who passed the test modeled after the Selective Service exam, HPD recruiters selected 70 cadets. However, only 50 of these graduated. Due to budgetary constraints, only 24 were actually assigned to duty as probationary officers. The remaining 26 were placed on a waiting list for future hirings and assignment as special police officers. The HPD remained too small to service the city adequately in the face of its exponential growth, which was fueled by the momentum of the Port of Houston and World War II–related industry.

Maintaining the same system of segregation originally practiced in small towns in the rural South was increasingly difficult in the rapidly modernizing city. Roger Biles has pointed out that "growing cities and an uprooted landless peasantry caused dissonance among some people with a strong sense of place."[59] Rapid, sustained growth in an urban setting placed heavy demands on the police to enforce the written and unwritten laws governing race relations in the Jim Crow South. Oftentimes, big-city police resorted to violence as they tried to maintain traditional Jim Crow values and order in the city. These acts of aggression shaped the community's perceptions of the police and created a chasm between the police and the black communities they served.

In the segregated South, the police hid behind ambiguities in the interpretation of the law that protected them from prosecution. Their repressive tactics were safeguarded by the customs supported by the elite and most white southerners. The southern elite defined the South's economic and political institutions as well as its social mores and attitudes. The lasting symbols of the social order the elite created—including the white Democratic primary, local control of voter registration, the exclusion of blacks from juries, and the enforcement of Jim Crow statutes—became targets of activists demanding social change and rights.

Black communities' perception that the police used brutality to support the elite and to defend segregation alienated many black citizens. The movement of African Americans to end racial segregation in Houston created social tensions that led to legal and public challenges to Jim Crow. As the gatekeeper of the social order, and as one of the institutions targeted for change, the police force was certainly caught in the middle of the civil rights movement, which began in the 1930s.

Spearheading the growing movement in Houston was the NAACP, Clifton F. Richardson Sr., and Carter Wesley. Richardson was the editor and an original partner of the *Houston Informer* Publishing Company.[60] By the late 1920s, the size of the population had created an independent black elite that was economically independent from the control of whites. This black elite represented one of two strains of emergent civic leadership, and members used economic and political influence to shape public policy. The other strain of leaders came from local black churches and labor organizations, which funneled a considerable amount of influence, labor, and money into the causes they supported.

Those in charge of public institutions viewed Houston's population growth as a liability in terms of the expansion of services. But private business welcomed the growth of the unskilled population and used it as a threat against organized labor, particularly black labor. In the 1930s and the 1940s, *Houston Informer* editorials written by its venerable editor, Carter Wesley, suggested that Houston's business establishment was using the black and that the black should, in turn, use the business establishment to improve their living conditions. However, requests for internal improvements in black areas were not heeded. While World War II–era prosperity created illusions of hope and dreams of economic prosperity for blacks migrating to Houston, it failed to offer an adequate solution to the housing problem.[61]

City officials' lack of concern united some blacks in a call for community self-improvement. Editorials in the *Houston Informer* tried to convince blacks to maintain good hygienic standards amid the deplorable conditions in which they were forced to live. They called on the citizens of the ever-growing wards to clean up their own yards and make the best of their situation.[62]

The situation only worsened, however, as blacks migrating to Houston were limited economically and culturally from moving into white neighborhoods. Although deed restrictions in a few communities did deny blacks access to homes, no municipal statute forbade blacks and whites from living together. Deed restrictions used the legal authority of contracts to enforce residential segregation patterns. Houston's segregated residential areas were more a result of custom than of law.[63]

Blacks who migrated to Houston settled in six major areas: the Third, Fourth, and Fifth Wards; Riceville; Acres Home; and Frenchtown. While most of the South experienced an outward migration of blacks during this period, Houston's black population grew at a faster rate than that of Dallas, New Orleans, and Atlanta. By 1940, Houston was the nation's second-largest Jim Crow city, after New Orleans, and the tenth-largest metropolitan area in the nation.

With Houston's sharp population increase came a sharp rise in the number of arrests of blacks, which caused some to fear contact with police. Vermel Cook, a longtime Houston resident who migrated to the city from Washington on the Brazos, Texas, in 1931, recalled that the police in the Fifth Ward were "frightful looking and did not play."[64]

Local politics alleviated any pressure on Houston's political establishment to extend services to blacks residing within the city's boundaries. Political and civic leaders simply sought to maintain order and continuity in Houston's poorer neighborhoods. Moreover, the rapid annexation of areas peripheral to the city made the growth of Houston's minority population negligible as a percentage of the total population. Robert Bullard emphasizes that "city services in older minority neighborhoods suffered severely as a direct result of the city's attempt to provide services to the newly annexed areas which were mostly white."[65]

Addressing the effects of annexation on the city's development, Jon Teaford has emphasized that Houston thwarted the political fragmentation of suburban growth by using Texas' liberal annexation laws to its advantage. As the white population grew, Houston's officials maintained political and economic control by annexing territories adjoining the city. Consequently, Houston grew from 66 square miles in 1940 to 446 square miles in 1967.[66]

Houston's growth in population and territory strained other already underfunded public institutions. Schools, hospitals, and street maintenance suffered from municipal neglect. Consequently, inadequate services for minorities created an ever-increasing activist stratum in the city, which accelerated the evolutionary process of change.

Despite such limitations, many migrants saw Houston as the place of dreams for their families. The city provided much more opportunity for them than the rural areas had. Education was the long-term vehicle for satisfying their dreams. However, most minority children attended dreadfully inadequate, segregated schools. William Kellar's work on the Houston Independent School District shows that the per capita funding of the district's black schools was one-third lower than that of white schools. And blacks and Hispanics in the Houston Independent School District were placed in horrendously overcrowded classes when compared to students in white schools. It appears that much of the success of these schools was due to black teachers and administrators who felt it was their responsibility to lift their students from the segregated conditions in which they were forced to live. Kellar suggests that these segregated schools, though underfunded, were among the best in the South for black students.[67]

The attitudes of the police also reflected national politics. As Nancy Weiss has argued, New Dealers did not choose to see blacks as racially disadvantaged, but, instead, as economically disadvantaged and in no need of special treatment.[68] The city would address only the needs of the voting majority, who in turn would extend ancillary benefits to the others. However, southern racial etiquette made this notion foolishly naïve.

The Houston Police Department, unlike other public institutions, was a visible guardian of traditional culture and had dubbed itself defender of the "southern way of life."[69] The maintenance of "place" became more illogical and difficult to maintain as the city changed in terms of demographics and economic growth. The old ways—of policing some citizens and serving others—were now questioned by those who felt persecuted. They demanded the same respect and protection from the police that others received.[70]

The position of traditional police in the South made them like the "man on a cliff" depicted by C. Vann Woodward in *The Strange Career of Jim Crow*.[71] Faced with rapid changes in their cities, their jobs, and their lives, police officers made value judgments that invalidated the rights of many minorities. This often placed the police on the wrong side of the law they had sworn to uphold while further straining the fragile relationship between them and minorities.

World War II unleashed changes in the social fabric of the urban South, where informal yet rigid racial customs were challenged by the economic need for black labor in defense-related industries. The latter set the stage for racial conflict in the South by forcing white southerners to work side by side with blacks and Mexican Americans, thereby raising questions about the basic tenets of Jim Crow.[72] However, the availability of jobs in Houston and the limitations on minorities helped avert some serious racial conflicts in the workplace. Yet workplace discrimination restricted salary and job advancement. Michael Botson's work on segregated labor unions in Houston's steel industry shows that "within jobs at Hughes Tool, blacks were paid one third of the salary of whites."[73]

Many white southerners felt that during the war, blacks were trying to upset the status quo. Some blacks, on the other hand, viewed the war's democratic promise as the launching pad for political and social change. Their increased activism placed them on a collision course with the conservative police, whose position as gatekeepers of southern racial customs and attitudes meant an eventual showdown over maintaining Jim Crow in Houston at any cost.

Houston's black leaders were frustrated with the slow pace of change that was acceptable to the NAACP. Letters from the Houston chapter of the NAACP reveal a chasm between local and national strategy during the war. Carter Wesley, a lawyer as well as a newspaperman, with the passion of someone living in the region and familiar with *Smith v. Allwright,* angrily requested permission to stir the legal fires. Nevertheless, the NAACP's legal counsel stalled and advised him to wait.[74] Police stepped up surveillance of black leaders in the city, intimidating and threatening them during nuisance arrests.

During this period, police brutality in Texas increased. During the height of the legal struggles, Wesley was beaten nearly unconscious by police in Conroe, Texas, approximately forty miles north of Houston. He alleged that he was assaulted by HPD officers who had followed him. Activists throughout the state were subjected to "private violence" that local police made almost no effort to prevent.[75]

Interesting twists developed in the city as blacks began to find their political legs. Leaders like Carter Wesley and Maceo Smith, of the NAACP, sought legal redress against the police. Now that the white primary was dead, they urged Thurgood Marshall and the NAACP to launch an inquiry into police violence against blacks. Disgruntled blacks sent letters and petitions demanding that the police provide adequate and sufficient services to the black community. This ran counter to the primary function of police in the South, which was to maintain law and order and harsh control over blacks. Violating this custom or publicly challenging police authority carried a heavy penalty, and the punishment was often painful for citizens who ran afoul of the law or just happened to be in the wrong place at the wrong time.[76]

Texas' conservative political climate reinforced institutional racism and harsh, confrontational racial rhetoric in the state. After April 3, 1944, when a headline in the *Washington Post* stated that "Negroes May Vote in Texas Primaries, Court Rules," many white Texans became greatly alarmed. Local conservatives, who believed the *Smith v. Allwright* decision would liberalize local politics, prepared for an assault from "communist inspired" black activists. State officials, fearing political fallout, publicly decried the ruling and retrenched as Attorney General Allan Shivers defiantly insisted that "the white primary was not dead."[77] In December, 1944, Harris County tax assessor and collector Jim H. Glass assured the press that registered blacks would not affect the outcome of the upcoming election. He added that "local politics would continue as usual."[78] This court ruling heated up the climate of hatred in the state and put blacks at risk, but it also helped change the political culture of the city after the war.

Reactions to the wartime migration heightened social tensions in the city and the nation. In 1943, these tensions boiled over into bitter race riots in other cities. While no such riots took place in Houston, major riots occurred in Beaumont, Texas; Detroit; Harlem; and Los Angeles. These riots illustrated the mounting frustrations over demographic changes and the potential threat of migrants competing for jobs and housing coveted by the white population.[79] They also revealed the police department's inability to control the rioting mobs.

In city after city where riots occurred, the police stood by and allowed marauding white mobs to victimize blacks and Mexican Americans. Moreover, when they did act, they almost exclusively arrested or shot blacks and Mexican Americans for looting.[80] War-era tensions revealed a vast cultural gap and an impending crisis between police and disenfranchised minorities in southern cities. In 1943, the rumblings of social change in the black community were increasing because of the growth of a sizable black middle class, and because the police reacted as they had in the past, by trying to keep blacks in their place.

The later years of World War II also saw the culmination of the effort of Houston's African American community to fight against political disenfranchisement. Darlene Clark Hine's *Black Victory* illustrates how political activism paid off in the spring of 1944, when the United States Supreme Court handed down the *Smith v. Allwright* decision, which rendered the Texas white Democratic primary unconstitutional.[81] The victory did little initially to alter Houston's political landscape, but it served as a launching pad for activism, paving the way for a new generation of African American who demanded a more inclusive part in Houston's political order.

As the political climate slowly shifted in the aftermath of the *Smith* case, blacks cautiously pressed the city for change. Hine suggests that the *Smith* decision created hope and eventually opportunities for blacks in the city.[82] Blacks without the vote had been completely marginalized, their needs defined for them by the venal political establishment. Blacks throughout the country saw the decision as a symbolic example of what they could do if they organized and fought. The Supreme Court's decision established the foundation for grassroots activism in both the urban and the rural areas of the country. Charles Payne cautions us to remember, however, that for those organizing the struggle after the *Smith* decision and the war, the South retrenched and became a deadly place for blacks.[83] The fear of violent repression by whites dashed the hopes of some blacks while opening the window to fuller access for others.

Samuel Walker, however, argues that police and community relations improved after the war. He adds that this was due to a combination of police professionalism stemming from training acquired at police schools and a shift in societal perception, which created a less tolerant public.[84] The perspectives of Texas blacks, previously limited residentially and controlled intellectually, were reshaped by the war. As a result of the hopes generated by the imminent Allied victory, local activism increased, and many blacks demanded full inclusion in society. These challenges to authority were logical outgrowths of this social transformation.

Houston's constantly changing political climate undermined the stability of the police department. Its leadership changed with every new administration— eight times from 1930 to 1945.[85] These constant shifts of administrative personnel were patronage-based promotions or demotions.

Efforts to maintain segregation within the HPD and on the streets of Houston were at odds with the impulse to modernize and to make the police department more professional and efficient. Houston's booming population and a growing demand for equality within its borders put postwar Jim Crow and the HPD on the ropes. However, both would fight to maintain traditional practice and custom in Houston.

Although the war brought out the patriotic spirit in most Americans, it reminded others of the gap between American ideals of equality and the realities of life for African Americans and other ethnic minorities. As these individuals tried to force themselves into the heart of the political and social mosaic, their actions clashed with the police. This activism was the beginning of the end of black political subservience. It also meant that a now politically viable black populace would have to be faced.

Jesse H. Jones, civic leader and Democratic Party power broker who helped ameliorate racism in Houston from the 1920s to the 1940s because it was bad for business. Courtesy Joe Pratt

HPD detective squad photo, 1940s era, which reveals the city's racial divide. From May Walker, The History of Black Police Officers in the Houston Police Department *(Dallas: Taylor, 1988), p. 7. Courtesy Houston Police Department*

E. J. Stringfellow traversed the racial divide of the 1950s and became the first African American city marshal. From May Walker, The History of Black Police Officers in the Houston Police Department *(Dallas: Taylor, 1988), p. 33. Courtesy Houston Police Department*

Oliver Brown tried to challenge the internal racial caste system and waited nearly fifteen years before he was promoted to the rank of sergeant, although he scored high on written exams. From May Walker, The History of Black Police Officers in the Houston Police Department *(Dallas: Taylor, 1988), p. 21. Courtesy Houston Police Department*

African American police pioneers circa 1959 or 1960, in front of the Wheeler Avenue YMCA. From May Walker, The History of Black Police Officers in the Houston Police Department *(Dallas: Taylor, 1988), p. 11. Courtesy Houston Police Department*

Police Chief Herman Short molded the police department in his own image and aggressively controlled the city in a period of social and political upheaval. Courtesy Houston Police Department

Students from Texas Southern College for Negroes and Freedom Riders in an HPD holding cell. Courtesy Houston Police Department

Mayor Louie Welch and Chief Short pinning a new officer. Ironically, Short was beginning systemic changes within the department via the hiring of white women. Courtesy Houston Police Department

TEXAS SOUTHERN UNIVERSITY
HOUSTON, TEXAS

DIVISION OF SOCIAL SCIENCES

March 15, 1967

Mr. Mack H. Jones
3550 Wheeler, #20
Houston, Texas

Dear Mr. Jones:

In conference with President Pierce and Dr. Tsiang, Head of the Department of Political Science, we were reminded again that the impending state of budget makes it advisable that we not anticipate addition of faculty members to the staffs of the various departments. We were also reminded that the Department of Political Science is unbalanced with people whose training is in the field of international relations and international law. Therefore, we find it necessary to reduce our number of persons in this area and secure one in another branch of Political Science. Since you are one of the most recent persons employed in the department and represent the area in which we must restore balance, it grieves me deeply to have to say that we find it necessay not to renew your appointment for another school year. Please believe that the regret is deeply implanted since the excellence of your scholarship and your great dedication to teaching forecast for the University a bright spot in its instructional program.

We do not expect to continue to be so tightly bound with regard to personnel and hope that you will find it possible to consider favorably any opportunity we may experience to have you rejoin us. Any recommendation that I can make personally in your behalf, I will be very happy to do so in light of my high regard for you as a person and as a political scientist.

Sincerely yours,

H. A. Bullock, Chairman
Division of Social Sciences

Approved:

Dr. Tsiang, Head of Department

Dr. H. A. Bullock, Chairman

Dr. Pierce, President

Dr. H. H. Hartshorn, Dean

Termination letter of Dr. Mack H. Jones from the Division of Social Sciences. Courtesy Mack H. Jones Archive

HPD police chiefs, 1963–2004. Courtesy Houston Police Department

Carroll M. Lynn was charged and later convicted of obstruction of justice and sentenced to federal prison. Courtesy Houston Police Department

Mayor Whitmire showed her political power and made an important step toward improving HPD with the hiring of Lee P. Brown, the department's first African American chief. From May Walker, The History of Black Police Officers in the Houston Police Department *(Dallas: Taylor, 1988), p. 3. Courtesy Houston Police Department*

C. O. Bradford was an angry sergeant when Brown challenged him to become part of the solution, not part of the problem. Bradford became HPD chief in 1996. Courtesy Houston Police Department

Mayor Bob Lanier restored entrenched elite rule to the city, but continued improving HPD by hiring former police officer and U.S. attorney Sam Nuchia as chief. Nuchia increased diversity and professionalism within the HPD. Courtesy Houston Police Department

In 1992, the lawsuit filed by Dorothy Edwards challenging the HPD's hiring and promotion practices changed the department's hierarchical order. From May Walker, The History of Black Police Officers in the Houston Police Department *(Dallas: Taylor, 1988), p. 51. Courtesy Houston Police Department*

Man, there was times when I thought I had to

choose between being a police or a Negro.

Well—I couldn't stop being a Negro.

—E. J. STRINGFELLOW

CHAPTER 2 "Almost the Law"

Black Police and the Ordeal of Jim Crow Policing in Postwar Houston, 1944–59

In 1944, the hope and promise of the impending double victory over fascism abroad and racism at home inspired many African Americans to reach higher for self-betterment. Immediately following World War II, institutional bureaucracies were among the most important and influential forces in the shaping of modern America.[1] As these individuals began to force themselves into the heart of the political and social culture, their actions clashed with those of the police who were sworn to serve and protect all citizens.

The optimism of the era encouraged many minorities to apply for nontraditional public-service jobs as fire fighters and police officers. Conversely, blacks in Houston had a changing set of expectations of the benefits that full participation in local society could offer by the end of the war. No better example of this hope existed than among the blacks employed as officers by the Houston Police Department between 1944 and 1959, arguably an era of great social, political, and racial transition for Houston and the HPD. Blacks who sought employment as police officers combined the hopes of economic improvement and self-betterment with a sincere desire to uphold the law. In reality, however, blacks serving as police officers were forced to make many difficult personal choices during this era, when many southerners viewed all blacks as potential criminals. These men served a Jim Crow Houston ruled by a small, white elite that controlled both the wealth and influence of the city.[2]

This chapter examines how African American police officers navigated through the difficulties of Jim Crow policing in which they worked and the world of Jim Crow customs in which they lived. Locally, as blacks made and won more significant victories in the battle against Jim Crow in the later years of World War II, the role of the police force took on even greater significance as it enforced segregation laws and maintained race-based customs. In contradiction, the HPD had to reexamine its own racial caste system, as the blacks on the force served in more than logistical or situational assignments. These officers, in turn, negotiated their own careers and tried to salvage vestiges of racial pride. The history of the HPD in this era of racial change illustrates the impact of early civil rights efforts on the city and its institutional entities.

As the city and the police both struggled to adapt to forces of modernization after 1945, tensions within the police department increased. In these years, Mayor Oscar Holcombe used the police force as a political hostage as he appointed reform-minded police bureaucrats to both control and to make the department more professional. The police formed the Houston Patrolmen's Association and looked toward unionization as a way to shield themselves from the damaging effects of political patronage. However, the strong antiunion bias of many police officers and a form of business progressivism in the city pushed and succeeded in getting the state civil service law, 1269M, passed. Law 1269M placed Texas' patrol officers under civil service protection rather than exposing them to potentially radicalized unions.

Houston's black police officers, who evolved from ghetto guardians to full police during this period, suffered from the lingering mental effects of Jim Crow. Although they had made significant strides toward equality on the job, they remained anomalies on the mostly lily-white police force because of the lingering limitations of Jim Crow. Blacks' legal and political activism in the 1940s was the beginning of the end of black political subservience in the city. It also assured that an increasingly active black populace would find its political voice.

In postwar America, overcrowded neighborhoods, inadequate city services, and hostile race relations shaped the lives of most blacks. Deed restrictions confined those who migrated to Houston in black island enclave communities in an ever-expanding sea of whiteness. This made ghettos of these already overcrowded communities. Economic realities relegated most blacks to menial or lower-paying unskilled jobs. The postwar economic prosperity that benefited society at large slipped through the grasp of the majority of abysmally poor blacks.

The modernization of the city made the maintenance of Jim Crow policing increasingly illogical. Therefore, maintaining a segregated police force in a large, modernizing city became both impractical and logistically unrealistic. Plus, as the city grew, social acceptance of institutional racism became less tolerable to minorities, particularly to economically independent black elites who were poised to negotiate with white elites for a say in how the city was ruled.

Despite Houston's growing ethnic diversity, Jim Crow customs reduced issues within the city to matters of black and white. The bittersweet memories of the Jim Crow past lived in the minds of those who survived this era and sought opportunities for self-betterment in a world regulated by legal segregation. A black former city councilman, the Rev. Ernest McGowen Sr., recalled that the heavy hand of Jim Crow required that all "Negroes had to fight against segregation," and that the "Negro policemen were treated as bad as, if not worse than, an ordinary black person."[3] Houston's black police found no privileges accorded to their status and were treated like other blacks: socially segregated, politically alienated, and as a servile class, because most of them were economically dependent on the city.

Ironically, racial groups were intimately bound by economics and proximity, which made it difficult to maintain traditional patterns of segregation.[4] Houston's urbanization ameliorated the stinging effects of Jim Crow, making it far less venomous than its rural counterpart. Although harsh in tone, urban Jim Crow was confronted by a wealthy and economically independent black elite that benefited from the size of Houston's black community. George Norris Green's political history, *The Establishment in Texas Politics*, reveals that it was Jim Crow establishment politics, not economic relationships, that promoted racially exclusive politics at the state level and supported forced racial subordination at the local level.[5] Black Houston understood that and demanded the right to vote in local elections earlier than did blacks in other sections of the South, in spite of strong white opposition. V. O. Key's groundbreaking *Southern Politics* emphasizes that "in its grand outlines, the politics of the South revolves around the position of the Negro . . . Yet it is far from the truth to paint a picture of Southern politics as being chiefly concerned with the maintenance of supremacy of whites over blacks."[6] The changing expectations of a democratic society led some blacks in Houston to believe that the dismantling of Jim Crow racial subordination was the only way to improve the overall quality of their lives.

The war's democratic promise eluded most of Houston's blacks, yet by the end of 1943, some windows of opportunity, including jobs in the HPD, had opened for blacks. Although few in number, more blacks became police officers. At the end of 1943, the HPD had 344 officers, including 7 blacks.[7] Houston's black patrol officers had the same legal authority and salary as whites according to their job classification. However, because of societal customs and attitudes and departmental suspicion of black officers, they were viewed with greater suspicion in their own community, "almost the law" in terms of the full exercise of their powers, and their peers viewed them as inferior. Moreover, functional limitations were imposed on them by the departmental custom that forbade black officers from arresting white citizens.

In 1940, the HPD's force possessed a rural mentality. Many officers had migrated to Houston from rural Texas, and their values clashed with those of Houston's ever-changing urban environment. White officers from rural Texas came to Houston with harsh racist stereotypes that defined social customs, even though race relations were somewhat different in the urban areas, if for no other reason than proximity. The perception among many in the department was that a general lack of respect for the police was growing. The HPD maintained order in the city through the use of brute force and intimidation, thereby hoping to achieve societal accommodation, respect for the law, and fear of authority.

Houston's modernization continued to clash with the traditional attitudes of the police and the city council. The latter continued to wrestle with the expansion of the force. Between 1940 and 1945, the HPD remained a small force for a city of Houston's size, averaging approximately 344 officers (see Table 2).[8] They staffed a city that had also grown in territory from sixty-six to ninety-eight square miles during the same period. Meanwhile, the population grew from 384,514

Table 2. *White and Black Racial Composition of Houston Police Department, 1940–80*

Year	Total Officers	No. White Officers	% of Total	No. Black Officers	% of Total
1940	344	337	97.9	7	2.1
1945	423	414	97.9	9	2.1
1950	570	557	97.7	13	2.3
1955	720	700	97.2	20	2.8
1960	1,159	1,123	96.9	36	3.1
1970	1,792	1,732	96.7	60	3.3
1980	2,971	2,731	92.0	240	8.0

Source: Approximate percentages based on actual raw numbers from Houston Police Department Annual Reports 1940, 1950, 1960, 1970, and 1980.

Note: Percentages may not add to 100 because of rounding.

to 458,100 and the police-to-citizen ratio worsened. Huge disparities existed in the ratio of black police officers to black citizens: 1 officer per 17,000 citizens, as noted earlier.

The movement of blacks to Houston placed them in contact with the police, who were often the only public servants they encountered, and both parties came to view each other as mortal enemies. Police services in general were woefully inadequate in the city, yet city officials did believe that enlarging the force was necessary. But the *Smith* decision eventually caused a gradual shift in the political makeup of the city and led some white and black leaders to form coalitions for the advancement of the city's development priorities. These coalitions rewarded black leaders for their political support and ensured that the economic relationships between merchants and blacks continued. Southern mercantile tradition exploited black dollars, but did not grant blacks access to public shopping areas. This tradition was altered, though not completely changed, because most blacks in the city were not informed about the agreement to integrate downtown stores.[9]

Houston's black population comprised approximately 20 percent of the population of the city between 1940 and 1944. The ratio of black police officers to black citizens was far lower; there were only 7 black officers out of a total force of 344 officers in 1940, approximately 1 percent of the police force. The 7 black officers usually functioned without a patrol car or with one that was rendered nearly inoperable by age. Their effectiveness was also constrained by racial attitudes within the department.

Moreover, nepotism and cronyism reinforced traditional attitudes on the force. These family and friendship ties may explain in part the resistance within the department to reform. The passing of leadership roles from one generation to the next also ensured white hegemony, as the civil service examination process began to exclude potential applicants.

Hostile racial attitudes on the force increased because of the open affiliation of some officers with the Ku Klux Klan.[10] Personal interaction with these factions created problems for black officers. E. J. Stringfellow, a longtime HPD officer and former city marshal, emphasized that "the forties and fifties were really tough; those white folks years ago used to throw everything that came their way at us."[11]

The breakdown of Jim Crow went forward in different ways in southern police departments and other institutions. According to Gunnar Myrdal in his classic 1944 study, *An American Dilemma*, the police officer "stands not only for civic order as defined by informal laws and regulations, but also for 'White Supremacy' and the whole set of social customs associated with this concept."[12] The importance of the policing function in the maintenance of Jim Crow made change regarding race issues within southern police departments a particularly touchy issue. Moreover, the nature of this change was of broad symbolic significance to society as a whole. An analysis of the breakdown of institutional racism and Jim Crow policies within the Houston Police Department is vital in understanding the nature of public institutional change.

Several retired black officers who went through the department's selection process felt that it was biased and that the interviews were highly subjective.[13] The personal interview was the major stumbling block for most minorities who passed the police entrance exam. Blacks who applied for jobs believed that HPD interviewers tried to drive them away through insults and petty racial references.[14]

The HPD's efforts to set and maintain base standards among the rank and file excluded potential applicants based on race and questions of character. This, coupled with other exclusionary employment rules, limited minorities in the department. The dual pressures of mistrust from the black community and disdain from the white community and other officers placed tremendous burdens on black police officers throughout the state. Seeking relief from the alienation in their communities and their work, blacks turned to unionization.

In 1935, HPD's African American officers and other black law enforcement officers from the area had formed the Texas Negro Peace Officers' Association (TNPOA). Leroy "Buster" Landrum recalled that "in the beginning their purpose was more social than professional."[15] The alienation that blacks experienced within the department was thus temporarily soothed through the common forum of the TNPOA, which was not a collective bargaining agency but a purely social organization. Unionization met the social and professional needs of black officers; it did not ease the stinging effects of Jim Crow. One black officer recalled feeling like "we were being watched all the time."[16]

By virtue of their employment on the force, blacks had to endure Jim Crow's "tragic duality" of being both a black and a police officer. Poet Paul Laurence Dunbar refers to this phenomenon as "wearing the mask"—or the broader surface acceptance of racial subordination by blacks as they face the harsh manifestations of racism.[17] As blacks in one of the South's largest cities, the HPD's black officers were second-class citizens; as police officers in the segregated South, they were sworn to enforce Jim Crow laws and customs that were a validation of their own oppression. Furthermore, in the larger sense, their presence revealed the impracticality of maintaining racial subordination in a modernizing city.[18]

Black officers' efforts to uphold the law often collided with the harsh realities of the segregated world in which they lived and worked, and it exacted a heavy personal toll on them and their families. Retired city marshal and HPD narcotics officer E. J. Stringfellow lamented that "there was times when I thought I had to choose between being a police or a Negro. Well—I couldn't stop being a Negro."[19]

The HPD's black patrolmen were an anomaly in the Jim Crow South. Within the department their presence caused tension and opened them up to blatant hostility from some whites. Moreover, they found themselves in a state where officials such as Govs. Allan Shivers and Price Daniel and local officials such as the police chief publicly endorsed black inferiority and created a work climate that isolated black officers and left them nowhere to turn for relief.[20]

As bad as work conditions were for black officers, it is important to note that their constant presence as police in Houston represented a major change in Jim Crow custom. Most southern police and fire departments did not hire blacks as officers or fire fighters until the 1960s. This early presence of blacks on the force thus made Houston one of only a few southern cities to use black police officers.

As rapid demographic changes in the city created a need for more Black police, the department resisted increasing their numbers. They filled a need for police protection and provided a vital service to a community that was both underserved and overpoliced by the HPD. Whereas black patrol officers provided increased police presence and minimally intrusive surveillance within the black community, whites who patrolled black areas had a reputation for brutality and overzealousness.[21]

Houston's explosive industrial and population growth during this period provided the city with a large, malleable labor supply and validated the need for more officers. It also increased racial tension. Economic prosperity provided a powerful stimulus for the thousands of migrants who poured into Houston in search of new opportunities, which helped transform the city from a large town to an emerging metropolis. The city's changing demographics forced a backward HPD to respond to the public demand for increases in public services, such as fire and police protection, as well as to grapple with how to protect the ever-expanding borders of the city.

The reelection of Mayor Oscar Holcombe in 1945 brought an aggressive expansion of police and fire services, over the objections of council members who saw no need to expand the police force.[22] However, because of his forceful personality and Houston's strong-mayor form of government, they yielded to Holcombe's call to increase the force.

Behind the scenes, a new political equation was emerging in the city that included blacks who had migrated to Houston before and during the war. They formed coalitions that yielded voting power years before many other blacks in the South succeeded in this quest. The Houston Police Department found itself caught in the middle of these changes while trying to maintain Jim Crow segregation.

Nationally, the twin phenomena of modernization and urbanization in Houston led to demands for increased and effective police protection. Locally, these issues were intertwined with civic leaders' need to control the movement for desegregation. The police and some civic leaders tried to link the protest movement to communism and outside radicalism, thus making the actions of blacks and any others who advanced ideas for change suspect. While civil rights protests were reflective of changing attitudes throughout the country, police viewed such protests as a decline in respect for authority, particularly when minority citizens called for police professionalization and accountability. The HPD was understandably alarmed by once-quiet and compliant black citizens questioning police authority.[23]

Part of the conundrum the police faced lay in the rapid growth of the city. It rendered the HPD's efforts to enforce traditional racial customs more impractical, as the city boomed and its black population grew steadily (see Table 1). Along with this growth came a diversity of opinion within the black community. James SoRelle suggests that the migration to Houston was "the darker side of heaven" for all blacks who migrated to the city seeking employment.[24] Therefore, necessity created a need for the HPD to maintain a continuous black presence on the police force to provide marginal police service in black areas of the city.

Mayor Holcombe had kept his campaign promise to change the police department in the 1930s, but his reappointment of B. W. Payne, who served as chief of police from 1933 to 1936, during Holcombe's first term as mayor, caused white factions to appear within the department.[25] White officers feared that the mayor would continue to fire or demote veteran officers, who unanimously called for civil service protection. These officers hoped to remove themselves from the effects of political patronage and the spread of organized crime that they thought was moving into Houston.[26] Although a competent veteran officer, Payne was viewed as an outsider by many in the department, and he was also regarded as Holcombe's boy.

Despite departmental objections, Holcombe's actions facilitated the dramatic expansion of the force. Table 2 summarizes the increase in the size and the racial composition of the HPD from 1940 to 1980. Between 1940 and 1960, the number of white officers increased by approximately 233 percent, and the number of black officers increased more than 241 percent.

The Houston Police Officers Association (HPOA) functioned as a police benevolent organization before 1945. But because of changing expectations and perhaps as a result of seeing the triumphs of other unions around the nation, it slowly evolved into a collective bargaining unit that included all police officers. HPOA efforts were in part focused on opposition to Payne's reappointment, but they were also a political move to attract new members during the expansion of the force. Nationally, labor unions were making steady gains in membership. Samuel Walker cautions that police unions were not supported outside of the rank and file and that they were not like private-sector unions.[27] Payne's affiliation with Holcombe was the HPOA's primary objection to his appointment. Its biggest fear was that Payne would replace or dismiss qualified officers who had not supported Holcombe's reelection. Unstated was the HPOA's opposition to control of the city by the "8-F group," wealthy businessmen who were allegedly the power elite of Houston.[28]

The HPOA modeled its efforts to attract members after those of national labor unions. Its members used political reform rhetoric to call for the insulation of police department personnel from the effects of political patronage, an end to firings and demotions of veteran officers by the mayor or his appointees, and implementation of a system of testing for promotions and advancement in the fire and police departments. They also demanded that field reviews and seniority be factored into standardized exams to improve their chances for promotion.[29]

The growth of the union was part of the national trend toward unionization and a carry-over of New Deal politics and the democratic promise of the postwar years. But the HPOA differed from other unions because of the conservative nature of the police. Its members did not view themselves as part of what they perceived as the left-wing shift of the American labor movement. Mark Haller believes that the trend toward radical police unions was exaggerated because they were essentially conservative and did not fit the myth that workers who unionized nationally were liberal or radical.[30] They certainly did not abandon racial segregation as a platform agenda item.

E. J. Stringfellow provides an example of the HPOA's integrationist limitations. As he recalled, "The union was segregated, and we [blacks] got anything we wanted as long as we stayed away from the union's picnic and any other function."[31] Labor reform efforts of the era were thus overshadowed by deep racial divisions within the ranks of the HPD. The conservative nature of the police associations pleased Houston's elite, which could count on the police to support its antiunion stance.

Don Carleton has written that "a power elite existed in the city, one whose members wished, among other things, to return the Republican party to power in Washington, purge the government of its New Deal inheritance, and keep the Russians, blacks, and labor unions in their respective places."[32] As he points out, the Red Scare caused a near-xenophobic desire to rid the state of communists and unions and to circumvent the elite's perceived loss of control over the black community.[33] The HPD used black police officers for surveillance in the community, and they were instrumental in the suppression of aggressive black activism of any kind.

The growth of trade and employee unions was the greatest source of concern for the political elite of Houston, which was the center for anticommunist activity in the state. Local groups remained vigilantly anticommunist and engaged in minipurges of left-wing labor radicals. Houston's patrol union did not fit the Red Scare model because of its conservative and racist tendencies, but fears throughout the state prompted swift action to ensure that local police patrol unions would not be radicalized. Such bars were unnecessary, however, because the association was so conservative that it alienated moderate members, who later formed splinter organizations.

In 1947, Gov. Beauford Jester yielded to political pressure for municipal reform when he signed HR 34, the Fireman's and Policeman's Civil Service—Cities of 10,000 or More law, commonly referred to as Article 1269M, Firefighters' and Police Officers' Civil Service Law. This law provided state protection to all municipal police officers and fire fighters beyond that afforded by existing city civil service law. While it fixed holiday pay, established the Civil Service Commission's authority, and created a classification system for police and fire fighters, it also protected nepotism within municipal departments. The law betrayed patrol unions by providing that blood relationships were neither illegal nor detrimental in the workplace. The hiring of family members within the police department was a source of contention among local politicians as well as police officers who were denied promotions.

The governor's action was intended to thwart aggressive unionization in the state. If he could control the pace of the patrol and fire unions' growth and activism, he would not have to accept their legitimacy as a collective bargaining unit. Using civil service reform, the governor thus exerted pseudo-control over the local political practice of patronage and, as an ancillary benefit, controlled municipal union activity as well.[34]

In theory, the law extended basic civil service protection to all officers. It sought to remove police officers and fire fighters from the impact of political patronage and it succeeded, at least on the surface. Black officers within the HPD, because of their marginalized status, however, viewed the new civil service laws with skepticism, as evidenced by the fact that few attempted to use the civil service to remedy individual job discrimination. Most officers I interviewed felt that it was fruitless to attempt to use the civil service because of the racist attitudes of those on the commission.

Some Black officers in the HPD tried without success to use the new law to challenge their second-class job status. Addressing the inadequacies of the civil service law, Oliver Brown, a black patrol sergeant who worked for HPD from 1958 through 1987, recalled, "We [blacks] tried to use civil service, but whites always seemed to get around it."[35] According to Brown, the law failed to guarantee blacks a fair chance at departmental exams. Retired Det. Sgt. Frederick Black stressed that "whites knew how to get away with things," suggesting that civil service was supportive of traditional attitudes and practices.[36] When asked if he tried to use the civil service law, Stringfellow replied, "Man, are you kidding? . . . For what?"[37]

Blacks had few if any allies in the state capital. Despite Governor Jester's moderate political stance, which displeased the state's ruling elite, he was no champion of minority rights. After his sudden death from a heart attack in 1949, he was succeeded by Lt. Gov. Allan Shivers, who was called the "Pied Piper" of Texas politics. Shivers's strident racial rhetoric as attorney general had helped him win the lieutenant governor's seat in 1948.[38]

The use of the special police officer position by the mayor and chief as a source of political patronage was another contentious point for HPD officers. Generally reserved for whites, those positions at any given time appeared to comprise no more than one percent of the police census. Their use in the twentieth century was generally based on patronage, not race, but when blacks were hired, it was to fill temporary needs in the black community. Most special police in this era were whites whose function suited the chief and the mayor. The special police, as explained earlier, were a pliant group that answered to the chief or the mayor alone and could be dismissed without explanation.

The arbitrary use of the special police created tension among the department's black officers, whose status was ambiguous. These tensions are even evident in HPD annual photographs between 1945 and 1958, which show clear racial segregation in the department. A group photo of detectives from circa 1958 shows white and black detectives in the same picture but sitting three feet apart. HPD annual reports also verify the ongoing presence of black officers in the HPD as regular officers.

Blacks seized the opportunity provided by political and social activism in the city and demanded more black police officers. Houston's black leaders used this issue to galvanize the black community and worked through clubs and organizations like the NAACP to underscore their demands.

Mayor Holcombe used his political savvy to avoid yielding to demands for more black police officers. In January, 1946, he stressed that "Negroes on the force would be increased if there were Negro jobs available. However, if traffic detail was the only job, then Negroes would not be hired—Negroes did not work traffic detail."[39] Blacks who worked for the HPD endured these types of limitations until the 1960s.

Societal fears of blacks as police officers originated in the late nineteenth and early twentieth centuries, when most whites felt that a black with a gun and supervisory authority over whites was immoral and unconscionable. Robert Wintersmith argues that the "strategy for the containment of Negroes, whether it was law enforcement or order maintenance, was lynching in the South, and mass rioting in the North. The thought of blacks over whites was unthinkable and morally repugnant."[40] This was exactly the strategy of the HPD, whose continued expansion included blacks as a crucial element by means of their status, even though their role continued to be ambiguous and limited by the department's racial culture.

In the fall of 1948, the new Houston Police Academy opened in the Sam Houston Coliseum at the corner of Smith and Walker Streets. The academy program included a four-month intensive regime of physical fitness training, firearms training, traffic control training, classroom training, and on-the-job training. Each class included at least two blacks; the numbers increased throughout the 1940s and the 1950s. Police department records from that period reveal no discussion about increasing the numbers of black officers to accommodate the city's growing population. The department's main concern was a practical one: how to provide minimum service to the black community without changing the racial composition of the force.

The blacks in the HPD's cadet class of 1948 were A. V. Young and J. Edwards. Edwards went on to graduate; Young withdrew from the first class but graduated with the second one. As he recalled, "I really did not know if I wanted to be a police officer."[41] After graduation, Young spent the majority of his police career in radio patrol. He was characterized by his peers as outspoken and he was never promoted, even though he had a master's degree and had passed the written exam with high marks.

Blacks who sought employment with the HPD usually heard of job openings by word of mouth or from local newspaper ads. Blacks in the city had long claimed that they were discouraged from applying or rejected after background checks concluded that they were of questionable character. The HPD yielded to pressure to hire more blacks to work black areas because of enlightened self-interest more than liberal idealism. Whites did not want to police black areas, and the police department thus needed more blacks as the city grew. Marjorie Duty was hired in the cadet class of 1953, making her the first black woman hired as a police officer. She was responsible for only black female inmates at the jail.

The application process for black officers was degrading. Stringfellow recalled in our interview that when he applied to HPD in 1954, "I went over and applied because I heard they were hiring, and I saw it in the paper. The first thing they said to me was, 'you is a little Nigger; them big Niggers in the Fifth Ward will whip your little ass.'" After assuring them that he could handle himself, Stringfellow was hired.

The HPD had a long-established pattern of hiring blacks from outside the city rather than from within the city. Al Blair, a native of Central Texas, recalls that when he applied in 1957, he was told by recruiters to go over to the jail. When he asked for directions, they laughed and said, "Boy, you must not be from around here. All Negroes from around here know where the jail is."[42] Since Blair's references checked out and he had no record, he was finally given directions to police headquarters located at 61 Reisner Street.

Notification of appointment came through telephone calls or letters. Blacks complained that their notification calls came late and their letters for employment came without advance notice. Frederick Black, another applicant, remembered, "I was out of town when my letter came. I did not know that I had been hired. When I returned to town around 2:30 A.M. Sunday morning, my landlady told me that I had a letter from the police department. I had to report the next morning."[43]

Oliver Brown relates a similar story. He was working as a cotton grader at the Houston Cotton Exchange when he got his acceptance notice at work. Brown did not object, however: "I didn't care how they called me to work. I was happy to get away from that job."[44]

The service of blacks on the force was both necessary and utilitarian, but racial custom limited some aspects of their training and their potential was seen as unequal to that of whites. Custom limited the opportunities and ability of black police officers adequately to perform some of their duties. Although the law said they were police officers, custom denied the full exercise of their duties in locations other than the segregated sections of the city.

Regardless of race, each officer entering the academy received three khaki uniforms for the summer and three wool uniforms for the fall. They purchased their own weapons (a .38 or .357-caliber) through a credit union account, with the cost deducted from their pay. All weapons were kept under lock and key except during firearms training and upon graduation from the police academy.

Classes began promptly at 7:00 A.M. The order of the day was physical conditioning and firearms training, followed by classroom training in the various phases of police procedure. Black recruits were paired with each other for physical training and buddy assignments. Recruits were assigned on-the-job training at no additional pay beginning in the last half of the academy. Most officers felt the academy was rough for all, black and white alike, though discrimination was also par for the course for black recruits.

The racial hierarchy was established on the first day of class at the academy. Custom prevailed, and blacks assumed their "place" in the rear. As Oliver Brown and the others recalled, "We were told to sit in the back of the class."[45] Although some resented it, they accepted it as the "way things were."[46] All of these officers recalled that incidents of racism or prejudice were both individualized and institutionalized. Black saw personal prejudice differently: "If they didn't like me, they didn't say it to me." He conceded, however, that separation within the department and training classes eased tension for all: "Plus, we did not like some of them any more than they liked us."[47]

Prejudice and racism were ever-present in the lives of black officers. Each of the black officers from this era whom I interviewed noted that the clearest expression of racism was the use of the word "nigger." "We were called nigger all the time," recalled Stringfellow.[48] They suffered insults throughout training. In training sessions led by Herman Short, then captain of burglary and robbery and later chief, trainees were forced to endure jokes about catching "a dumb nigger burglar" who did not have enough sense to run when he saw the police approaching.[49] Some whites laughed uncomfortably at the racist jokes while others saw them as part of the culture—*their culture*!

The pressures of the academy were difficult for everyone, as noted earlier, but blacks had to choose which fight to take on, since to fight every insult would have been impossible. Moreover, this job was their economic livelihood. Every day each black officer made choices regarding how far he or she could go to abide Jim Crow.[50]

The pervasiveness of Jim Crow made breaks and lunches an ordeal for blacks attending the academy. Black cadets were segregated at lunch and required to enter through the rear of the cafeteria. Black officers were told that they could have any food they wanted as long as they ate in the kitchen. But black patrolmen collectively refused to enter through the rear door until 1960. As Brown explained, "We didn't go to lunch anymore."[51] Some whites did question why blacks did not eat lunch in the cafeteria, but none challenged the custom of lunchroom segregation. Although their boycott of the cafeteria was seemingly insignificant on the larger political level, the black recruits settled for small personal victories and used this personal and much safer vehicle for protest.

After graduation from the academy, each officer received a duty assignment as patrol officer in the various divisions. blacks were almost always assigned to patrol black residential and business areas.

Limitations placed on black patrol officers severely curtailed their authority as law enforcement officers. Their role was defined by custom and dictated by traditions that forbade blacks from arresting whites. Their movement was restricted, and they had to receive permission to pursue suspects if they ventured out of their duty areas. Some of the most painful incidents for black officers revolved around the use of their discretion as law enforcement officers. Whites could and often did question arrests made by blacks, and could override a black patrol officer's authority.[52] A. V. Young frequently complained that this was a misuse of power that made black officers look bad in the community. His complaints obviously went unheeded, and he was passed over for promotion and choice assignments for most of his career, as noted earlier.

By the late 1950s, things seemed to be changing. Black recalled that "white cops would not let a man that a black officer arrested go in front of you like the they did in the old days, when they did not care. They might let them go when they transported them to the police station."[53] This was done to establish rank, place, and custom so that black patrol officers would remember who was in charge.

All duty assignments had a numerical coding. Black codes all ended in the number seven; therefore, anyone listening could determine the race of officers by both the car number and radio transmissions. Blacks routinely patrolled Houston's red-light districts. Brown recalls, "I was working my beat downtown when I saw this white fellow that was drunk and staggering. I arrested him and transported him back to the station. The fellow just looked like he had seen a ghost. I mean, a black man arresting him."[54]

Overt objections by any black officer to racial injustices were rare, even though these officers were mostly veterans of the desegregated army and had some difficulty adjusting to segregation at home. Some officers did resist, but when blacks violated a custom or stepped out of line, they were subject to dismissal and reassignment to such menial tasks as elevator duty at HPD headquarters.

The most vocal of the blacks received assignments that kept them out of sight and away from information sources. Robert Crain, a barber and landowner in addition to being a police officer, allegedly defied custom by arresting whites. He was punished by being assigned to elevator detail. His economic independence, however, allowed him to push against the barriers of racial subordination.[55] Officer Brown received a peripheral assignment after he violated a racial taboo in what he called the "Bowen bus incident." As he remembered it:

> I was assigned to a detail downtown on Prairie and Texas streets. There was a side of the streets for blacks and one for whites. I tried to be fair and uphold the law and I arrested a drunk white fellow. The owner of the Bowen Bus company reported me for harassing the customers of the downtown businesses. The Captain called me in and started in on me about the complaint against me. I got so mad that I started to cry. The Captain thought I was crying because I was scared of losing my job. I was crying because I wanted to knock the fool out of him, but I knew they would kill me! The Captain

comforted Brown and said "Brown, your badge is the same badge that any other officer carries. You are no less than any one of us. But, be careful because you know how things are."[56]

Motor patrol units in black areas were rare, given the department's lack of adequate units and the prevailing sentiment that white neighborhoods needed the cars more. Black motor patrol units were available, but they were limited to the black wards and business areas. Inadequate equipment allocations and geographical limitations restricted black officers' effectiveness and lowered their morale. "Negroes were assigned the worst cars for patrol," Stringfellow recalled. "Man, we had one patrol car that had bad rings, which caused it to smoke real bad. The windows did not work either and when it rained, we had to stick our head out of the window to see."[57] There were even times when some watch commanders told black officers to use the bus to transport prisoners.

Blacks were not allowed outside their duty areas for any reason unless called as backup or so ordered by a supervisor. This severely limited the use of discretionary power, making black officers function as 'almost the law' at times. In contrast, white patrol officers had free range within their duty assignments. Some had latitude as a roving unit and often came into black areas to inflate their arrest statistics. Police sweeps and random arrests in minority neighborhoods remained a contentious point in police/community relations until the late 1970s.

The low ratio of black officers, especially, to citizens encouraged them to rely on fear as a method of policing. Brown recalled that "you had bad officers, black and white, and they would beat and harass citizens" rather than act professionally. Moreover, "some white guys did not want to work in black areas and they showed it when they came in raising hell."[58]

Black patrol officers and their lack of resources were often the butt of white officers' jokes. Patrolman Brown added, "If your cars [those assigned for prisoner transport] wasn't [*sic*] working, then you called on the Gamewell box and they sent a car to transport the suspect."[59] Each ward area or quadrant had a Gamewell telephone call box, which was a direct line to the police station. Once the call was received at the station, the radio dispatcher sent a car to transport the suspect. Brown remembers that one time a call came for him to check a Gamewell box on Lyons Avenue, located in Houston's Fifth Ward. He searched and did not find the box. When he called to report, they all had a laugh and said, "Boy, look up the pole."[60] According to departmental folklore, a former sergeant had the box installed on the pole outside the window of a bordello he frequented while on duty in the 1930s.

From the 1940s to the late 1950s, most blacks at the HPD's academy received no training for traffic detail and were given only limited access to motorized patrol units. When the subject of traffic control came up in class, blacks were excused. Frederick Black did receive some traffic training in 1957, but, as he recounted, "we were trained" in traffic but "we welcomed being told that we could sit out traffic training at times."[61]

Although custom in the city barred the use of blacks as traffic officers, in the mid-1950s, the department, under Chief Jack Heard, began training blacks in traffic control to handle emergency situations. However, the city's changing political climate spelled doom for Heard, who resigned as chief in August, 1956, to take a job with the Texas Department of Corrections. On August 16, 1956, Mayor Holcombe appointed Carl L. Shuptrine as chief of police. The constant turnover in the chief's position, as it had in the past, undermined the integrity of the HPD's efforts to expand and stabilize the force. Moreover, social and political changes in the city hardened some racial attitudes during this period.

In spite of the racial climate in the city, black patrol officers had salary parity with whites. In 1956 and 1957, the average salary for a patrol officer, excluding overtime, was $350 a month.[62] Although black and white officers earned comparable salaries, most pay inequities grew out of the availability of overtime and extra work. As Officer Black revealed, "You got overtime sometimes, but depending on who you were and who your supervisor was."[63] Most blacks got overtime only when special or nonpatrol assignments were available.

From 1943 to 1959, opportunities for promotion for blacks existed in theory, but in practice they were quite limited. W. Marvin Dulaney argues that such opportunities for black police officers were nearly nonexistent in the United States.[64] Blacks were systematically denied promotions and discouraged from applying for supervisory jobs. In fact, they were discouraged from taking departmental examinations for promotion. The denial of access to information regarding promotions also hurt blacks, who felt that they "were informed of openings too late to apply or when all available examination slots were filled." Brown added, "They not only did not tell us about promotions, we were frequently scheduled to work on exam days." Officer Black supported Officer Brown's claim, adding that "we were denied vacation days to take examinations or we would receive special assignments that would have us working late hours that would keep us from being or getting ready for the test." Black remembered being scheduled for an all-night assignment to watch an industrial accident spill in the Clinton Park section of Houston on the day before the sergeant's examination. He recalled, "I got off too late to take the test." These practices were common and were accepted by some whites as fair and a normal part of the job.[65]

Low job performance ratings from white supervisors also killed any hopes of promotions for black patrol officers. Blacks routinely received lower performance scores than whites, which limited career advancement. "We were always rated lower than whites," Brown noted.[66] Most blacks felt that these arbitrary evaluations robbed them of promotions. Many whites did not view blacks as equal, and most did not want to recognize them as fellow officers. The HPD's internal caste system gave whites an inordinate amount of power in determining whether blacks on the force would advance. Regardless of the method of exclusion, however, promotional opportunities were systematically denied to blacks.

While difficult to document with precision, nepotism and friendship ties among whites also hindered blacks from being promoted. According to Stringfellow, "One of those ole boys told the other one, who was his son or brother, the answers to the tests."[67] Nepotism hurt whites as well, but they could eventually become part of the dominant police culture.

The HPD solved the problem temporarily by reclassifying some blacks to the detective grades. Detectives had the same grade and rank as a patrol sergeant, but no supervisory authority. Blacks were not viewed as supervisor material largely because of the potential reaction of white officers. This arrangement was nonthreatening to status and kept some of the black patrolmen content. Little changed in how black officers worked or in their status, however, since blacks still policed the ghetto as detectives—a job few whites wanted or would accept.

Detectives had a specialized function, were paid more, and did not have the headache of being supervisors. To the rank and file, the detective squad was an elite assignment. The HPD's use of this position illustrates a desire to address the needs of the black community without losing control, thereby maintaining the department's Jim Crow tradition. Blacks who passed the exam and became detectives worked in the black communities. Most welcomed the move from patrol to detective and considered the job a promotion rather than a lateral placement. Moreover, they knew all too well that Houston's immutable social conditions would hinder them from exercising the full extent of their power as black detectives. Lateral moves and reclassifications were common in police departments throughout the nation at this time. Dulaney views this as an effective practice, since the Houston Police Department did not have a black sergeant until 1974.[68]

The sergeant is the most important link in the police department. Information for most blacks was filtered through the sergeant-in-charge. Since no black was promoted to the rank of sergeant before 1974, blacks were not privy to insider information some white received in conversations with their peers. None of the black police officers I interviewed attributed the lower ratings they received from their white supervisors to racism. Officer Black stated that that "was just the way things were back then."[69] Whites looked out for their own.

The denial of promotions become a divisive issue for the TNPOA. Having no real power as a collective bargaining agency, it functioned as a clearinghouse of ideas for local affiliates. The Houston group argued about how to improve officers' chances of being promoted. Most of Houston's black officers wanted to compete fairly in the departmental promotional system. But a small minority, led by Scobbie Williams, a veteran juvenile officer, advocated a separate system that would give blacks a supervisor of their own race. Williams's demands divided the group, fracturing its already fragile cohesion. According to Brown, "He [Williams] wanted the department to give us a black sergeant and that we should test and compete among ourselves for promotions."[70] This divergence of opinion among the black officers was reflective of the divisive nature of Jim Crow society and the heterogeneity of the black community.

Conditions for blacks in Houston were not as bad as in many other parts of the South. Yet in their capacity as police officers, they faced the same discrimination and mistrust as black citizens. Wherever they were assigned, blacks were more than police officers. To some black citizens they represented what a black man or woman could do if given the opportunity; to others they were brutes, snitches, and traitors—or pliant tools of the whites.[71] Similar assessments are made by Nicholas Alex in *Black in Blue*.[72]

More recent studies suggest intragroup suspicion and class prejudice among middle-class blacks at the time, who respected black officers but did not view them as their social equals. Most blacks accepted blacks as police officers. When asked how black police performed, one black Texas native who visited Houston between the 1940s and the 1950s told me that "the police were at times lowdown suckers."[73] In fairness to blacks on the force, they could carry out their job only as well as they were trained to do.

The HPD's black police officers understood their nebulous position and mounted no substantial organized challenges to improve it during this period. As black officers on a white force that did not accept them, and as black police officers in a community that did not fully trust them, they were caught between a rock and a hard place. They viewed their job with the same hope and promise as whites did theirs, but the heavy burden of dual status as black and police officer placed tremendous stress on them.

The HPD's black and white officers, separated by traditional racial customs, were strangely united by professional ignorance and unprofessional practices. Officer Black stated that "we were taught not to take any mess." "Not taking any mess" meant using as much force as necessary to ensure that everyone respected the law.[74] The issue of police brutality and misconduct generated protests across racial lines. Oliver Brown suggested that both blacks and whites used force and intimidation to maintain law and order.[75]

Black officers had an immediate impact on crime in the communities they policed. Black precincts had both the highest crime rates and the highest arrest rates. Many of these arrests were due to officer bias and notions of racial superiority by white officers, who often inflated their arrest statistics. Because of personal bias and segregated residential patterns, many police departments targeted minority areas. A review of HPD arrest rates in the 1950s reveals that three times as many blacks as whites were arrested for "sin" crimes such as vice, prostitution, and gambling. Black police officers were required to overlook white transgressions while aggressively confronting black misconduct.

The custom of selective enforcement of the law caused credibility problems for black officers in their duty areas. Black citizens, regardless of class distinctions, felt that the laws were applied only to them, and that some whites were free to do as they pleased. Black patrol officers wanted to arrest whites who had violated the law, but they could have lost their livelihood or their life for violating Houston's racial customs. Their inability to impose the full authority of the law compromised their effectiveness. While occupying a fragile position within the HPD, black officers were called "traitor" or "Uncle Tom" in their own neighborhoods. In the department, they served a vital and useful function as overseers of the black community.[76] With little to work with, they were isolated in a world of blackness from other men in blue. These limitations on their authority made them appear to be pseudo-police.

Interestingly, black police officers believed as whites did, that they served one class while overseeing the other, according to Officer Black: "We [the police] served the elite."[77] The control of the masses was important for the harmony of the police/establishment relationship. Houston's business environment supported a power elite that was progrowth and maintained, with few if any major changes, traditional relationships in various communities. This elite moderated the harsh effects of Jim Crow in Houston because it was bad for the city's image, and black police officers served an important part in controlling crime. The use of black police, though practical and beneficial, did, however, threaten white control and custom within the force. Therefore, racism within the force continued to be a problem for the city.[78]

The social tension of the 1950s and a growing fear of increased narcotics-related activities prompted the HPD to use blacks as undercover operatives. Consequently, black officers became valuable agents of police repression within the communities they served. They were always present at civil rights demonstrations and arrests. Stringfellow recalled a peaceful civil rights protest in downtown Houston in the 1960s: "Man, we were called to arrest some dudes that was protesting. I picked up the Reverend Bill Lawson during the protest. Lawson, who was thin said, 'Stringfellow, do not drop me,' and I said, 'I ain't, Bill.' They were peaceful and nobody resisted. The sergeant called me over and chewed mc out for not roughing them up."[79] The police generally used extreme force against black social agitators in the 1950s and the 1960s.

During the Red Scare, the HPD created the Central Intelligence Division (CID) to gather information on alleged communists in the city. Police attributed the increased activism within the black community to communist agitation. In order to control activism and abate public protest, the HPD began in 1958 to use black officers as infiltrators and surveillance officers. Al Blair and Elston Howard were the first blacks used as CID officers. Blair declined to address the specifics of his job for me and did not criticize his role. He felt that it was a regular part of police work. One officer who wished to remain anonymous said, however, that "they knew what they did was wrong." The use of blacks as watchers or intelligence gatherers suggests that the HPD feared that social agitation by blacks was a communist-led activity.

Growing racial tensions in the 1950s also increased the need for more blacks on the force. External issues such as *Brown v. Board of Education of Topeka, Kansas,* the Red Scare, the boycotting of downtown merchants, and the emergence of multileveled civil rights activism propelled the HPD toward change. It helped that activism in the city was not aggressive, as in other parts of the South. The absence of aggressive social agitation was due in part to Houston's favorable economic climate, which assured employment for most blacks. The absence of a harsh racist image or a central rallying issue, such as police violence, also moderated activism and made it difficult to galvanize the community, as happened in Birmingham, Alabama.

By the end of the 1950s, local attitudes among young blacks were changing. According to Thomas Coles in *No Color Is My Kind,* the biography of tragic civil rights activist Eldrewey Stearns, "white Houstonians were not used to young blacks demanding their rights in public."[80]

Change and complacency collided in 1959, however, when black officers Al Blair and Charles Howard were confronted by a white sergeant for arresting a white suspect. This confrontation revealed the complexity of maintaining Jim Crow policing in a city with changing policing needs and functions. Moreover, state officials were trying to neutralize and control black organizations like the NAACP and other activists.

The CID's black officers and intelligence information gathered by blacks proved beneficial to the department. This did not prevent a sergeant from publicly ridiculing Blair and Howard and informing them that "he had not seen Negroes arrest a white and that he would have to check out their arrest." In full view of the prisoner and other people the sergeant warned, according to Blair, "You boys are outside of your place."[81]

Upon hearing of the incident, the CID's shift captain became enraged at the sergeant. He issued an oral order that the practice of blacks not arresting whites should stop immediately. Furthermore, any officer who attempted to impede black officers from carrying out their duties would be severely reprimanded. The motive for the captain's decision is unclear; however, it was very practical. With a large and growing black community that had become increasingly hostile to police, internal surveillance by blacks would be critical in assessing strategies for containing and controlling the black community.

The work of Blair and Howard as intelligence gatherers in black communities proved invaluable to the department. The HPD had firsthand surveillance in the communities without compromising the integrity of community leaders, on whom they had relied for information in the past, or placing a white officer at risk. The CID helped make the HPD's intelligence-gathering apparatus, which had relied on undependable paid informants and disgruntled community leaders, more professional. The lingering effects of the practice of not allowing black officers to arrest white suspects did not dissipate immediately, however, and some blacks chose not to arrest whites in order to avoid being hassled by white officers or out of fear of losing their jobs.

As the 1960s approached, the subtle demands to integrate Houston of the late 1950s gave way to more aggressive agitation for social change. Police officers and city leaders were thrust into the middle of Houston's racial transformation, which had begun during the city's amazing period of prosperity in the 1950s. They all tolerated, rather than genuine accepted it, and although the city changed somewhat, the police, tragically, dug in in their efforts to maintain tradition and custom and to preserve law and order. For the black officers who had struggled through the stinging effects of Jim Crow, being "almost the law" would become a thing of the past.

I joined the force when Herman Short came on television and said the reason that there where no Negroes on the police force, was because they could not find any qualified Negroes to apply.

—JIMMIE DOTSON

CHAPTER 3 Circling the Wagons

Police Department Retrenchment in a Time of Social Change, 1960–73

The maintenance of segregation in America was challenged in the 1960s by the various components of the civil rights movement. At the same time, the Houston Police Department was vainly trying to maintain the last vestiges of the Jim Crow hierarchy in the city. This chapter examines the HPD's reaction to the growing racial tension between city officials and minority communities. As more minorities rejected racial subordination and demanded greater accountability from public-service institutions, they specifically targeted the police department. Its historical aggression toward minorities and the tensions it created culminated in the Texas Southern University (TSU) riot on May 16–17, 1967. The violent confrontation between the police and black students became the defining moment in race relations in Houston and set the stage for the rise of other activists and protests in the city. Former Houston mayor Fred Hofheinz agrees: "TSU Riot created a lot of politicians."[1]

During this era, the HPD reacted defensively to the external pressures for change created by modernization, social agitation, and unrest; however, the fallout from these incidents forced internal changes. Initially attempting to stop change simply by reacting forcefully to such pressures, the HPD's chief of police, Herman Short—the Houston version of Birmingham's Eugene "Bull" Connor—eventually understood that the department should try to control the pace of change and steer it in a safe direction. His racial and political views at the time, nonetheless, reinforced the public view that the HPD was either unwilling or unable to alter practices and attitudes formed under Jim Crow and become more responsive to the entire population of Houston.

Paradoxically, despite Short's aggressive resistance to social change, the Houston Police Department under his leadership made significant steps in its painful process of transformation. After Short left in 1973, a truculent police department had to reassess its attitudes, values, practices, and policies.

The national movement for civil rights reached its apex in most cities, including Houston, as minorities' impassioned demands for social change shocked the nation. From the outset, police agencies across the country clashed with protesters. The role of the police as protectors of the law and guardians of social order was born of racist traditionalism rather than modern police techniques.

Two agencies helped shape most of the policies and procedures that influenced police behavior and attitudes in the 1960s: the Federal Bureau of Investigation, led by J. Edgar Hoover; and the International Association of Chiefs of Police. These organizations regarded social activism and the civil unrest it brought as egregious assaults on the existing social order. The HPD circled its wagons and retrenched, clinging more tightly to the old method of maintaining order. Social protesters challenged the department to reassess its attitudes, values, and practices, and it became even more conservative and reactionary. The HPD's members personalized broad changes as direct threats to the public safety and set out to destroy social activism in the city.[2]

As was true of most police agencies throughout the country in this era, the Houston Police Department drew its leaders from the World War II and cold war generations. Their patriotic conservatism and anticommunist sentiment made them unwilling to compromise with what they regarded the liberalization of Houston's culture and as an indication of the softening of society rather than as a logical consequence of modernization and urban social evolution. The police found it difficult to accept the changing social values of the minority community, which no longer tolerated racism and police brutality.

Traditionally, the impulse for change within the HPD had come from internally guided, pragmatic rank-and-file actions, but the social and political tensions of the 1960s thrust external pressure for change on the department.[3] These pressures required a higher and more consistent level of professionalism and bureaucratic functioning than existed within the department.[4] These broad forces combined in a powerful alchemy of change that was beyond the pale of HPD understanding, authority, and functioning.

Four things signaled the coming of dramatic change in the city: the presidential election of 1960; the federal census; the rising crime rate; and the aggressive social activism of blacks in the city. The election of John F. Kennedy renewed hope for the dispossessed, who had overwhelmingly voted for him. In Houston, the election served as a political awakening of the growing black masses. Approximately 75 percent of the registered black voters supported Kennedy. The 1960 census revealed the immutable fact that Houston was an enormous, ethnically diverse city that had benefited from the sustained effects of modernization and urbanization. It was, by 1960, the fourth-largest city in the country, and blacks constituted more than 22.9 percent of its population. The rising crime rate and escalation of social activism outraged the majority of citizens, who demanded police protection.

In a symbiotic motion, these factors clashed with the conservative values of police managers, who coveted the support of elites. Using the fear of rising crime and racial upheaval to legitimize police aggression for the public good, local authorities turned their backs as the HPD clamped down on activism. The department's reaction to social upheaval was similar to police attitudes found throughout the nation, and police and community relations were under close scrutiny by social and political activists.[5]

A generation gap in perspective and attitude between new recruits and older officers produced tension. Like other police departments, the HPD was mired in traditionalism, and it refused to accommodate modern attitudes or opinions. This led to difficulties between line staff or the rank and file that began to penetrate the previously impenetrable core of departmental custom and the police subculture's code of silence.[6] Although some segments of society demanded changes in police conduct and service delivery, the HPD's management retained the support of the majority of Houston's growing population, who feared 1960s-type radicalism.

In 1960, the population of Harris County exceeded one million. The major stimulus for this population growth was industrial development. Employment surged as manufacturing output in the city reached record levels. The Houston ship channel continued to be one of the premier ports in the nation and ranked fourth in tonnage shipped in 1960.[7] The petrochemical industry remained the primary growth sector for the entire Gulf Coast region. Industrial output made Houston the showplace among southern states. The city was led by Mayor Lewis Cutrer, who served from 1958 to 1963, and Harris County was headed by the eccentric Judge Roy Hofheinz, who was helping make Houston Space City, USA, by encouraging the aerospace and petrochemical industries.[8]

The city's annexation of new territory also fueled population growth. The state's liberal annexation laws helped increase the city's area from 75 to 390 square miles. Houston aggressively sought the lucrative tax dollars of the surrounding communities. In fact, Mayor Cutrer committed political suicide in 1963 when he announced his opposition to more annexation. Understaffed police and fire departments were overwhelmed by annexations between 1954 and 1967. Moreover, the city council failed to provide appropriate guidance. It was divided over the issue and only slowly appropriated funds to increase public services in the late 1950s.

In 1960, Carl Shuptrine was chief of the police department, which consisted of 740 police officers, 97 percent of whom were white males whose ingrained patriarchal attitudes favored the use of traditional police practices and the maintenance of traditional attitudes and customs. The expansion of the department also increased the HPD's bureaucracy, which in 1960 consisted of eight bureaus and ten divisions, with an annual budget of $8,344,600.[9] The department also included 20 blacks and 30 female officers who believed that police service was a steppingstone for professional advancement.[10] Although such numbers were significant for a southern police force, the department's demographics still did not reflect the city's diversity. When measured by the FBI law enforcement standard of 2.3 police officers per 1,000 citizens, the size of the force continued to be inadequate for the population of Houston.

The growth of the city eventually benefited the police department. The average patrol officer's salary was $385 per month in 1960, which compared unfavorably with industrial salaries in the Houston area. Police service was viewed as a job for those who could not do anything else. What applicants found most appealing as they tried to join the HPD was job stability and authority. Low salaries, however, affected morale.

Amid the glittering haze of prosperity stood the antiquated notions of Jim Crow and the belief of some in unquestioned police authority. The city council and police had difficulty fathoming even the simplest of changes. For example, in June, 1960, Councilman Johnny Goyen had to convince the city council to approve the issuance of cotton shirts for police patrol officers to wear during the summer, instead of the year-round wool uniform.[11] This issue suggested how difficult it was for the city to accept even the simplest of changes within the department.

Houston was in fact two cities: one rich and prosperous and the other desperately poor and violent. The evolutionary changes of the prospering city were on a collision course with the HPD's role as the self-appointed guardian of morality and the patron saint of Jim Crow practices. John L. Cooper notes that "the role of police in the ghetto is beset with ambiguities, not the least of which is: What should be their function?"[12] As I have noted, it was particularly difficult for the HPD to accept change of any kind, but change in the area of race was especially hard.

As societal expectations changed, the department's attitude that it was the upholder of society's morals created problems for the force. Some minorities in the 1960s were looking for a new police force, one that could prevent crime while maintaining standards of justice and fairness for all the citizenry. Police conduct fell more and more out of step with prevailing attitudes. Members of the force increasingly came under fire for brutality and corruption.

The first storm of controversy in the 1960s again revolved around the issue of police brutality. The HPD had a reputation for brutality and aggressive behavior toward suspected violators of the law. Chief Shuptrine told a Harris County grand jury investigating police brutality related to traffic violations in 1962 that a policeman "ought to have the wisdom of Solomon, the nobility of a saint and the brawn of Hercules." That same year, the HPD claimed that there were 102 cases of aggravated assault against police officers. A concerned U.S. attorney, Woodrow Seals, told an HPD cadet class in April, 1962, that "the protection of individual rights is the foundation of the Constitution; if you don't uphold the Constitution, we have no democracy." Prominent Houston defense attorney Leon Jaworski had reminded another class in 1960 that "policemen must protect the poor as well the rich, the good as well as the bad."[13] The HPD, however, failed to heed these admonishments. Orderly and sufficient service extension for the poor would have to wait.

In June, 1963, Chief Shuptrine resigned amid mounting pressures over his inability to reduce the crime rate and sharp criticism over a shortage of officers. Understanding his limitations, he left to take over as head of the Port of Houston police. He was temporarily succeeded by Hobson "Buddy" McGill, the night police inspector, who did not want the job permanently. While this drama played out, inspector of police Herman Short waited anxiously for his chance to lead the force. As Short waited, the HPD nearly doubled in size, from 740 officers in 1960 to 1,216 in 1963, or 1.20 officers per 1,000 citizens. Yet despite this impressive growth, the police-to-citizen-ratio was less than half the FBI's recommended standard of 2.50 police per 1,000 citizens. When Houston's police ratio was compared to that of 36 other cities of 300,000 or more, it averaged 1.75 officers per 1,000, while the five cities as large as Houston averaged 2.91 police per 1,000 (see Table 3).[14] This was a historical problem for the HPD, which saw large budget increases during the period but could not attain the recommended ratio or solve the crime problem (see Table 4). Houston became one of the most violent cities in America in terms of its murder rate.

The pressures of Houston's modernization created an estrangement between the police and society. The alienation felt by the police caused them to begin creating a police subculture that was armed with an impenetrable code of silence and an ambiguous understanding of the law and their changing role in society. One local historian recalls a former CID captain saying that "we don't break the law protecting society, but we do push it to the limit."[15] According to Ed Cray, the police wanted complete control of law enforcement and to be unfettered by civilian oversight.[16] When confronted with outsiders interfering with their function, the police set themselves apart from the society they served.

Table 3. *Ratio of Police Officers to Citizens, Houston, 1968–77*

Year	*No. Police Officers*	*No. Police Officers/ 1,000 Population*
1968	1,438	1.22
1969	1,578	1.31
1970	1,662	1.35
1971	1,788	1.42
1972	1,969	1.52
1973	2,146	1.62
1974	2,253	1.67
1975	2,491	1.80
1976	2,671	1.89
1977	2,840	1.97

Source: Tax Research Association of Greater Houston and Harris County, "Houston Police Department," September 1977, vol. 30, no. 8, 2.

In the 1950s, it had become clear to police professionals that a police subculture had emerged. The idea was first articulated by Chicago's police superintendent, O. W. Wilson, who argued that the code of silence and alienation felt by police separated them from ordinary citizens.[17] The police believed that society was moving in a direction they did not care to go, so they developed a police-against-the-world mind-set.

Each municipal area had its own variant of police culture. The head of the HPD's Technical Services, who was responsible for radio's operational and support equipment, Insp. Larry Fultz, observed, "I don't think the community image of a policeman has a damaging effect on a policeman's personality. I think he lives in the narrow perspective of his role in the community and the democratic demands made on him."[18]

James Q. Wilson suggests that the pressures of a changing society made police feel the need to develop a police "subculture" or "code" that helped them fight their feelings of alienation. Wilson sees two major causes for this alienation: "The Pariah feeling and the man in the middle feeling. The Pariah performs a social function of the highest importance but he will not be given an appropriately high status even if successful."[19] Police personalized the shift of societal attitudes, and their actions suggested that they loathed some segments of society. In Houston, alienation and a growing conviction among some police officers that they were upholding moral standards in an immoral society led to volatile confrontations and the repression of the rights of some groups.

Consistently understaffed and under closer public scrutiny, police forces nationally and HPD in particular circled their wagons when they perceived an outside threat. Jerome Skolnick, an expert on police violence, suggests that "police had a negative view of the communities they policed. Moreover, police broadly viewed crime and narrowly viewed societal pressures that led to crime and disorder." In other words, the police saw many of those whom they policed as rotten apples, as inherently criminal. Low morale, changing expectations, and inadequate numbers and resources only exacerbated such feelings.[20]

By 1963, fears of a rapidly rising crime rate plagued Houstonians, who demanded more police. In a vain effort to soothe public fears,

Table 4. *Annual Appropriation, Houston Police Department, 1960–73*

Year	*Appropriation*	*% Increase*
1960	$7,164,894	
1961	$7,508,420	4.8
1962	$7,948,485	6.1
1963	$8,432,167	6.1
1964	$10,708,227	7.3
1965	$11,489,445	10.3
1966	$12,667,302	9.8
1967	$13,909,222	25.7
1968	$17,485,997	11.2
1969	$19,437,062	19.8
1970	$23,276,145	3.4
1971	$24,078,819	15.1
1972	$27,722,185	15.2
1973	$31,941,289	15.4

Source: City of Houston, General Budget, 1960–73.

Mayor Cutrer proclaimed that he would like to add 200 cadets a year to the force. The *Houston Post* pointed out that because the HPD lost an average of 60 officers per year, his plan would mean a net gain of only 140. The mayor was harshly criticized by the city council for failing to increase the size of the force to acceptable levels. To his credit, however, the force actually doubled between 1960 and 1963, but by now he had fallen from grace with the press for some of his controversial positions on annexation, the police, and water rights. Thus the sharp rise in violent crime weakened Cutrer's chances of reelection in 1963.[21]

The mayoral race that year boiled down to Cutrer and former councilman Louie Welch. In a futile effort to garner support from the police department, Cutrer responded to the fears over the rising crime rate by appointing police inspector Herman Short as interim chief. Welch, the veteran politician, however, won the election. A master of political double-talk, Welch was adept at the politics of control and complacency. While on the city council, he had been a painful thorn in Cutrer's side as he constantly criticized the mayor's actions or inaction and made the public skeptical of Cutrer's ability to continue to lead the city.[22]

In 1964, Mayor-elect Welch, a "strategic moderate," was personally and politically a middle-of-the-road Texas conservative who understood the benefits of being politically ambiguous on issues. The mayor needed the support of the police to protect vital interests in the city, and he, astutely, affirmed Herman Short, a right-wing conservative, as the forty-third chief of the Houston Police Department. This ensured Welch's control of the city and the loyalty of the department. Short was a "pragmatic racist" who at times resembled Houston's version of Eugene "Bull" Connor, but he distinguished himself from the latter by understanding the need for the police department to direct its own transformation, rather than have change imposed on it by outside forces.

Short was born in West Virginia and moved to Houston at age seven with his parents. After graduating from Milby High School in the Houston Independent School District, he served a two-year stint in the U.S. Coast Guard before joining the HPD in 1946. He worked his way through the ranks to captain and then inspector of police.[23] He was viewed by his men as hard but fair, though at times he was uncompromising and stubborn. Yet in his own way, he possessed tremendous political savvy in handling Houston's elites. Through manipulation and coercion, he maintained control of the police force longer than any chief before him. In a department marked by complacency and traditionalism, he won the unquestioned loyalty of many of the white officers. Although well respected by many officers, he was equally despised by others who served under him.

Short brought unprecedented stability to the HPD's management. His law-and-order, no-nonsense approach and his insistence on traditionalism, however, ultimately led to controversy in a city beset with social change. In spite of Short's aggressive resistance to racial change, the Houston Police Department under his leadership made some positive strides in its painful process of transformation. It refined its bureaucratic structure, increased its tactical-weapons strength, added more officers, and experienced several dramatic increases in its budget, all of which did little to lower the city's crime rate.

Like many bureaucrats of his generation, Short attempted to control or moderate the effects of change on the department. His passivity in the face of repressive actions by the HPD reinforced an emerging public perception of police antipathy toward some of the communities they served. As the civil rights movement challenged the archaic system of racial segregation throughout the South, the HPD revealed a steadfast unwillingness to alter traditional practices and attitudes formed under Jim Crow. The police department drew a line in the sand and resisted societal demands for greater accountability, largely because deeply entrenched racial attitudes could not allow for negotiating with minorities.

The fears generated by the rising crime rate conflicted with the demands for social change and greater police accountability. During this period of high social volatility, many in the city's growing minority community saw the police as provocateurs rather than protectors, as enemies rather than allies. In a shrewd manner, Short used the rising crime rate to minimize the legitimacy of local protests. Interestingly, he was able time and time again to secure increases in appropriations and moderate increases in the number of police officers.

Short's aggressive rhetoric and promises to control crime initially pleased the business elite. He pledged to provide additional police protection and encouraged businesses to use trained police as off-duty security. As the crime rate rose in the city in the 1960s, police clamped down on some citizens. These methods angered some and created socially volatile situations. As time passed, more citizens levied allegations of brutality against the police department, accusing it of being unresponsive to the entire population. Like his predecessors, Short took no decisive action to curb police violence. He shrewdly attributed crime to the erosion of morality whenever there was an adverse reaction to police indiscretion.[24]

During this era, fear gripped America as the social and political climate quickly shifted and riots erupted in city after city. Racial violence in 1964 in Watts and in 1965 in Newark indicated discontent.[25] Following Watts and Newark, police chiefs from all over the country feared violence and destruction. The notion of extending civil rights to blacks was difficult for police officers to accept as well; the fine line between basic constitutional rights and liberty was obscured by police perceptions of the movement as unlawful.

Potential urban civil disorder was the central theme during the 1964 meeting of the International Association of Chiefs of Police, in Louisville, Kentucky. Pres. Daniel D. C. Liu, chief of police for Honolulu, Hawaii, apocalyptically emphasized to the body that "the social fabric of the United States is bound to be strained dangerously in the next few years by the implications of the new Civil Rights Law now on the books. For our American way of life to continue, for freedom to continue, security must be maintained by the legally constituted authorities."[26] In a paper entitled "Crowd Control in a Period of Social Change," Cincinnati's police chief argued that "the social unrest forming in the wake of the desegregation movement in our nation amplifies the challenge the police address in the maintenance of law and order."[27]

Nationally, police viewed social change as a subversive threat to democracy. Their reaction to the country's changing social mood revealed the ambiguity surrounding the policing function and a growing sense of alienation in the ranks. As Skolnick has argued, police forces functioned as either "peace officers concerned with public order or patrolmen detectives concerned with enforcing the law."[28]

Nationally, by 1964, municipalities had prepared for potential civil disorder. Locally, police simply tried to maintain law and order, giving little thought to the prevention of crime. Houston, like other major cities, instituted riot control training. Harris County district attorney Carol Vance published the "Handbook for Civil Disorders," outlining the laws and legal procedures for local authorities to follow in the event of riot conditions. In keeping with the national training initiative, the HPD required all officers to undergo in-service training unless their shift prohibited them from attending. Chief Short declared to the press and the city council that he had total control of the city—and its "Negroes"—in the event of unrest.

By 1964, black communities in the larger metropolitan areas had exclaimed to America with violent clarity that they were changing the focus of their struggle. This phase of the movement clearly divided the nation along generational lines. Some youths quickly and violently raised their struggle from the gradualist legal discourse for equality to a de facto war for dignity, respect, and empowerment within their respective communities.

In 1964, local tensions began to surface in Houston. The pressures of generational demands for change boiled over in a minor rock-and-debris-throwing incident at Houston's Texas College for Negroes, now known as Texas Southern University. The HPD quickly dispatched police to the scene and, with an extreme show of force, arrested 512 students. More important, they indelibly stamped in the minds of protesters the cost of civil disobedience. Fortunately for Short, the local movement had not yet developed a central focus, and aggressive police action suppressed the students. His actions affirmed to the city's leadership that he could control the "Negroes."

By the late 1960s, societal discontent had reached its apex. Minor complaints and grievances exploded into passionate protest that brought violent police repression. The escalation of the Vietnam War, the antiwar movement, anxiety over the draft, and social and political alienation among minorities and youths in general served as a powerful undercurrent for change.[29] Each one threatened cultural homogeneity and Jim Crowism and caused a dramatic shift in the consciousness of the nation.

In response to liberalism, police nationwide became a more reactive force hell-bent on controlling the pace of change. Locally, however, Houston's constant growth and the ever-increasing need for labor, as well as the willingness of the business elite to compromise in order to keep protest at a minimally intrusive level, helped spare the city from destructive social unrest. Houston's favorable economic conditions and fragile coalitions between white and black elites kept protest and protesters within limits acceptable to conservatives. Moreover, most blacks had jobs, though they were lower in status and pay than those of their white counterparts.

Houston's emerging black leaders, however, challenged the supremacy of gradualists like black millionaire businessman Hobart Taylor and civic leader Quinton Meese, who had helped control the community through coalitions with white business elites during the 1950s. Taylor and Meese had considerable influence during the 1950s and the early 1960s, forging agreements through biracial coalitions with members of the downtown merchants to quietly integrate select business establishments there. That deal, as discussed earlier, denied full access to most minorities and was a pact with the devil that bought segregationist time and spared the city the damaging effects of an economic boycott.

In 1967, however, many of the city's institutions that had quietly integrated saw more direct contact or socialization between the races, which, for the most part, remained segregated. Local establishments still discriminated against blacks and Mexican Americans. Some stores refused them the right to try on undergarments in women's departments and hats in some men's stores. Younger blacks also complained about being followed through stores by clerks and security as soon as they entered the door. In addition, they were angry over the quiet agreement made by the earlier biracial coalitions. Local newspapers had agreed at the time not to report the agreement, thus averting the spreading of the news to the masses. This action took part of the momentum out of the local movement in 1960.[30] Now the younger generation challenged discrimination at another level, which, if effective, would force merchants to understand black buying power.

Between 1966 and 1967, blacks publicly complained about police injustices and brutality. The police scrambled to understand why blacks were now so vocal and hostile toward the law. In March, 1966, Mayor Louie Welch said that he "would seek ways of resolving problems in police relations with Negro citizens." He agreed to a meeting with community leaders after a new group of black leaders emerged, questioning the city's commitment to integration. Among the new leaders was the Rev. D. Leon Everett II, pastor of the New Jerusalem Baptist Church and head of the Metropolitan Council of the NAACP. After meeting with the mayor, Everett said, "I think the meeting was good, and that a confrontation of sorts happened. There was communication, I think that more meetings, not necessarily with the same people, would be a help." Another community leader, the Rev. John Sanders, rector of St. James Episcopal Church, said, "I think there was recognition that there is more unrest among Negroes than the administration heretofore was willing to admit." He added, "The idea was getting across that there could be another Watts."[31] Houston's leaders did not want a race riot, and they embarked on a campaign to control or neutralize all social agitation.

At the heart of the platform of the emerging leadership was their political alienation from city politics and the abuse of blacks by the police. Despite the dialogue, Mayor Welch did not see the same problems. He stated that "hunger and unemployment have a great deal to do with unrest" and suggested that those factors were not present in Houston.[32] His comments reveal the serious gap in perception that existed between whites and Negroes in the city.

Despite poor police-community relations, Houston, as noted earlier, had avoided most of the destructive demonstrations and civil unrest that had occurred nationally. Nevertheless, racial and social tensions escalated. As blacks discovered their political power, they worked harder to rally the community around central issues. Concerned city officials responded to community pressures in March, 1966. Welch publicly acknowledged that "43 cases were cited where disciplinary action had been taken against white officers in handling black cases."[33] Although no specific details were given regarding the officers' actions, this was an obvious public relations ploy to ease tensions and pacify blacks. It failed, however, as community-police relations continued to deteriorate.

National events helped shape local attitudes and actions, but until 1967, there was no hard racist image of the city to galvanize support for black leaders. But poverty, police abuses, and political alienation served as powerful stimuli for social agitation. As Robert Bullard has shown, blacks in Houston were disproportionately poor and less likely to own their home in the 1960s.[34] The federal census of 1970 reveals that over 70 percent of blacks in Houston still rented their homes, compared with 43 percent of whites. Even though more blacks were voting in Houston, they still did not have political influence because of the way the city had created at-large voting districts, which left blacks vulnerable to policy decisions by white politicians who could easily win citywide elections.[35]

The contrast between the abject poverty of many blacks and the unimaginable affluence of some whites more adversely affected younger blacks. Their frustrations generated feelings of powerlessness and fostered perceptions of hopelessness. Seeing no way out, and ignorant of their political and economic options, violence became the black youths' feeble cry for change—immediate change. Police inability to control the crime rate angered the black community as well as the white community. On June 17, 1966, the *Houston Chronicle* reported, "Houston Ranks Fifth in Top Murder Cities" of the fifteen largest cities surveyed in the first three months of the year. Only Dallas and New Orleans had smaller police forces. Blacks displayed ambivalence by demanding effective police protection while at the same time calling for protection from police persecution. Many blacks complained that the police "concentrated on protecting the white communities rather than the minority communities in which residents are more likely to be victims of crime."[36] Complicating matters was the HPD's failure to create a positive relationship with Houston's black community.

Police fears of an angry black community forgetting its "place" were actualized between 1967 and 1970. But police perceptions of a homogeneous black community proved wrong. By 1967, a serious rift had developed in most civil rights organizations and had splintered communities. Police efforts to pressure activist leaders simply accelerated the rage of the larger black community, which was now increasingly fragmented by age and politics.

From March, 1965, to September, 1967, the National Advisory Commission on Civil Disorders reported 104 urban riots/civil disorders, which led to 130 killings, over 3,500 injuries, 29,000 arrests, 5,434 convictions, and approximately $450 million worth of damage in the United States. Nationally, the major cause of the riots during the period was frustration with economic realities and extreme hopelessness. Blacks constituted 21,770 of the 29,000 persons arrested in association with the riots. Of the 130 people killed, 78 were black, most of whom were young males shot by police.[37] This led to immediate demands for change from blacks and whites.

These conditions led to even more militant demands for immediate change from youths, and their impatience served the civil rights movement well. Young people, still linked to the organized movement through reverence and respect, focused their rage on visible images of Jim Crow racial subordination. Nationally, the passionate impulses of black youths led to their rejection of both gradualism and theoretical nonviolence.[38] But for the charisma of Martin Luther King Jr., the youths would have completely abandoned the movement. Legislation had failed to provide constitutional guarantees and had not immediately changed their present realities. According to Norman Coombs, "it soon became clear, . . . the passage of the civil right acts was not the victory which would end conflict."[39]

In their hostile resistance to the extension of liberty and justice to blacks, the police demonstrated to black youths that they could not be trusted. The black community's changing perception of self led to a demand for respect. This shift in perception legitimized black rage and created the subtle nuances of a new form of black pride.[40] Out of this grew the "Black Power chant," which served as the anthem of the youth movement and led to an explosion of anger and rage.

"Black Power" was a motivational chant introduced by Stokeley Carmichael in 1966.[41] Young blacks in the cities and on college campuses began to define their own identity. Many rejected being called "Negroes" and identified their black identity through the birth of Black Pride and Black Power. Black Pride and Black Power could not be given to them; it had to be earned. Consequently, youths around the country sought to change their own realities by expressing a new militant sense of black consciousness.

Black consciousness also reflected the national law enforcement reaction to urban protest. James Baldwin writes that the police "move through . . . like an occupying soldier in a bitterly hostile country."[42] In response to this type of repressive police presence came the motivational chant, "Black Power." The "new Negro" and the "old police" were well acquainted with each other. When the police clamped down on black activists and activism, they only made things worse.

The black community was invigorated by the emergence of new leaders and an apparently fearless ground swell of new activism; however, the change in tactics and attitudes also ignited the fears of Houston's white community, which had reacted violently to liberalism in the past. Although the new activism was more rhetoric than substance, it touched off the primal fears of white Americans and raised to new heights police resolve to destroy it. It also reawakened the patriarchal desires of the older black community to control black youth because they feared that white allies would hold them accountable for the actions and rage of black youth.[43]

On May 16–17, 1967, the new Black Power collided with traditional police power as students at Houston's Texas Southern University clashed with the Houston Police Department in an incident later referred to by the HPD as the "TSU Riot."[44] The events began as a demonstration of frustration and ended in a police riot that would forever change the city. The fears of the community at large validated the HPD's repressive reaction to activism.

Many older leaders in Houston's black community fretfully tried to understand the basis of the youths' militant protest as they also tried to assure the city's white leaders that they could handle the problems in their communities. But the dynamics of the relationship between those who desired to lead and those who led changed from accommodation and marginalization to confrontation. Tragically, older leaders who had paved the way for the present struggle often became objects of scorn and indignation for the new generation, which viewed them as timid and too afraid of white folks to push for change now!

The roots of confrontation took hold as the university experienced a change in leadership. In the fall of 1966, former TSU president James Nabrit had retired and interim president J. A. Pierce had assumed control. Like many from his generation, President Pierce did not question the authority of whites. In the American South, black leaders had come to understand the penalty for forgetting their place. As a result, some blacks of his generation accepted the limits imposed on their reality by those who ruled in order to ensure economic support for their institutions. Deferential to whites, Pierce was characterized by the radical students as reactionary, rigid, and inflexible. Former student Donald Jefferson recalled that those were "some angry Negroes."[45] University registrar John Westbury recalled that the "student body was tremendously diverse but most of the students were from the Houston area."[46] There were few students from other states or countries, so the uneasy climate on the campus could not be attributed to outside agitation.[47]

The administration's desire to control the students caused it to ignore and trivialize their grievances. Pierce believed that he was acting in the best interests of TSU, as he simply wanted to maintain control and save himself and the university from embarrassment and the scorn of the ruling white elite. His rigid, heavy-handed leadership set the stage for confrontations between students and the administration. Clearly generational in nature, his perception of how whites would view unrest at TSU represented a larger problem in the black community: some older blacks were more worried about what the ruling white elite in the city would think than about the legitimacy of the issues that precipitated the students' actions.

The first sign of the impending conflict appeared when students calling themselves the "Friends of SNCC" organized in the fall semester of 1966.[48] On January 7, 1967, the group sought official recognition as a campus organization for the spring semester. On January 20, 1967, James B. Jones, dean of students, responded by advising the three organizers of the Friends of SNCC that they must first secure a faculty adviser.[49] According to university regulations, the organization would receive official recognition from the university if it met the conditions set forth in a letter from dean of students Jones: "We require that organizations seeking approval supply the following: 1. Copy of proposed constitution which must specify requirements for membership, dues to be paid and the regular meeting schedule. 2. List of officers and a faculty sponsor."[50]

The students chose political science assistant professor Mack H. Jones as their sponsor. As a student at Southern University in Baton Rouge, Louisiana, Jones had been suspended for his involvement in civil rights protests. He transferred to Texas Southern, where he received his undergraduate degree and also participated in acts of civil disobedience. Jones was hired at Texas Southern in the fall of 1966 by Henry Bullock, chairman of the Social Sciences Division, over the objections of the aging chairman of the Political Science Department, Henry Tsiang. As Jones recalled, "I came to TSU to work with Bullock, [who] I felt really cared for the students."[51]

According to Jones, the students really were not that politically active prior to 1967. He accepted the position of faculty adviser of the Friends of SNCC, which was led by F. D. Kirkpatrick, Millard Lowe, and Lee Otis Johnson. Kirkpatrick was a graduate student in sociology, and Millard Lowe was a decorated Vietnam War veteran. Lee Otis Johnson was characterized by some as "the kind of brother you take to a fight with you" and by others as a "loudmouth." Jones characterized Millard Lowe as "the kind of brother that you need when you are organizing a movement, because he could really rally the students with his loud rhetoric." Kirkpatrick, the most colorful of the trio, came to the university as a former member of the militant Deacons for Defense in Louisiana. Jones remembered that "Kirk [Kirkpatrick] was a likable brother, but hard to figure where he actually stood on issues."[52]

The administration automatically singled out these men as potential troublemakers. Although the TSU administration allowed the Friends of SNCC to meet on campus, it never officially recognized the group. The administration helped keep surveillance on the group for the police department by allowing Friends of SNCC to hold public meetings in the Religious Center on campus.

Much of the fear surrounding the group was unwarranted, because it had no mass following and did not attract other radicals at Texas Southern. The tensions leading to the unrest were systemic and had little to do with the actions of the organization. The unrest was, rather, the result of fear on the part of the administration and black students' frustration over conditions at Texas Southern and in Houston. Vernon Hunt, a TSU student in 1967, recalled that "most students didn't pay them any attention."[53]

In 1967, black students and urbanites all over the country were stepping outside their fear of the police, which, to the black community, increasingly represented the enforcement arm of the oppressor, not the benevolent arm of the protector. This was certainly the case in Houston, where the police under Chief Herman Short had a history of brutality against blacks. Now a group of students inspired Houston's black community to demand "Police Protection without Brutality or Contempt."[54]

On March 8, 1967, the Friends of SNCC called for a mass meeting to be held near the TSU campus at the YMCA on Wheeler Avenue. The topic of the meeting, according to a memorandum announcing it, was "Police Brutality Throughout the State of Texas." The group accused the "state highway patrol" of beating four gospel singers. According to the memorandum, one of the singers alleged that during the beating "the trooper remarked that he had killed one Nigger and was dying to kill two more Niggers."[55]

The student memorandum was indeed inflammatory. After all, black communities knew all too well what police brutality meant. This action would increase the level of institutional fear among students, who sought to broaden the protest to include community and antiwar issues. In the flier, the students exhorted the black people of Houston to join in the fight against police brutality:

> Week after week our people are slaughtered like cattle in the butcher pens and the highway patrolmen, city and county policemen are the slaughterers. Everyday hundreds of our own black brothers and children are drafted to fight in a war, thousands of miles from home; while at home another form of violence is perpetuated by white Americans against the Negro people. Police brutality is a threat to each of us from sunup to sundown, while driving to work and play. Police brutality

means the deadening pain of our mothers, wives, brothers and children. It is the hurt and anguish in the heart of men beaten for no reason and forced to pay for it with taxes.[56]

Even though the meeting was off campus, the university responded via letter, dated March 11, 1967, from Dean James Jones's office asking that the "Friends of SNCC and Mack Jones meet for lunch to discuss the March 8th rally." Following the meeting the organization was banned from using university facilities.[57] Mack Jones recalled that the meeting "was a joke. They [the administration] already had their minds made up."[58] The group was also permanently barred from using university property. The administration seemed to pull farther away from the community of which it was a part; the students believed that their destiny linked them to the larger black community.

On March 15, 1967, in an effort to avoid future problems with the Friends of SNCC, the administration also fired its faculty adviser, Mack Jones. In the termination letter, it informed Jones that, "due to budget reductions and the hiring of too many political scientists with international relations specialities, they would not be able to renew his contract."[59] This action only widened the gap between the university and the students. It also prompted more student activism in the wider Houston community. Ironically, on March 10, 1967, Jones had already accepted the job as head of the Political Science Department at Atlanta University. Although he had expected to be fired, when he heard of the dismissal, he "was still shocked nonetheless at the administration's lack of professionalism." He recalled that "the administration tried to hold us [the faculty] responsible for what the students did . . . I could not control them and more importantly I would not [have] anyway."[60]

The suspension of the Friends of SNCC and the firing of Mack Jones made things worse at TSU. The students circulated a flier condemning the dismissal. Even students and faculty who had remained relatively quiet for most of the academic year questioned the president's actions. Jones's firing sparked activism among faculty members, who openly confronted the president over the action. In a meeting on March 30, 1967, a faculty committee headed by the chairman of the Art Department, John Biggers, unanimously passed a motion demanding a review of the facts in Jones's dismissal.[61] It also radicalized the students, spurring many who had not been involved to action.

The administration again stalled while frustration grew on campus. Police stepped up surveillance, detailing every move of student activists. On the morning of March 8,1967, students closed the university for two hours by boycotting all classes and by lying in on Wheeler Avenue, effectively closing the street to traffic.[62] The administration hurriedly tried to fix the problem. Dean Jones again stalled the students and avoided a full boycott of classes on March 29 by agreeing to reconsider Jones's fate, but the administration failed to act.

On April 1, the disappointed students boycotted classes, locked the exit doors in campus buildings, and blocked Wheeler Avenue again. The majority of the students on campus refused to participate in the boycott, even though they sympathized with their fellow students, because they feared the consequences of their actions.[63] Ironically, much of the credit for ending the boycott went to the fired professor. Mack Jones told the students, "I am concerned that things could develop in a manner that we would not be proud of." He gently reproached them when he said, "You ought not let yourself to be led around," and "I hope you conduct yourselves so you do not leave yourselves open to any violence by the police."[64]

Nervous city leaders called Chief Short, who assured them that things were under control. After consultation with Short, Mayor Welch approved warrants for the arrests of the leaders of the class boycott. Justice of the Peace Jack A. Treadway signed vaguely worded warrants based on a complaint signed by Acting President Pierce, which requested the men's arrest.[65] These warrants infringed on the students' First Amendment right of free speech. On April 3, 1967, despite only minor damages and minimal support from the student body, Short arrested the leaders of the Friends of SNCC who were present at the boycott, along with Franklin Alexander of the DuBois Club.[66] In an even more inflammatory action, the court set a bond of $25,000 for each man. Although suspended campus organizer Lee Otis Johnson was not present at the earlier boycott or rally, an arrest warrant was also issued for him. He was arrested as he led a march of approximately 750 students and activists on the Harris County Jail on April 4, 1967.[67] His fate became a symbol to students and others of a police department out of control.

Jones stated that "on the next day [April 5] the administration was called on the carpet by the Mayor's office."[68] The Houston Police Department increased its presence in and around TSU with undercover and plainclothes officers. Short's provocative actions had angered the students. The Rev. Bill Lawson the pastor of the nearby Wheeler Avenue Baptist Church suggested that "this action by the police was designed to control and deter the students, but it only made matters worse."[69] TSU students began to throw debris at passing motorists they felt were staring at them as they drove down Wheeler Avenue.

On April 5, 1967, Justice of the Peace Jack A. Treadway and District Attorney Carol Vance informed the *Houston Post* that they were "ready and willing to proceed Thursday on the question of whether three jailed leaders of the Texas Southern University student protests will continue to remain in jail under $25,000 bonds."[70] The hearing shook the men; the threat of remaining in jail and even of being convicted frightened them.

Lee Otis Johnson had actually been released on a $1,000 personal property bond prior to the hearing, which raised questions concerning the legitimacy of the original charges against him. According to him, after his release from jail, "we had already accomplished what we set out to do on campus. This was not just a campus movement. This is a city and state movement that reaches all across the nation. This is a liberation of the black mind. The black mind has been white-oriented."[71] Johnson was correct; it was a movement of the black mind. While the men were in jail, the students of TSU continued to protest.[72] On the morning of April 7, Kirkpatrick and Alexander were each released on $1,000 peace bonds. Under the conditions of the peace bond, the men had to refrain for one year from activities that would lead to arrest.[73]

Then on May 12, 1967, Stokeley Carmichael spoke to a crowd on TSU's campus. Kirkpatrick claimed that he had invited the fiery leader, but it appears that Carmichael was on a national tour to test support for a united black front. After a stop at the University of Houston, where Carmichael electrified the integrated crowd, he spoke at Texas Southern, where he left the campus as he had found it. He did not push the students beyond controllable limits. According to Barbara Jones, the "students were already ready to explode" and "Stokeley could not have stirred the fire any hotter than it already was at TSU."[74]

On May 16, groups of TSU students demonstrated at two locations, Northwood Junior High School and the Holmes Road dump. The Reverend Lawson recalled that the police really got rough with the protesters at both sites. Lawson himself was arrested at the Holmes Road protest. According to him, Mayor Welch had assured the city council earlier in the day that the students would be controlled if a conflict broke out.[75]

On hearing of the arrests at the earlier protests at Texas Southern University and the dump, students angrily roamed the campus as if looking for direction. The HPD angered the crowd when officers arrested Douglas W. Waller, a known student leader, who was found with a weapon in his possession. The arrest came as he tried to rally students around 10:30 P.M. to protest at the Holmes Road dump. Waller was charged with "loitering and possession of a weapon."[76]

In a more provocative move, Short placed patrol units on the periphery of the campus and ordered them to drive through the campus at regular intervals. They had been on campus long enough to understand what type of reaction their presence would cause. Former police officer Bobby Blaylock said, "For two or three months, I spent more time at TSU than I did at home."[77] Another officer, Al Blair, recalled that "we knew everything they were doing on campus before it happened."[78]

As the students roamed around TSU's campus, the police prepared for a potential assault on the protesters. At approximately 8:00 P.M., the HPD assembled the troops in full riot gear near TSU, at Jeppessen Stadium on the University of Houston campus. As the police presence increased on campus, the students threw debris and watermelon rinds at the police cars and at curious whites driving through campus. The police were already dressed in riot gear and stationed a few blocks away when the order came to move in. The campus was sealed off around 11:30 P.M. The police drew their line in the sand. A battle was sure to come, but when? Mack Jones stated that the "police were ready for a fight, not a truce."[79]

As a last-ditch effort to avert the riot, the mayor released William Lawson, Earl Allen, and F. D. Kirkpatrick from jail. They were to be taken to a dormitory on campus to talk to the students. But they "never reached the dormitory," according to Lawson. The "police started shooting before we went in." Lawson further stated that the "police ran over our backs charging the dormitory."[80]

HPD officers fired over five thousand rounds into the dormitory. One officer was killed and another wounded in the gun battle. Officer Ronald Kuba, a rookie only thirty-four days out of the police academy, was initially reported to have been shot in the head by a sniper, but later investigations revealed that he was actually hit in the forehead or right temple by a ricocheting bullet fired by another police officer. He was struck and lay in a pool of blood near Lanier Hall. The *Houston Post* headline on May 18,1967, "34 Days," rallied public support around the slain officer. Miraculously, no student was seriously injured during the mêlée.

Police responded with heightened aggression following the shooting of Officer Kuba. As they entered the dormitory that had been barricaded by the students, they went berserk, destroying everything in their path. HPD's official, nonpublic report insisted that "the students at TSU destroyed their own personal effects."[81] Kirkpatrick, one of the leaders of the Friends of SNCC, did not join his fellow students. Instead, he legitimized the HPD's actions on the night of the riot by telling the *Houston Chronicle* that the police "did the right thing, the only thing that they could do." Eyewitnesses, however, contradicted him, saying that the police smashed property and beat students at random. Bob Wolfe, a local television cameraman, reported that "police treated those who didn't resist fairly, but heaven help those that did."[82]

Although police actions during the assault on the dorm were reprehensible, mainstream press coverage of the incident provided the community with misinformation and vilified the students. The selective reporting of the facts validated police conduct in the eyes of the public. Whites felt that the police were justified in their assault on the dorm in order to restore order. On May 18, 1967, Rep. George H. W. Bush entered the fray by suggesting that "our police department acted swiftly and prudently Tuesday night to quell a disturbance which has upset our entire community and caused the death of one of our fine police officers."[83]

The African American press and city officials were openly hostile toward each other. According to the mayor, blacks were creating fear of and hostility toward the police and the city. Therefore, he did not allow representatives of the black press into city briefings. When a white writer for the *Forward Times*, the city's second-largest black-owned newspaper, questioned the mayor regarding the exclusion of black journalists, Welch accused the black press of fanning the flames of discontent. The anger of the black press was evident, but it was no more inflammatory than the white press. Bill Lawson wrote in the *Forward Times*, "It has been called a riot, but most of the ingredients of a riot were absent. There was no evidence of looting . . . there was no evidence of widespread resistance to arrest, even though brutality by police was painfully obvious."[84]

Nationally, police actions and reporting of incidents were similar in areas where other student protests occurred. Police responses on other black college campuses had deadly results. On February 8,1968, the police killed three black students and shot twenty-seven others at South Carolina State College in Orangeburg. Then on May 16, 1970, police killed two black students and wounded twelve at Jackson State College in Jackson, Mississippi.[85]

Local reaction in the wake of the riot heightened tensions in the city. Short labeled the students as criminals and pushed for the speedy trial of the "T.S.U. Five": Charles Freeman, age twenty; Douglass Waller, twenty-one; Trazawell Franklin Jr., twenty-one; John Parker, twenty; and Floyd Nichols, twenty-five. They were arrested and held on $10,000 bond for inciting a riot that led to the death of Ronald Kuba.[86] They were charged under the riot statutes of the Texas Penal Code, which held that those who incited a riot could be charged with any and all crimes that occurred as a result. This rarely used statute was broadly written and vague as to the responsibility of police. Moreover, the preemptive action of the police actually served as a catalyst for the events of the night. On June 10,1967, Dr. Pierce informed the *Forward Times* that "25 students including the five charged have been suspended or expelled since the riot because their performances were not in the interest of the university."[87] Following the riot, only the semester break saved the university from the angry students.

The state pressed its case against the TSU Five, charging them with inciting a riot. In 1968, Charles Freeman was tried in Victoria, Texas, on assault charges for the injuries that Officer Blaylock sustained during the riot. The trial ended in a mistrial, and the judge dropped the "inciting a riot" charge. None of the TSU Five served time for the events of May 16–17, 1967. They faded into obscurity, but paid a heavy emotional and personal toll for their militancy. Moreover, the justice system sent a clear and unmistakable message to young black activists: if you engage in social agitation, you will be taken off the streets.

The aftermath of the riots transformed many communities of Negroes into communities of black people striving for self-determination. Don L. Lee stated the aims of black radicals in a poem entitled "Integration": "I seek the integration of Negroes, with black people."[88] Some young blacks saw themselves as different from the established leadership within their community, and by 1967 they were identifying themselves as black. However, to many within the HPD they were still "niggers" whose protests could not be allowed to exceed acceptable limits as defined by the traditions of Jim Crow.

Police response to social conditions in Houston also carried with it a desire to maintain a system of racial subordination. Blacks who wanted to stop police violence worked through the formation of grassroots organizations. The police found that they were no longer impervious to criticism by blacks and responded with increased levels of brutality after the TSU Riot. The HPD tried to stymie future protest by imposing a near–police state in minority communities; however, as allegations of brutality increased, Chief Short was reported in the *Houston Post* as saying that the HPD had disciplined sixty-seven officers for uttering racial slurs and being offensive to minorities in August, 1967.[89]

The issue of police brutality polarized the city. Many whites felt that police conduct was appropriate, and they validated police violence as a necessary consequence of ensuring safer streets. The use of intimidation by police was an extralegal means of controlling society, and many segments of society, especially blacks, grew more distrustful of it. While they desired police protection, they wanted it free of abuse. This spurred the creation of loose organizations that applied subtle but persistent pressure to prevent crime, but also to ensure respect from the police who served their communities. Yet many police officers believed that all blacks hated policemen, despite James Q. Wilson's findings that "the single most striking fact about the attitudes of citizens black and white toward the police is that in general these attitudes are positive, and not negative."[90]

Police were myopically responding to an emerging vocal minority throughout the nation that was "composed of the young," who felt the sting of police "justice" as police around the nation responded aggressively to social change.[91] Their actions reflected the generation gap alluded to earlier. Police forces could not comprehend why society was changing so rapidly. They were specifically angered by the limitations placed on them by the U.S. Supreme Court in *Mapp v. Ohio* (1961) and *Miranda v. Arizona* (1966).[92] The Court sought to end what it viewed as egregious violations of individual rights. Police across the nation responded with dismay and contempt for what they felt was a liberal swing of the courts that gave undue rights to the criminal. The High Court's affirmation of individual and civil rights created a new social reality that broadened democracy's promise and placed new expectations on the police. The rise of societal intolerance of aberrant police behavior required a higher level of professionalism in departments where it did not exist. The police shifted the blame for this solely onto radicals.

In 1968, the mood of the nation changed as graphic and horrific scenes of the escalating Vietnam conflict created a tempest of social unrest at home. Local politicians legitimized police violence by publicly calling rioters "lawbreakers and mad dogs."[93] In response to aggressive social unrest, some states implemented a shoot-to-kill policy for looters, but Mayor Welch issued no such order, insisting that "it is up to the police to handle lawlessness as they see fit."[94]

The Houston police acted on these feelings of alienation by using increasing levels of brutality. Public indignation over police brutality was slowed by rising fears about the city's crime rate, but in the aftermath of the riot at TSU, the police engaged in acts of brutality that caused a gradual reassessment of the policing function. On December 7, 1968, HPD officers allegedly beat two handcuffed suspects in front of witnesses. After an investigation, Chief Short suspended the officers involved, but they were exonerated by a Harris County grand jury on September 9, 1969.[95] A second case, on December 7, involved Mexican national Manuel Romas, who alleged that the police beat him during the arrest of his wife for a misdemeanor charge. The officers were again acquitted. Some Mexican American activists decried the injustice of the jury's decision.

The beating of Johnny Coward, a black youth approximately twenty years old, from Houston's Third Ward, raised the question of police brutality within the white community. He was also alleged to be a member of the People's Party Number II, the local Black Panther affiliate. Three things were different in the Coward case: his age and prior history with the HPD; the level of brutality; and the involvement of the FBI. In 1968, Coward was kicked so hard during a scuffle with police that he lost sight in his left eye. Two officers were charged, and Coward was charged with assaulting a police officer. (Countercharges served as offsetting liabilities in cases of alleged brutality.) The savagery of the offense and a national outcry over police abuses prompted the FBI to act. Its investigation led to the officers being charged, although they were later acquitted.

The community's fear level rose and fell with the police's ability to control crime. Using a media blitz, Short tried to shift most of the responsibility for the rising crime rate onto the community. In commenting on the case, he defined crime as the source of moral degeneracy, with control of crime dependent on good citizens controlling their children. Following his remarks, there was an increase in vigilantism among business owners. The local press reported that citizens were arming themselves to protect their homes and businesses. By August, 1969, Short's frustration was showing, as he blamed the rise in crime on the decline of morality in Houston. The HPD published local crime statistics to incite fear and to gain support by showing the high arrest rates in minority areas of the city.[96]

Rising crime was a national problem directly attributable to the rising poverty rate. In addressing the issue, James Q. Wilson claims that "during the 1960s we were becoming two societies—one affluent and worried, the other pathological and predatory."[97] The FBI reported on August 13, 1969, that crime rose 28 percent during 1968 in the Houston area. As control of the city eroded because of crime and social malaise, police methods clashed with modernization and police training lagged behind new expectations. The police went to extraordinary lengths to control some segments of local society and even broke the law to remove some activists from the community. Moreover, a generational problem within the HPD became evident as older officers who had received little or no in-service training were transferred to new duty areas that included minority populations.

The arrest and conviction of Lee Otis Johnson, a student leader at TSU who was convicted for possession of marijuana and sentenced to thirty years, provides an example of police injustice. Johnson, a vocal opponent of racial subordination and a fiery orator for black rights, paid a high price for challenging the system. On May 18, 1969, the *Houston Chronicle* revealed that many whites in Houston felt the thirty-year sentence was justified, while younger whites and blacks felt it was politically motivated. Blacks responded by increasing pressure on the mayor to fire Short. *Houston Post* writer Bob Tuft wrote on May 20, 1969, that "Welch sees no cause for Short's resignation."[98] Councilman Bob Webb blamed Welch for the police shortage and claimed that something had to be done about crime.

Chief Short approached the city council for funds for a helicopter and more tactical weapons. The council approved the expenditures over the objections of Webb, who felt the money and helicopters were a waste of city resources. But Short used the fear of crime and social unrest to generate support for his proposed expenditures. Despite his efforts, however, he was unable to increase the size of the force significantly, though he continued to receive increases in appropriations from City Council (see Table 4). The HPD even reduced the requirements for police recruitment in order to attract more minority police officers.[99] The police force increased from 1,438 to 1,578, but it was still too small to control the city.[100] The chief particularly raised community fears of the rise of Black Power and the appearance of the Black Panthers, a loosely knit group of affiliated organizations around the nation that joined to challenge the police and local authorities.

Police departments responded to threats and chants of Black Power with increased surveillance, covert operations, and increases in tactical-weapons strength. Black Power was reviled by the local establishment, which was willing to push the limits of the law to control it. The police feared the rhetoric of Black Power, which, like other youth-led movements, heightened the fears of local communities. Moreover, the apprehension of parents validated the use of violence by police, who used any means necessary to restore order. A by-product of the rise in black consciousness, Black Power invigorated neglected urban youth, moving them to action. Police reacted as if local blacks who aligned themselves with Black Power had violated their personal space.

Allen Matusow argues that the Black Power movement was all but dead by 1969 and lacked cohesion as early as 1967,[101] but it left a legacy of important cultural and political symbolism. It inspired those who subscribed to it and brought black nationalism to the consciousness of many who feared it while empowering others to stand up and demand their rights.

National reaction to the Black Panthers manifested itself through hero worship or mind-numbing fear. Some blacks even considered them a sinking ship of angry fools, and whites thought of them as a menace to the decency and morality of America. Their self-determination aim, however, was lost in rhetoric, and their effectiveness was destroyed by infighting and a failure to understand the visceral reactions they created in traditional America.

The police went to extreme lengths to monitor, control, and neutralize left-wing radicals. Through the use of undercover operatives, illegal wiretaps, and informants, they gathered data on blacks and other so-called radicals. Police CID and undercover operations were stepped up during periods of high social agitation with the full support of the U.S. attorney general and the instruction of the FBI.[102]

The HPD was no different as it increased surveillance of minority communities between 1966 and 1972. This surveillance, which was mostly carried out by undercover operatives and informants, provided valuable information about the community and its actions. Houston's affiliated Black Panther Party, or the Peoples Party Number II, was led by twenty-one-year-old Carl Bernard Hampton, a native of Pleasantville, Texas, an enclave community along the Houston ship channel.[103] When the Panthers boldly warned the city that they would not yield to disrespectful police on the public streets, Short verbally sparred with them and insisted that the "citizens of Houston will have full and free access to all public streets."[104] Nationally, the Black Panthers' rhetoric challenged police and showed contempt for their authority, leading some black leaders to cooperate with the police out of a dual fear of radicalism and angry verbal attacks on them by the young radicals.

Herman Short saw Black Power as an egregious assault on the police and on the moral order and decency of the city. He received the green light to control the Panthers and other radicals from a citizenry worried about their potentially violent nature. He and the police CID commander used surveillance and informants to detail every move of the Panthers. They gained keen insights into the group's daily activities from its 2828 Dowling Street headquarters. When a warrant was issued for Hampton for possession of a weapon, Short and Mayor Welch made the decision to arrest him and disrupt the activities of the Peoples Party Number II.

The press made members' home addresses and family histories front page news. Right-wing organizations such as the John Birch Society and the Sons of the American Revolution publicly offered their unqualified support to the police. Chief Short received the Man of the Year award from the Sons of the American Revolution in 1970. According to Chandler Davidson, "perhaps the best indication of Short's legal philosophy was the statement by his personal friend, Governor George Wallace of Alabama, that Wallace would install someone like Short as FBI director if he became president."[105]

Police brutality surfaced as the catalyst of conflict between black revolutionaries, other local leaders, and the police. The Panthers underestimated the determination of the police to control the community. Through use of effective surveillance, the HPD was aware of their every move, as noted earlier. The HPD and the Peoples Party Number II engaged in a series of small conflicts, which led to "the fatal shooting of the group's chairman, 21 year old Carl Bernard Hampton."[106]

The July 27, 1971, the "Dowling Street shootout," as it came to be called, climaxed a cycle from violence to repression of black radicalism.

Late Sunday, after church services, police fired from St. John's Baptist Church in Houston's Third Ward, mortally wounding Hampton in the abdomen. Four others were shot and fifty-two people were arrested, most of whom were onlookers.[107] The police were extremely harsh in rounding up citizens who may have witnessed the event.

Black nationalism frightened blacks and whites alike in Houston, but the Dowling Street shootout led to a politically more aggressive black citizenry. Blacks were no longer content merely with election to local school boards and now broadened their political focus. They began successfully competing for state and local offices. Local attorney Barbara Jordan and Curtis Graves had started in 1966 to press local election officials to change the at-large system in Harris County. Short advised the police to keep an eye on Jordan for her own good. She had been unsuccessful in earlier runs for public office, but won a seat to the Texas Senate in 1967. Her election set the stage for a new breed of bolder political leader.

The political rise of blacks was a result of the energizing changes created by civil protest and grassroots activism in Houston. In 1971, the citywide election of Judson Robinson Jr., a black man, to the city council shocked the establishment. As Chandler Davidson points out, "the target for most Negro leaders' wrath was Herman Short."[108] Barbara Jordan, Robinson, and black state representative Curtis Graves pushed Mayor Welch to remove the chief. Welch refused, however, dismissing any talk of removing Short as "incoherent babbling."[109]

Robinson's election opened the door for the fight for local reapportionment and the rise of minority political power. By 1972, Welch had decided not to seek reelection, in part because of his sense that he had lost black support. The HPD's overzealousness and aberrant conduct in some communities had hastened a shift in the level of community acceptance of police racism and brutality on the part of public servants.

In 1973, Herman Short resigned after the election of liberal Mayor Fred Hofheinz. Short did not trust the mayor-elect and the coalition that helped elect him. Moreover, Short had completely lost touch with the community, as he believed the city was in the hands of communist-led liberals. His nearly ten-year tenure as chief ended when he felt that he could no longer effectively control the changing city without being questioned and without the full support of the elites who now distanced themselves from him. His continuing right-wing affiliations made him, in the view of the city's elites, a political liability. Although he had loathed federal interference in local affairs, his conduct had opened the department up to FBI scrutiny and hurt the image of Space City. Short left the department in 1973, convinced that he had done his best and that the city was on its way to hell if it did not regain its moral strength. To his credit, Short had been a capable and efficient police administrator. In his mind, the department was his to control and the city was his to protect at any cost. In the end, he failed to compromise and became a prisoner of his own racist convictions as a new set of political demands to end racial subordination were presented.

After Short's resignation, the HPD's leadership was tentative and unstable. Five men served as chief between 1973 and 1980. The demands for greater police accountability and cooperation were seen as "antipolice" by the HPD, which became increasingly reactionary. In the absence of strong and flexible leadership, the department could not move in a different direction. It spun out of control, without dynamic leadership and with a dwindling supply of political allies, creating an inescapably negative image to overcome.

I can truthfully say that there is no more racism in the Houston Police Department.

—POLICE CHIEF B. G. "PAPPY" BOND

CHAPTER 4 "What a Mess We Have Here"

Chaos with the Breakdown of Leadership in the Police Department, 1973–78

The police in America were besieged in the 1970s with demands for change from outraged citizens, who felt that the police had lost control. At times, the violent reactions of police departments to social change set the stage for dramatic and brutal confrontations. The HPD was no different; it was as if they were about to lose their minds.

While traditional racial attitudes within the HPD continued to shape practices and procedures, some police officers internalized these racist attitudes and projected them outwardly at a wider sampling of citizens. Herman Short's retirement left an unstable, unprofessional, and unfocused bureaucracy, which led to a series of controversial and sensational developments that grew out of the department's maintenance of traditional attitudes and racist practices. Minority communities responded by calling for an end to police repression and brutality. Many within the HPD commiserated with one another, however, about the development of what they regarded as antipolice attitudes in the city. They refused to see these as a logical reaction by an informed and enlightened citizenry appalled by continual violent police behavior.

This chapter examines the HPD from 1973 through 1977, one of the most turbulent and chaotic periods in the department's history. Aggressive and brutal behavior by the police led to a series of local controversies that redefined the department's public image. These tragedies dramatically altered the public's perception of the department, changing how some viewed the authority of the police. The HPD unraveled at the highest levels when Police Chief Carrol Lynn was convicted of felony obstruction of justice and bribery charges. Assistant Chief W. L. Williams was convicted of income tax evasion on earnings he received from a contract security job he ran from his HPD office. The shootings of two white suburban youths, Billy Keith Joyvies and Randy Webster, and the ensuing cover-up raised questions about police procedures and training. In both shootings, the officers used throw-down guns to hide procedural mistakes.

The most highly publicized case of police brutality occurred with the savage beating and drowning of José Campos Torres. During the investigation, police antipathy toward the Mexican American community led to the Moody Park riot. This event served as a catalyst for Mexican American activism and political organization, which found a common voice in protests against an unyielding HPD.

During this period, the HPD lost any sense of restraint. It acted like an alienated "Big Brother" gone wild, conducting illegal surveillance on both "mainstream elected and appointed officials, along with more ordinary folks."[1] Improved methods of mass communication increased public awareness of official misconduct, and the police reacted. They also came under closer scrutiny by the press, federal crime commissions, and the FBI.[2] Public concern about police attitudes and practices was aired in federal court and congressional committee hearings. In the face of mounting pressure for reform and impending changes, many top police bureaucrats resigned rather than face a political culture in chaos.

During the 1973 mayoral election, political moderate and attorney Fred Hofheinz emerged as the front-runner in a race with Dick Gottlieb. Many within the HPD viewed the upcoming election as a referendum on the police and cast Hofheinz in the role of liberal reformer.[3] This prompted some whites in the department to campaign against him; however, he prevailed with powerful backing from the business elite and black voters. Indeed, Gottlieb angrily asserted that Hofheinz was "a desperately ambitious young politician" who focused his campaign on the black community. By campaigning and talking to black leaders, Hofheinz had, according to Gottlieb, actually emulated Welch's campaign style from the 1971 race for mayor, which Hofheinz had lost to Welch.[4] By suggesting that police reforms were imminent, Hofheinz convinced the city's black voters that he would be sensitive to their needs. Whites, especially southern white politicians and racists, had long feared a monolithic black vote. They believed that the black community was homogeneous and its vote could easily be manipulated.

Chief Short made it clear that he would resign if Hofheinz was elected. According to Louis Marchiafava, Short "seemed to have lost interest in the job, leading up to and during the campaign." He was a noticeably changed man "following the death of his wife in an auto-pedestrian accident."[5] Some HPD insiders intimated that the chief was working an extra job as a real estate agent in his last months in office.[6]

Short's last years as chief revealed a serious generational issue in American culture, one that placed World War II–era police managers at odds with the changing needs of society. Some managers, who had served from the 1940s through the 1960s, resigned to pursue other avenues or stood firm in tough law-and-order stances in defense of police professionalism. Such was the case of Chief William Parker of Los Angeles, who became known as the "J. Edgar Hoover of municipal policing."[7] Short emulated Parker's war on crime, and local minorities were the enemy.

In 1973, Herman Short resigned as chief of the Houston Police Department, ending the department's longest period of stable management. A competent administrator, Short was at the same time one of the most loathed and most respected individuals in Houston's history—a polarizing figure in a polarized time. Former Mayor Fred Hofheinz characterized him in an interview as "a real bad man."[8] A former mayoral adviser and political lobbyist, George Strong, recalled, "When we were campaigning, I felt that Short was an evil racist. But after we had been in office and I was assigned the police department by the mayor, I realized that Short was a racist in some things, but he held the police department together."[9]

Short's resignation created a leadership void that deteriorated into chaos, managerial incompetence, and nasty controversies that worsened the HPD's image. Like many other police managers in other cities, Short had lost touch with the changing social and political reality. He had been particularly unwilling to meet with minority leaders, because he felt it showed weakness and because "most minority leaders were mostly cowards."[10] His stubbornness and racial biases had helped make the HPD a caldron of racism. Thus, he and his department became a political liability for some of the people who had supported them. When, in 1973, Mayor Louie Welch, a longtime Short supporter, announced his retirement from city politics in 1974, a liberal shift began in local politics, which indirectly led to Short's resignation.

Despite his racist reputation, Chief Short's retirement was an ominous sign for the city. Even though he was an unyieldingly conservative "law and order" proponent, he had been extremely effective at maintaining some control of the police force and had made significant strides in HPD's bureaucratic development. No other chief until the 1980s could control the police department and advance its public image.

On January 3, 1974, Mayor Fred Hofheinz appointed Carrol Milton Lynn as the forty-fifth Chief of Police of the Houston Police Department.[11] According to George Strong, "the mayor was trying to find someone that did not have skeletons in his closet that would hurt the city, and would work on changing the force."[12]

A bureaucrat for most of his career, Lynn was regarded by the press as a "moderate reformer" like mayor-elect Hofheinz. Lynn had joined the force in 1960 after service in the army. He moved through the ranks to captain, settling in personnel at the police academy.[13] Many officers on the force felt that he was weak and corruptible. He had neither Short's political savvy nor the respect of the force that he needed to control the fractious Houston Police Department. Mayor Hofheinz later reflected, "As I tried to democratize the police department, the chief acted like a crazy man."[14]

Lynn's mental state affected his approach to managing the force. He knew his officers viewed him as incompetent and perhaps even paranoid. As Strong recalled, "The chief would call me and ask me to meet him in an alley to discuss problems. I asked him why? He said they were out to get us."[15]

The size of the force had dramatically increased since 1964, the first year of Short's tenure. When Lynn assumed command in 1973, the HPD consisted of 2,146 police officers and 698 civilian employees (see Table 3).[16] Yet the growing population required an ever-increasing police-to-citizen ratio to meet the FBI standard. Houston's population topped 1.4 million in 1974, and the city's area increased to approximately 503.33 square miles, making the existing police force woefully inadequate.[17] The perennial problem of too few officers to serve a growing population became critical as crime continued to spiral out of control. This prompted a rise in citizens' fears and raised important questions regarding police competence and accountability.

More by accident than by design, a more racially and ethnically diverse force emerged in the 1970s. As a direct result of the city's changing demographics, the HPD experienced a dramatic shift in the number of nonwhite males—especially Mexican Americans—on the force. Women and blacks also benefited from the relaxing of the HPD's height and weight requirements, first in 1969 and again in the 1970s.[18] Minorities were still limited in terms of internal advancement. Blacks turned to the Civil Service Division, which became an important vehicle for change (see Table 5).

In 1973, Dorothy Edwards, a black patrolwoman, sued the department, alleging that the HPD's promotional and testing system discriminated against blacks. Her complaint charged that the testing methods were biased and that whites had an unfair advantage because of the sharing of answers and the wording of entrance and promotional exams. In the early 1990s, she won her suit, paving the way for more

Table 5. *Houston Police Officers, by Race, 1970–80*

Year	*Total No. Officers*	*No. White Officers*	*% of Total*	*No. Black Officers*	*% of Total*	*No. Mexican Officers*	*% of Total*
1950	354	338	95.5	13	3.7	3	0.08
1960	1,158	1,117	96.5	36	3.1	5	0.04
1970	1,662	1,589	95.6	60	3.6	13	0.08
1980	2,481	1,820	73.4	240	9.7	421	17.0

Source: Houston Police Department, Budget, 1950–80. The term "Mexican" was used by the department to refer to all officers of Latin heritage until 1980.

Note: Percentages may not add to 100 because of rounding.

significant change in recruitment, training, and retention of minority applicants.

George Strong remembered one conversation with police officials regarding the exams, and, according to him, the police asked questions that had nothing to do with being a police officer. He added that "they were trying to exclude minorities with probing and deceptive questions."[19] Clarence Bradford, an African American who became chief of police in 1997, said that the "Edwards case was the most important labor-relations case in the department's history."[20]

Although the Edwards case was not decided by the courts for over ten years, it prompted the HPD to begin promoting minorities. In an apparent effort to ameliorate a potential court mandate to settle the suit, the HPD promoted the first blacks to the rank of patrol sergeant in 1974. These men, J. C. Hartman and R. C. Humphrey, became the first blacks to have supervisory authority in the department. Many other blacks followed their lead and took promotion exams that they might not have taken otherwise. Sgt. Freddie Guidry, an African American, said that his attempt to secure a promotion was "a mental thing; you have to want it, you have to hunger after it."[21]

During the growth and diversification of the force, Lynn tried to present himself as a capable administrator in order to win allies. He emphasized that he wanted to "change existing policy for promotions in order to give younger guys a chance." His policies affected the promotional opportunities of some members of the department who felt that he had abandoned the traditional practice that had favored whites. He also alienated others in the local law enforcement community and the establishment. *Houston Chronicle* staff writer Phyllis Splitter recalls that "during Lynn's tenure as Chief, he had scrapes with Sheriff Jack Heard, city councilmen, the Houston Police Officers Association and the news media."[22]

Lynn's actions also reopened the dormant jurisdictional battles between the HPD and the Harris County Sheriff's Department. Sheriff Heard had police work in his background. In the 1930s, his father, Chief Percy Heard, was one of the first police reformers in Houston, and the sheriff himself had worked for the HPD in the 1950s, before he left to work for the Texas Department of Corrections. There was bad blood between the Houston Police Department and the Harris County Sheriff's Department, which had squabbled for years over control of law enforcement in Houston. However, as the city grew through annexation, the Sheriff's Department lost any hope of controlling law enforcement in Harris County because of urban sprawl.

Lynn's personal feelings of alienation brought out his insecurities and revealed his deep resentment toward those in the Houston law enforcement community who he felt did not respect him. His inability to overcome his personal animosities doomed his career. His choice of enemies also isolated him. Lacking the support of the media, which had covered the police positively during most of Short's tenure, and the HPOA, which had deferred to Short, Lynn had no effective advocates on his side.

On February 15, 1974, Chief Lynn placed HPD patrolmen Wayne Jones and Jack Heard Jr. (the sheriff's son) on indefinite suspension without adequate evidence to support allegations of sexually abusing a prostitute.[23] A dismayed Jack Heard Sr. said of the chief's actions, "The entire matter should be taken to the grand jury." He added that his son and Jones "were being charged in a rape in which there is no complaint, and they are being treated as criminals when no criminal action is being taken."[24]

Lynn's insecurities and long-held hostilities toward some on the force and the Harris County sheriff led him to pick the wrong fight. He could have waited for Harris County district attorney, Carol Vance, a friend of the sheriff, and HPD investigators to levy charges against the men. His actions—directed at Sheriff Jack Heard Sr.—severely damaged the decades-old coalitions between city and Harris County authorities. The chief's haste placed the department in an adversarial position with the county and alienated those who might have supported him when his own personal and legal problems arose.

Lynn's social limitations and lack of bureaucratic savvy were only part of the problem. He had inherited the serious problem of managing an unruly and institutionally racist department that wanted to maintain its traditional behavior. The fragmentation of the force actually began during the last years of Short's tenure, when the number of HPD substations and bureaus increased. The growth of the force and the creation of subspecializations through bureaucratization pitted some divisions against others. The creation of Master Districts revealed how police were deployed by district. This reorganization increased tensions in the department, because each substation tried to outshine the others.

The officers' lack of respect for and trust in Lynn, combined with his insecurities and abrasiveness, weakened his credibility and gave the HPOA a much-needed forum in which to air its grievances. Lynn's weaknesses and managerial infighting breathed new life into the union, which had been ineffective as a collective bargaining unit until Lynn's appointment. All other issues in the city, including the demands for black police officers, became subordinate issues to the force.

While the union argued with management, low morale produced a powerful undercurrent of tension between the rank and file and management. Race again became an issue when the HPOA protested the promotion of minorities they regarded as unqualified.

Nothing fueled the flames of discontent, however, as much as the internal bickering of the HPD's managers. Lynn foolishly attacked some managers, vowing to replace some and reassign others. The chief was expected to make appointments, but many officers felt that Lynn had cast aside protocol. Many in the department believed that he had replaced competent officers with officers who were less qualified. Lynn tried to control dissension by indiscriminately firing and disciplining officers for improper conduct, but he infuriated many on the force, who felt he denied the fired officers due process. He was in fact removing his critics and trying to force the department to accept his authority.

On February 2, 1974, Lynn shocked the force when he reassigned Assistant Chief Harry Caldwell to night command from the police academy. Lynn alleged that Caldwell "would use the night position to conduct a study of how area police agencies are working together." The chief shuffled other positions, but none of his actions seemed as vindictive as Caldwell's replacement with T. D. Mitchell as head of staff development.[25] Caldwell had been placed at the helm of the training academy in 1971 by Short, who later lamented that he "regretted putting Caldwell in charge."[26]

The replacement of Caldwell, who was both a veteran officer and an academic, hurt the department's training programs. Under his direction, the department had made significant strides toward improving training and methodology. Caldwell also had refined practices that ran counter to the changing social mores of the community. Under his leadership, a pressing issue for the department had been to find more applicants with college credits, in an attempt to improve the performance and situational/discretional responses of officers. Most important, the HPD had opened its new state-of-the-art training facility, the L. D. Morrison Police Training Academy, at Rankin Road and Aldine-Westfield Road.

The chief continued to make questionable staff reassignments. On August 17,1974, he suspended Deputy Chief W. L. Williams for insubordination. In a highly publicized series of events, Williams, who had never been disciplined, said he "was surprised to hear that he had been suspended from the press." A stunned Williams informed the media that "there is not so much as an oral reprimand in my file."[27]

Although these personnel actions were within the scope of the chief's authority, they were the first in a quick succession of events in which Lynn exercised poor decision making. His desire to exert control over dissenters within the ranks and to win supporters backfired, however, because he was viewed by some in the HPD as a person who challenged traditional practices. But the chief broke the law by gathering information on his officers and local politicians with illegal wiretaps. Mayor Hofheinz recalled that "the chief recorded folks' conversations without their knowledge."[28] Although the practice was widespread in law enforcement, Lynn was singled out and held personally culpable.[29]

In the meantime, external pressures for police reform accelerated across the nation. Locally, the new police academy gave the department time to make reforms by creating new programs and employing new technologies. This was particularly helpful for the HPD, since the new Texas Commission on Law Enforcement Officer Standards and Education (TCLEOSE) and the federal Law Enforcement Assistance Administration (LEAA) were developing guidelines to eliminate police training inconsistencies and to determine the probable causes of urban clashes between citizens and law enforcement. The dual issues of police misconduct and inadequate training concerned officials at the national and state levels, and the two organizations were trying to explain the relationship between police misconduct and citizen unrest.[30]

Through the LEAA, federal authorities tried to implement industry-wide training standards and guidelines for all police forces. Stuart Scheingold reports that the federal government committed over $30 billion for crime prevention, research, and training programs from 1978 through the 1980s.[31] Nationally, police agencies accepted federal dollars to support their war on crime. This invited federal oversight into local affairs, something that Herman Short had vehemently opposed: "I do not want any money from the federal government because they will try and run your department."[32]

Following the riots of the 1960s, however, many southern law enforcement agencies, which had avoided federal assistance, actively sought federal grants. In the 1970s, many municipal police forces' reform efforts were nothing more than shrewd ploys to extract funding from the federal government rather than sincere attempts to implement change. One problem, according to James Q. Wilson, was that the LEAA advisory committees were almost exclusively composed of academics whose idealism made them gullible.[33]

The availability of federal dollars caused Texas to address its reform issues through TCLEOSE, which set new standards for law enforcement officers in the state.[34] Training and development dollars were awarded by federal officials who were trying to find ways to curb rising crime. In the past, the HPD had avoided federal aid, but now it began to covet it. However, along with the aid came federal oversight and guidelines. The department's negative image, shaped by its brutal legacy and criminal acts by some on the force, attracted the attention of federal authorities.

In spite of the HPD's superficial efforts at reform, criminality at the highest levels shaped the department's image and drew federal authorities into HPD affairs. Perhaps because of his zeal, Lynn's actions led to serious legal troubles that overshadowed any effort to change police practice. With few friends left on the force and no allies in the city, he set himself up for the hardest fall of any HPD official ever. On April 20, 1978, Lynn was charged with extortion and obstruction of justice.

In 1976, Lynn had been reassigned by the mayor after overwhelming evidence was discovered, in the form of tape-recorded conversations, that indicated that Lynn might be guilty of obstruction of justice and extortion. His open antagonism toward the mayor's requests for reasonable changes in the department contributed to his reassignment. He had refused to step down as chief while he under investigation, even though his colleague Harry Caldwell urged him to do so. Lynn's so-called friends and confidants testified against him at trial, and he was found guilty and sentenced to ten years in federal prison. After serving approximately eighteen months, Lynn was paroled to Houston and became a paid consultant for Harris County commissioner Squatty Lyons.

In 1976, B. G. "Pappy" Bond succeeded Lynn as the forty-sixth chief of police.[35] Bond was an affable old gentleman, well liked inside and outside the HPD. When he assumed control, he was confronted with lingering stereotypes about the department that hindered its efforts to attract minorities. When questions arose from concerned minority leaders, Bond boldly and disingenuously proclaimed that there "is no more racism in the Houston Police Department."[36] Voicing disappointment with minority recruitment, Bond stated that he had thought he would gather "a lot more cooperation from within the minority community."[37] His lament reveals the complexity of the HPD's racist past. While the department had all the trappings of a modern police force, it was unable to adapt to changing social expectations.

During his tenure as chief, Bond deferred to the force rather than controlling or regulating it. His deliberate manner and attempts to be fair to officers involved in controversial incidents made him appear indecisive. His management style and ability to avoid controversy led him to resign in 1977. The *Houston Chronicle* reported that he was leaving to run for office. George Strong stated that "Pappy Bond was a real nice guy, with a lot of political knowledge."[38] Instead of running for office, however, Bond became head of Tenneco Corporate Security.

On June 5, 1977, Mayor Hofheinz appointed Harry Caldwell as chief of police. Caldwell was perhaps the ablest and most qualified insider to direct the HPD when he succeeded Bond. Caldwell had been a classmate of Bond in the 1953 police academy class. Caldwell was working on his doctorate at Sam Houston State University when he was appointed chief. A jubilant Caldwell stated of his appointment, "All of a sudden, there you are, baby."[39]

He was bright, articulate, deep-voiced, and, according to Strong, "arrogant."[40] He was also a competent administrator and understood the need for accountability. As assistant chief, he had implemented reforms in training and imposed a system of general orders that informed the officers of policy changes and required them to sign a statement affirming that they had read them. He immediately assumed the unpleasant task of purging the department of criminal elements and fired the officers involved in the Torres, Joyvies, and Webster cases. The most embarrassing firing was that of former chief Lynn, who, to protect his pension, had refused to retire after being indicted on felony charges of obstruction of justice and wiretapping. The firings angered many in the department.

Politics again affected the department when Hofheinz chose not to seek reelection. Each modern-era Houston mayor has passed the baton to the next. Hofheinz lent his full support to downtown Chamber of Commerce chairman and businessman Jim McCann. With the backing of the elite and the support of Hofheinz, McCann won the election in

1978. He was forced to respond quickly to the fallout from the police department.

While management irregularities and incompetence surely hurt the department, brutality defined its public image. Once a department whose primary mission was to maintain racial subordination in the city, the HPD was now an entity whose racist attitudes and practices affected all segments of society. During the 1973–77 period, a pernicious wave of criminality engulfed the department, including twenty-eight fatal shootings by officers. The whole department was involved in damage control, as officer after officer was arrested for illegal activities.

The shooting of Billy Keith Joyvies on July 11, 1975, brought police violence to white suburbia and changed the public's perception of HPD aggression. The episode began when the HPD responded to a call for assistance from Harris County reserve deputy constable R. J. Morrow, who had witnessed someone stealing a toolbox from a truck on the North Freeway. Morrow reported, "I shined my bright lights on the suspects and the chase ensued." The suspect led Morrow and the HPD on a thirty-mile chase along the southeast side of the city, at speeds that exceeded ninety miles per hour. The chase ended along the Gulf Freeway at 11:00 p.m, when two officers shot what they said was an armed suspect, later identified as Billy Keith Joyvies.[41]

Accompanying Joyvies was his fifteen-year-old girlfriend, Della Lee Weise. She initially claimed that Joyvies was unarmed, but the officers testified that they feared for their lives because Joyvies fired at them during the chase. Although she would later recant her story, Weise did give legitimacy to the police claim of self-defense when she corroborated police allegations by acknowledging that "Joyvies owned a gun, but she did not know that he had it with him."[42] Although the shooting was originally ruled justifiable, questions lingered for two years. Only pressure from Joyvies's parents kept the case alive.

The HPD promised the Joyvies family a thorough investigation and reassigned the officers involved to desk jobs. Their case, however, hit a dead end and was all but closed when another shooting under similar circumstances occurred on February 8, 1977. This episode resulted in the death of Randy Webster, a white eighteen-year-old.[43] Webster's death renewed interest in the Joyvies investigation. On April 22, 1978, U.S. Attorney Tony Canales said that the FBI was conducting an independent investigation of the 1975 police shooting of Billy Keith Joyvies.[44] The combined effects of the two cases stunned the local community. The department responded by firing the officers involved in both cases.

On the night of the Webster killing, the Park Place substation of the HPD received an auto theft call. Officers Danny Mays and Norval W. Holloway responded, pursuing the suspect in a chase. Mays had served most of his career with the HPD as a traffic officer. He had only recently been transferred to Park Place from the Traffic Division.[45] He had not received any retraining and had not been properly trained in arrest procedures following a high-speed chase.[46] During the long chase, the radio operator told officers involved in the chase that he did not know if the suspect had a gun. However, the officers responding to the call believed that they had heard the dispatcher say that the suspect did have a gun. Adrenaline was high as the chase reached speeds of over eighty miles per hour along Houston's southeast side.

The chase ended when Webster wrecked his van. Officer Mays was the first on the scene. When he approached the van with his weapon drawn, he yelled at the suspect to put his hands out the window. Webster either refused or was too slow in reacting. Also at the scene were Officer Holloway and Sergeant Olin, who approached the van with their weapons drawn. The three men instinctively tried to wrestle Webster to the ground. Sergeant Olin tried to hold his midsection while Mays struck at Webster's head in an effort to subdue him. Mays swung his pistol to strike Webster, whose head whipped around toward the officer. The weapon discharged, striking Webster in the side of the head. The officers panicked. They knew they had shot an unarmed adolescent and that they had made a terrible mistake.

If the incident had ended with the shooting, the officers would have been guilty of negligence. At this point, the event, though tragic, was not feloniously criminal. However, the events that followed made the officers criminally culpable. They sought to cover up the mistake with a throw-down gun. This opened the department up to charges of libel and brought an onslaught of criticism. Moreover, this was the second offense by officers of the Park Place substation in which a white teen-aged male had been shot following a chase.

This time, external pressures on the HPD intensified, as both the FBI and the Texas Rangers responded to demands to look into the facts surrounding the Webster case. According to one officer, the FBI seemed to "investigate us [the HPD] as if we were guilty."[47] A former FBI agent in the Houston area acknowledged that the "HPD had a bad reputation, and the bureau was a bit biased when they came into a case."[48]

Outraged citizens, tired of police brutality, called for a review board to address police actions. According to Monrad Paulsen, the police "have been given a job to do, but we haven't told them what the rules are."[49] The rules of racial etiquette had become obscure to the HPD, whose attitudes and brutal practices, once directed at minorities, now victimized whites. This case also came at a time when the courts began to hold the police culpable for such actions.

These shootings raised critical questions regarding the use of deadly force by the HPD. They also brought the use of throw-down weapons to the attention of the public, which, naturally, questioned the practice. Using deadly force on a suspect fleeing the scene of a crime at night was a long-standing practice within the HPD. Moreover, only recruits were trained in the new procedures, and this lapse was partly to blame for the shootings. Also in the mix was the department's long tradition of aggression.

The HPD was by no means alone in its aggressive use of force in this troubled era. The U.S. Justice Department handled 10,000 complaints between 1970 and 1979 alleging excessive use of deadly force by the police.[50] The proliferation of throw-down guns also reflected changing attitudes on the part of the police and society. In the decade between 1960 and 1970, police killed 1,428 citizens in the line of duty nationally. Many in police work believed that society had lost its respect for authority. In many instances, this meant simply that some citizens refused to passively accept aggressive police procedures and violently resisted, with deadly consequences. Thirteen HPD officers were killed in the line of duty between February 28, 1960, and January 31, 1970. Many police officers responded to the potential threat of overly belligerent prisoners who might resist arrest by carrying extra backup weapons.

The police use of backup weapons as a legitimate response to growing societal violence dates to the 1920s and the 1930s. During Prohibition, police came to fear gangsters, who seemed to have more firepower than the officers did. As the fear became more prevalent, officers began to carry pocket or boot guns as backup weapons. The widespread practice reflected their fear of overly aggressive criminals and the survival mentality of patrol officers.

This was not illegal and, under the circumstances, was quite understandable. Most police officers who carried backup weapons did so out of self-preservation. As the urban population grew, so did the probability that police officers might be involved in fight and lose their primary weapon during a scuffle with a suspect who had lost all fear of authority.

During the 1960s and the 1970s, the mental fallout over changing social values began to weigh on local police forces. Coupled with a perceived decline in respect for authority came heightened expectations of police. These changes in expectations caused many officers to move from self-protection mode to overt criminality. Rather than accept responsibility in a changing social environment, some covered their mistakes and occasional criminal acts with the sinister practice of using throw-down weapons. Police fears were validated in their minds as the courts extended the rights of the accused.

Many police officers entered the 1970s afraid of losing their lives, their jobs, and their freedom if they made mistakes on the job. Many police practices remained the same, as training and retraining lagged behind the needs and expectations of society. Therefore, use of the throw-down gun grew more out of the combination of alienation, fear, and occupational isolation than criminal intent.

Previously, police officers could discharge their weapon in pursuit of anyone who committed any offense at night. But the rules of pursuit changed in the 1960s, before training in most departments offered effective situational solutions for the officer on the street.[51] The HPD used general orders to notify patrol officers that the department had changed the night firing policy: no longer could officers arbitrarily fire at any fleeing suspect; the use of deadly force was permitted only if the officer's life was threatened.[52] These new orders were written and supported by changes in state law limiting the use of deadly force. Although each officer had to sign a statement that he or she had read the policy, no retraining accompanied the general orders. Therefore, only rookies received the appropriate training in weapons discharge; the older officers' practices and methods clashed with new circumstances.

In this changing environment, in 1979, the Joyvies family sued the city of Houston and the police department for negligence in the death of their son. The U.S. attorney tried the case as a civil rights violation. Attorneys for the department put on an effective defense that implied that the officers' perceived threat of death had caused Joyvies's death. Moreover, they asserted that the throw-down gun hid a mistake, not a murder. Their argument was effective enough to convince the judge and sway the jury that Joyvies must have been guilty, because only the guilty run from the police. But the biggest bombshell was that the attorneys convinced the jury that the practice of using throw-downs was not widespread. Additionally, U.S. District Judge John V. Singleton Jr. instructed the jury that it must acquit the defendants on charges of civil rights violations, because the youth was dead when the cover-up occurred and, therefore, they could not have violated his c ivil rights. Joyvies's parents were livid. His mother exclaimed that she could not believe what she had heard.

The Joyvies case would never have come to trial if the police had not replicated similar events in the shooting of Randy Webster on February 8, 1977. Houston's urban sprawl brought unintended consequences, and Randy Webster's case was a classic clash between suburban and urban. Webster's family, unlike the Joyvies family, was awarded a multimillion-dollar settlement, and the officers involved were fired.

As the drama over the Webster and the Joyvies shootings was unfolding, another highly publicized case of police violence rocked the city, and its aftermath signaled a major change in police control in Houston. The Webster and Joyvies cases created an atmosphere of mistrust in the larger community of the police department. People now questioned the integrity of the entire police force, calling them killers and thieves. However, the most profound change was that many white Houstonians mistrusted the police as much as the minorities did.

You take these handcuffs off, and I'll whip all of your asses. You are just a bunch of pigs.

—JOSÉ CAMPOS TORRES

CHAPTER 5 The Storm Clouds of Change

The Death of José Campos Torres and the Emergence of Triracial Politics in Houston, 1978–80

As the drama over the Randy Webster and Billy Keith Joyvies shootings was subsiding, another highly publicized case of police violence rocked the city of Houston. On the night of May 5, 1977, the arrest, beating, and drowning of José Campos Torres brought the storm clouds of change to the city.[1] Torres's death galvanized the politically fragmented Hispanic community, much as the Texas Southern University Riot on May 16–17, 1967, had helped create a more dynamic class of leaders in the African American community.[2] The tragic insignificance of Torres's life catapulted him to martyrdom. He became the ultimate symbol of police racism, injustice, and brutality. His death prompted Houston's mayor, Fred Hofheinz, to say that "something is loose in the city that is an illness, that has infected the police."[3] His death also prompted Vance Muse to observe, "Houston cops—by many standards, are the worst cops in the nation: They are disorganized, corrupt, poorly trained and most pertinent to your fears, over armed and brutal."[4]

Torres's death raised several questions: Did his race play a significant factor in his death? What kind of respect did the police have for Mexican Americans? Did police training and procedures validate this kind of aggression? Why were Torres's actions construed as a threat to police authority? What was the police code of silence? But the most important question was What did his death do to transform Houston's racial ethics?

Torres was born in Houston in 1953 to José Luna Torres and Margaret Torres. He served three years in the army in the Vietnam era, from 1973 to 1976, and was a member of an elite combat unit until his heavy drinking led to repeated arrests. Those who knew him suggested that the more he drank, the worse his temper got. His first sergeant, Donald Myers, observed that "Torres had the potential to be a good soldier, but alcohol got the best of him." Torres's attitude, like that of many returning veterans, was angry and hostile toward authority due to his treatment by a racist society when he returned home. He was particularly angered by the police, who, he felt, harassed Mexicans.[5]

The Mexican population's sustained growth forced the Houston police to make quick, systemic adjustments. The police department had had a "Latin Squad" in the 1930s, but that name had slowly evolved to what the force called the "Mexican Squad" by the 1960s. From 1930 through 1970, the number of Mexican Americans on the force grew faster than the number of African Americans, although it is statistically significant that most of these officers were Mexican or Latino in surname only. Herein lay the root of most of the tensions between the police and the Mexican American community: the Latino officers had no sense of community identity. Furthermore, some of these officers lacked experience and training. Manuel Crespo, for example, was a mortician who was hired and trained as a special detective in the 1930s, but did not follow the promotion track from patrolman to detective. Officers like Crespo provided valuable surveillance and a minimally visible police presence.

Mexican Americans and Mexican nationals frequently felt the sting of the law, particularly from the old Latin Squad. Police in Houston's barrios were, for the most part, reputedly aggressive and brutal. Their presence aroused fear and mistrust. This historical mistrust had intensified by the 1970s. When the city's murder and robbery rate increased in the late 1970s, Chief Caldwell attributed much of the crime to Mexican nationals.[6] Such anti-Mexican attitudes homogenized all Spanish-speaking people into one group—Mexicans—with little distinction among American citizens, Mexican citizens, and people from various other Latin American nations.

The fate of José Campos Torres must be examined within this context. On the night of his arrest and death, Torres had been drinking heavily at the 21 Club, a hole-in-the-wall bar located at 4700 Canal Street, near the Houston ship channel. Torres had been on a twelve-hour drinking binge that put him in a rage. He and the bar manager, Antonio Bela, scuffled when Bela told him to leave and banned him from the bar. During the fight, Bela asked someone to get the police. At approximately 11:35 p.m. the first officer on the scene, M. G. Oropeza, arrived. When he entered the bar, he immediately joined the fracas with Torres, who still refused to leave. The next patrolman, Carless Eugene Elliot, recalled, "We entered the bar and found another officer tussling with the actor, who I later learned was Jose Campos Torres." It took three officers to subdue Torres, whose tenacity and strength, despite his diminutive stature, "turned the arrest into a wrestling match."[7]

The fight with Torres enraged the officers. Jerome Skolnick reminds us that "when a citizen makes an officer sweat to take him into custody, he has created the situation most apt to lead to police indignation and anger."[8] Once subdued, Torres was handcuffed with his hands behind his back and put in the patrol car.[9] Still in a drunken rage, he continued to curse and yell at the officers. Patrolman Joseph James Janish had suggested earlier that they should teach Torres a lesson. As Patrolmen Stephen Orlando and Elliot transported Torres, their adrenaline-fueled rage gave way to seething anger that negated their professionalism. They verbally sparred with the drunken Torres on the way to the police station.

Patrolman Orlando made an impulsive decision to stop the patrol car on the way to the jail. The officers pulled over at 1200 Commerce and ordered the handcuffed prisoner out of the car. This area was later described as a "dead zone or hole, which is an area in cities where police [and other public servants] hideout to relax while on duty."[10] Orlando and Elliot were joined by Patrolmen Terry Wayne Denson, Janish, Louis Kinney, and Glenn Lee Brinkmeyer. Officer Elliot later said that he "thought the men had made a wrong turn." But as they surrounded Torres, who cursed and spit at them, it was clear what they intended to do. Elliot later recalled that he turned away so as not to see the beating of Torres, but emphasized that "they really hit him hard."[11] The officers then placed the suspect in the car and took him to jail.

The patrolmen were still angry when they arrived at the city jail with Torres around 1:15 a.m on May 5. After the jail's duty sergeant made a visual inspection of Torres, he refused to take custody of the prisoner until he had been checked out by a doctor. He ordered them to take Torres to Ben Taub Hospital to have his bloody nose and the cuts on his right leg treated. The HPD had recently changed its policy on accepting wounded prisoners because of allegations of brutality committed by police officers on prisoners who later died or reported serious injuries while they were in the jail. This change in departmental policy was an attempt to reduce the potential liability for mistreating prisoners who were already injured when they entered the jail.

The HPD's reputation for aggression against prisoners was well documented. In fact, several recent and highly publicized events at the jail had spotlighted the need for effective checks and balances by jail administration. Thus, the order to take Torres to the doctor was given to minimize the city's potential liability.

It was late and the angry and tired officers did not want to take Torres to the city's charity hospital and sit all night waiting to see a doctor. They simply wanted to book the suspect and leave. The officers disobeyed the directive and decided to let Torres go after they taught him a lesson. According to the officers, Torres allegedly refused to go to the hospital and be checked by a doctor.[12]

To the officers, Torres was an unruly Mexican who needed to be taught respect. After leaving the jail, Officer Orlando made the decision that proved fatal to Torres, who by now had been reduced to a subhuman level by the officers' prejudice, anger, and ignorance and his intoxication. Orlando radioed the others and told them that they should meet back at 1200 Commerce. There, at the bayou's edge, they intended to give Torres another painful dose of respect and then let him go. According to defiant patrolman Glen Brinkmeyer, "I really wanted to teach Torres a lesson about respecting the law."[13]

The overuse of extreme force during the 1970s to convey the will of the law was an integral part of policing in the United States. The police in general felt that they were being attacked from all sides—the courts, citizens' groups, and the federal government. Police response to protesters continually placed them at odds with the communities they served. The racist attitudes of the officers who arrested Torres grew out of the attitudes that had been fostered during the tenure of Chief Herman Short. This approach was largely reserved for blacks.

The officers assumed that it would be better to punish Torres themselves, since the charges against him were at best only class "A" misdemeanors. Patrolman Denson would later complain that he was tired of seeing the guilty go free and that he felt he had ensured that justice would prevail in the Torres case.

When the officers drove back to the hole along the murky waters of Buffalo Bayou, they betrayed the public trust, and their subsequent actions breached human decency. Officer Denson said that they took Torres to the bayou "to talk to him, reason with him." Once there, they took Torres from the car and took the handcuffs off him. He stood motionless for a moment, and then the officers whipped him for approximately five minutes. Afterwards, they told him that he could go if he could swim his "wet-backed ass across the bayou."[14] They lost all sense of reason as they exhorted Torres, drunk and badly beaten, to swim across Buffalo Bayou. Suddenly, in a flash of rage, Patrolman Denson either pushed or forced Torres to jump into the bayou. The officers spotlighted the water to see if they could locate him and then got in their patrol cars and left.[15]

Rage and prejudice had impaired the judgment of the officers, who apparently did not even consider that Torres was too intoxicated and injured to swim.[16] The lethal combination of alcohol and the severe beating served as Torres's summary execution. After he entered the water and the police lost sight of him, they assumed that he was hiding in the water until they left. When the officers returned to the station, they said that they had let him go because he did not want to see the doctor. Torres was gone, and there was no record of his arrest.[17]

After a little soul searching, rookie patrolman Elliot went back to search for Torres. As Elliot recalled, "I did not see him and feared the worst." He said that he was told by the other officers involved to "keep quiet, because he was as guilty as the others."[18] The code of silence demanded that he remain quiet to protect his fellow officers and not compromise police unity.[19] Torres therefore became a casualty in the war of police against the community, and Elliot became an unwilling accomplice to the murder.

As a web of lies began to envelope the police department, the Torres family, in an ironic twist, called the HPD to report him missing. His aunt, Delores Pérez, called on May 6, and was told by the jail attendants that Torres was not in custody.[20] This was a half-truth in a chorus of lies, but for the moment it was the closest thing to the truth that the Torres family would receive. Because the officers involved had all initially lied about Torres's whereabouts, he was just a missing person. An internal investigation later revealed that the patrolmen gave conflicting accounts of the events that led to Torres's death. In general, those involved said that they had let him go, or they claimed that he had never been in custody in the first place.

Had the officers let Torres go, they would have violated a myriad of internal rules and state laws; thus they were tripped up by their own lies even before the case was made against them. An administrative change in jail procedure would trap the officers, who had forgotten that they had signed Torres in on the Jail Blotter when they went to book him on the night of his death. The Jail Blotter revealed that the officers had lied and that Torres had been in custody.[21] The men had also violated police department procedure and the Texas Code of Criminal Procedure, which states that a prisoner must be brought before a magistrate if arrested for a crime.[22] Thus their discretionary powers ended once they arrested Torres at the 21 Club.

Three days passed before Torres's body was discovered. On May 8, at 1:30 p.m, David Bazer Rzasl, a tour boat operator, discovered a bloated body "floating face up in Buffalo Bayou about one hundred yards upstream from the McKee Street Bridge."[23] Rzasl used his boat to tow the body to shore. Torres "was wearing a T-shirt, green army-type, fatigue pants, jump boots and a belt with an Indian buckle."[24] Because the officers had thrown Torres's wallet in the water after him, there was no identification on the body. Only persistent calls from his relatives alerted authorities that the body might be his.

After hearing a report on the local television station that a body was found in Buffalo Bayou, Torres's aunt called the morgue. She and her husband arrived at the Harris County morgue at 10:30 p.m on May 8 to give a description of the clothing Torres was wearing on the day he disappeared. Due to the body's advanced decomposition, the investigators took the Pérezes' statement but would not let them visually identify the body. Ultimately, Torres was positively identified through fingerprint analysis by the Harris County Sheriff's Department.[25]

The discovery of Torres's body caused an immediate stir in the city. On the morning of May 9, Houston was rocked by the findings of the Harris County medical examiner, Dr. Joseph A. Jachimczyk, whose preliminary coroner's inquest report concluded that no one as drunk or beaten as badly as Torres was could have swum across the bayou. According to the report, Torres died from body asphyxia due to drowning. The cause of death was determined to be "drowning homicide." He had suffered a laceration to the right shin, as well as recent contusions of the right temporalis muscle, dorsum, or right, hand at the wrist, and on both shins. The severity of the beating was evident despite the advanced stages of decomposition of his body. The report further revealed that Torres had been subjected to a savage beating that had caused his body to be bruised from his head to his shins.[26] Dr. Jachimczyk concluded that Torres had died shortly after he entered the bayou.

After the medical examiner ruled Torres's death a homicide, a stunned Houston Police Department administration, on May 10, quickly suspended five of the officers involved. In an even more astonishing move, the Harris County district attorney, Carol Vance, charged Terry W. Denson and Stephen Orlando with murder. The indictment of the three other officers soon followed.

The city was tense and tired of police brutality and impropriety. A contrite chief, B. G. "Pappy" Bond, finally acted: "I have made a decision that I will form a permanent Internal Affairs Division."[27] The new division would investigate allegations of police wrongdoing.

External pressure mounted as officials from the U.S. Justice Department came to Houston and met with Chief Bond on the day of the announcement. A federal mediator, Robert F. Greenwald, explained that "we are telling people that we are here and why we can be helpful. If they decide, we can be helpful to the city."[28] A truculent police department did not want federal interference, however, and began damage control. The FBI had been investigating the HPD throughout the 1970s because of allegations of corruption, but tensions between the FBI and the HPD actually went back to the days of Herman Short. J. Edgar Hoover was allegedly angered when then Alabama governor George Wallace touted Short as a possible replacement for Hoover as head of the FBI if Wallace was elected president in 1972.[29]

The Torres case therefore not only brought the Justice Department into another area of local politics, but, most important, it also helped the political momentum of the Mexican American community's leaders, who had actively called for federal intervention. As Mayor Hofheinz later recalled, "Torres, like the TSU Riot, created a lot of politicians in the city."[30] Mexican American activists called for quick and decisive action by Harris County assistant district attorney Sam Robertson, who was initially assigned the case.[31] Chief Bond and Mayor Hofheinz received an angry letter from Hispanic political leader and state representative Ben Reyes, who called for a civilian oversight board.[32] The League of United Latin American Citizens (LULAC) and other Chicano groups that had opposed each other's civil rights strategy called for decisive action by the city.[33] Local political aspirants were very concerned about this turn of events, because they viewed the growing cohesion in the Mexican community as a threat to status quo politics in the city.

Torres's death created negative political fallout for Mayor Hofheinz. The mayor, who had been virtually assured reelection before Torres's death, became a casualty of negative press coverage and shifting public opinion. He waffled and contradicted himself during the investigation of the incident. He initially denounced the police, then supported them. He lost their support as a political body, as well as the support of most of the conservative voters in the city, who would have followed the lead of the police union. One of his advisers, George Strong, told me that "the mayor was really [politically] hurt by the Torres incident."[34] Former councilman "Big" Jim McConn, the mayor's chief political rival, gained a tremendous political advantage because he was not in office at the time of the incident. In the end, Mayor Hofheinz, in direct response to the Torres case and the almost certain loss of minority coalitions that had helped elect him to his first two terms, decided not to run in 1978.

Internally, the HPD began to unravel. Chief Bond tendered his resignation effective November, 1977, though the mayor thought he had talked him into staying.[35] Without warning, Bond stepped down on June 10 to assume a job as head of corporate security for Tenneco Oil. He was replaced by a longtime HPD insider, assistant chief Harry Caldwell. Bond tried to pick his successor, but the mayor reached down through the ranks of assistant chiefs to pick Caldwell.

On June 28, 1977, Caldwell's first major action as chief was to terminate five of the six officers involved in the Torres case. The officers had been on indefinite suspension since May 12. Caldwell felt that the case was a blot on honest police officers who did their jobs properly every day.[36]

On that same day, a Harris County grand jury indicted Terry Denson, Stephen Orlando, Glenn Brinkmeyer, Louis Kinney, and Joseph Janish. Denson and Orlando were charged with murder; Brinkmeyer, Kinney, and Janish were charged with misdemeanor counts. Officer Carless Elliot returned to patrol duty, because no criminal charges were filed against him.[37] Chief Bond had tried earlier to fire him for dereliction of duty to punish him for telling on the others. Denson retained Robert "Bob" C. Bennett as his attorney and posted a bond of $10,000. Orlando hired Mike Ramsey.[38]

Reacting to the firings, police department personnel expressed an unofficial vote of confidence in Caldwell, who also had the full backing of the new mayor, Jim McConn. The mayor defiantly said, "The only vote of confidence that matters is mine."[39] McConn was a conservative who used the city's political fragmentation to his advantage and worked to slow the investigation and any proposed changes or reforms in the political culture of the city. He was also trying to salvage the city's image in the wake of the Torres case.

The accused police officers initially stonewalled investigators from the district attorney's office by hiding behind the code of silence.[40] Then pangs of conscience, or fear of jail, began to take a toll on the officers. The lies began to unravel when one of the men expressed remorse over his part in the alleged murder. As falsehoods and contradictions swirled around the investigation, rookie patrolman Carless Elliot broke rank, but the other officers continued to deny any culpability in Torres's death. They continued to display little or no remorse for the events that led to Torres's death.[41]

The officers' attorneys got the trial moved to Huntsville, Texas, the seat of Walker County, some sixty miles north of Houston.[42] This tactic had been used in an earlier case by defense attorney Richard "Racehorse" Haynes, in a wrongful death case against two HPD officers accused of beating an inmate who died in the Houston city jail in 1971. Haynes stated that at the time, "he knew he would win an acquittal when the last bigot was seated on the jury." The *Houston Post* reported that the trial of the officers in the Torres case was moved from Houston to ensure an impartial jury, but many in Houston, including Mexican American activists and community leaders, believed that the Harris County district attorney moved the Torres case to Huntsville in order to get acquittals.[43]

Famed trial lawyer Percy Foreman accused prosecutor Carol Vance and his predecessor, Frank Briscoe, of "white washing every charge against police." This, Foreman contended, created an atmosphere of police violence.[44] Huntsville, home of the Texas Department of Corrections, was known as a conservative law-and-order city that would be biased in favor of any police officer accused of a crime in the line of duty. Harris County district attorney Bert Graham insisted, however, that he would vigorously prosecute the case. He and Ted Poe, the county's two best prosecutors, would try it.[45]

Before the trial began, federal authorities let it be known that civil rights charges in the Torres case might be filed if the state courts failed to convict. U.S. attorney Toney Canales believed that the same policies, or lack thereof, that had led to the killing of Randy Webster and Billy Keith Joyvies in the mid-1970s were also responsible for Torres's death. Canales emphasized that a "search and kill policy was once used" and that it must "stop at all costs."[46] Particularly concerned over Torres's death were the leaders of the local LULAC chapter, who felt that police treatment of Mexican Americans was reprehensible but who continued to push within the system to secure justice through the courts. They exhorted the Justice Department to prosecute Torres's case as a violation of the civil rights statute. They were supported by District Attorney Vance, who also wanted federal authorities to try the accused officers. This opened Vance and the DA's office up to harsh criticism later that they did not prepare and try the case vigorously. Federal authorities refused to get involved in the case until the Harris County grand jury finished its deliberations.[47]

Legally, Torres's case was stronger than the Webster and Joyvies cases, at least on the surface. The facts in the Torres case were undeniable. The beating that he received prior to his death significantly deprived him of his civil rights by causing his death. Nevertheless, the trial at the state level revealed the difficulty of convicting police officers for wrongdoing. It also highlighted the attitudes of white juries toward Mexican Americans and other minorities when the case involved police. Many in Houston felt that the officers would go free. The most serious obstacle for the prosecution to overcome was the state's Code of Criminal Procedure, which required the DA to prove "intent to commit murder." As Bert Graham later explained, "we wanted to try the case under the federal statutes, which carried life in prison and you didn't have to prove intent."[48]

The Houston Patrol Officers Association helped provide legal support for the officers. Denson and Orlando, as already noted, had two of the best trial lawyers in Houston, Mike Ramsey and Bob Bennett. Ramsey had won an acquittal in another highly publicized case of police brutality in 1972 that resulted in the death of Bobby Joe Conner from a ruptured spleen. Ramsey had moved the case to New Braunfels, where the men were acquitted of murder in 1972.

While the HPOA did not condone violence, it insisted that Denson and Orlando were innocent until proven guilty and that it should provide sufficient legal counsel for the men. The HPOA's move was political in that the association used controversy such as this to increase membership by playing on police fears of alienation. Some white officers, in particular, joined the union because they felt that it would give them a homogeneous voice in times of race-related trouble and change. They also joined in reaction to the increasing presence of minorities on the force. Some white officers feared that minorities were displacing them. The union thus provided white racial homogeneity and group strength for white patrol officers who felt increasingly alienated.

When the accused officers' murder trial began in state court, it had all the trappings of a sideshow. Sam Houston State University officials lobbied to have the trial held on campus in their new mock-court classroom. Legal officials, aware of pretrial publicity, wanted to avoid any suggestion of undue influence as a result of negative publicity. Prosecutors knew they had a tough case to prove. They had to show intent to commit murder in order to ensure a conviction. They also had to convince the seven women and five men on the jury that the police, the supposed guardians of democracy, were capable of murder during the discharge of their duties.

The trial started in September, 1977. Both sides dramatically presented their cases. Ted Poe was the lead prosecutor and opened with a witness who helped establish a context for understanding the events that transpired on the night Torres was killed. Poe skillfully caught the officers in lie after lie, and on one occasion forced Orlando to read his perjured testimony to the jury regarding whether he had seen what Denson actually did on the night Torres was killed. Poe concluded his cross-examination of Orlando by insisting, "You lied." A shaken Orlando responded, "I guess I did." Orlando concluded his testimony by saying, "I really didn't see him."[49]

Bert Graham grilled the officers, who answered in a straight, tough, and unemotional style. During the trial, Graham displayed Torres's weathered boots as a visual reminder to the jury that Torres was a real person and not a monster. Poe artfully illustrated that the men showed more concern about Officer Kinney's new nickel-plated pistol than they did about Torres's life. When asked why they admired the gun so, one officer replied, "It is the tool of our trade."[50] The prosecution was superb. Prosecutors felt that, at the very least, they had proved manslaughter.[51]

Defense attorneys Ramsey and Bennett conceded that their clients were present at and in some way culpable for the events that led to Torres's death. The defense's case revolved around the intent clause of the murder charge. Ramsey emphasized that the state must prove intent to commit murder to get a conviction. At the trial, he opened by admitting that his client was somewhat culpable in Torres's death, but then put Torres's character on trial. Torres was skillfully demonized as a drunk with a chip on his shoulder. However, Judge Warren thwarted Ramsey's attempts to parade a string of witnesses who would testify to Torres's aggressive behavior. During defense examination, Ramsey allowed Denson to testify that he was frightened of Torres. His testimony was then used to establish self-defense as a possible motive for the officers' actions. Ramsey reemphasized that the officers' actions were wrong but that this was not murder, just a bad situation that got worse. He also questioned whether Brinkmeyer's testimony against his fellow officers would have been as forthcoming had he not been granted immunity from prosecution.

Ramsey's argument was a semantic masterpiece. He interjected whenever he could that his client did not push Torres or drag him screaming to the bayou's edge. Denson, according to Ramsey, "walked Torres to the water edge." His subtle legal rhetoric offset the negative characterizations of his client that the prosecution had painted.

On October 4, Judge Warren instructed the jurors that they must either acquit the defendants or convict them of one of four possible charges: murder, if they felt that the officers "intended to do bodily injury" to Torres and caused his death through actions that were "clearly dangerous to human life"; involuntary manslaughter, if Torres's death was caused by the officers' reckless; negligent homicide, if they felt that the defendants knowingly ignored the dangers that led to Torres's death; or simple assault.[52]

On October 7, after three tense days of deliberations by a jury that was nearly deadlocked twice, the officers were convicted of the misdemeanor charge of negligent homicide. Judge Warren sentenced them to probation and fined them one dollar each.[53]

The verdict opened painful wounds in the city. The *Houston Post* masthead read, "Murder Is Not a Crime: If You Are Police Officer." Minorities felt cheated, and politicians, fearing angry voters, demanded swift action. Mexican Americans demanded justice and fair treatment by the police. They formed coalitions across race lines as Houston's ministers and black community joined with Mexican Americans to protest the injustice. Federal authorities, under pressure from community groups and the Harris County DA's office, finally brought charges.

The federal trial opened on January 23, 1978, in the Fifth Circuit Court in Houston, with Judge Ross N. Sterling presiding. The accused men faced a four-count indictment that read,

> Men acting under the color of Texas law conspired to injure and intimidate Joe Luna Torres, Jr., and that the conspiracy resulted in his death, in violation of 18 U.S.C. § 241 (Count I); struck and assaulted Torres (Count II); pushed him into the bayou or aided and abetted that offense (Count III); all of which denied Torres his constitutional right not to be deprived of liberty without due process of law; and that they conspired to prevent another person from communicating information about these violations of federal law to an agent of the Federal Bureau of Investigation (Count IV).[54]

The federal prosecution team was headed by Mary Sinderson, the first chief of the new Civil Rights Division of the U.S. Attorney's Office, and assistant U.S. attorney Brian McDonald.[55] Also charged in the federal trial was conspirator James Joseph Janish, who was represented by Mike A. Andrews. Denson and Orlando were again represented by Ramsey and Bennett, respectively. On February 8, after a fifteen-day trial, the jury returned with a verdict of guilty on Counts I and II.

On March 28, 1978, Judge Sterling sentenced Denson, age twenty-seven, Orlando, age twenty-two, and Janish, age twenty-four, to one year in prison on a misdemeanor count for beating Torres and he gave them a ten-year suspended sentence, probated over five years, for conspiring to violate Torres's rights, resulting in his death. Sterling downplayed their crime as a "a situational offense which these defendants will never encounter again."[56] Sterling's sentence was almost identical to the sentence the state court had handed down.

During the federal trial, the HPD was involved in another embarrassing incident. On April 10, 1978, assistant police chief Carrol M. Lynn was arrested on a federal charge of obstruction of justice. Lynn, formerly the police chief, still had $25,000 in bribe money on him when he was arrested outside the home of a Houston oilman from whom he was allegedly extorting the funds. Mayor Jim McConn responded to the arrest of the former chief by promising that "we're going to clean the department out from our own end as far as we can by demanding resignations and by firing people."[57] The police department sacrificed the unpopular and clearly corrupt Lynn because his sins were far less egregious than those created by the officers responsible for Torres's death.

Against this background, tensions surrounding the lenient treatment of the convicted officers in the Torres case quickly led to the Moody Park riot on May 7, 1978. A mixed crowd of approximately fifteen hundred people, mostly from Houston's Mexican American community, now angry, militant, and politicized, gathered in the park to celebrate Cinco de Mayo and to commiserate about the sentences handed down in the Torres case.[58] The Houston Police Department vowed to watch, photograph, and keep a record of those who were present at the protest. During the rally, some Chicano youths, who by now completely rejected the gradualist strategy of the moderates, demanded immediate changes in the existing police structure.[59]

The HPD's intimidation tactics only challenged the Chicano youth and activists. Travis Morales and Richard Vara, the demonstration's leaders, could not contain the Moody Park crowd once it was provoked. Some verbally sparred with officers from the HPD, who had set up a perimeter around the park during a protest meeting and ignored the importance of not being viewed by protesters as provocateurs.[60]

The celebration turned angry as participants discussed the light sentences handed down for the officers responsible for Torres's death. As the crowd hurled insults at the police, someone allegedly started a fight, and the police officers moved in.[61] The protesters moved from the park, marched angrily down Fulton Street, and churned through the business district, smashing cars, then looting and burning businesses. The disturbance spilled into the north side business district, causing several million dollars in damages.

The police had completely failed to maintain order. It was apparent that the HPD had not learned its lesson from the TSU Riot or the Dowling Street shootout. Jerome Skolnick reminds us that police attitudes toward inner-city citizens are slow to change.[62] The police presence on the periphery of the park and the department's aggressive public statements regarding controlling and photographing the demonstration pushed the already tense situation to the boiling point.[63] Although the law was clearly on their side, the police did not use sound judgment in the Moody Park incident, particularly as increasing segments of the city's population regarded them as criminal and the court system as unjust.

On May 16, 1978, the Justice Department asked the U.S. Fifth Circuit Court of Appeals to review and overturn the suspended sentences and requested reinstatement of the ten-year felony civil rights violation sentence.[64] Judge Sterling's decision was immediately appealed to the three-judge tribunal. On May 19, the Department of Justice filed a request for a writ of mandamus ordering Judge Sterling to correct the illegal sentences entered in this action. Furthermore, the defendants had been convicted by a jury of a violation of federal code 18 U.S.C. 241 with death resulting, an offense punishable by life imprisonment. The complaint alleged that Judge Sterling had placed the officers on probation "without authority to do so, because Federal Probation Act, 18 U.S.C. 3651 *et seq.*, authorizes federal courts to suspend imposition or execution of sentences and to grant probation only upon entering judgments of conviction for offenses not punishable by death or life imprisonment."[65]

Judge Sterling was livid. He claimed that he had violated no law and that the Justice Department was out of line. He later wrote that the challenge was "an almost intolerable attempt to interfere with the independence of the court." In April, the Justice Department asked Sterling to reinstate the sentences, but he refused.[66]

In October, 1979, the Fifth Circuit ruled that Judge Sterling's lenient sentencing was in error but found no sufficient grounds to overturn the sentences he had imposed, thus ending the legal aspects of the Torres criminal trial.

The Torres case may have ended, but its political legacy in Houston was just beginning. Blacks and Hispanics together constituted 27 percent of the voters in 1970 and 32 percent in 1980 (see Table 6).[67] In the 1960s, African Americans had challenged the political supremacy of the local white elites. Although largely unsuccessful, they made moderate gains in terms of officeholding, beginning with Curtis Graves and

Barbara Jordan. Local demographic changes had begun to affect the social and political culture of the city by the mid-1970s. Nevertheless, local politics remained largely unchanged because of political gerrymandering and block voting.

In the 1980s, however, minorities across Texas aggressively challenged white political control of the state, and their challenge ultimately altered the context within which the HPD and other police forces operated. Chandler Davidson notes that in the 1980s, Mexican Americans were the big winners in the state's political lottery. They were elected to 1,427 statewide offices, while blacks held only 228.[68] The state Democratic Party's image was redefined as more minorities used it as a vehicle for their political transformation, particularly in urban areas, beginning with the election of Henry B. Gonzales, of San Antonio, to the U.S. House of Representatives in 1968.

Race-based politics in Houston gradually changed with the election of Judson Robinson Jr. to the city council in 1971.[69] He was a resident of the Fifth Ward and the son of Judson Robinson Sr., a former labor leader, former housing authority official, and one of Houston's most

Table 6. *Minority Voting Percentages, Houston, 1940–90*

Year	Black Voters		Hispanic Voters		Combined Black & Hispanic Voters
	% of Population	*% of All Voters*	*% of Population*	*% of All Voters*	*% of All Voters*
1940	22	2	5	1	3
1950	21	9	6	2	11
1960	23	13	7	3	16
1970	26	22	12	5	27
1980	28	24	18	8	32
1990	28	30	28	10	40

Source: Thomas and Murray, *Progrowth Politics*, 209.

Note: Voter registration data are estimated from voter counts in the predominantly minority precincts. Population data from 1940 to 1990 are from the U.S. census.

successful black entrepreneurs.[70] Robinson was a polished individual who had been educated at Fisk College in Nashville, Tennessee. He was also a community activist in the Fifth Ward who had experienced run-ins with the police before entering politics.

He was considered diplomatic and politically astute and his impact was immediately felt on the council. When race-related problems arose in the city's housing authority in 1971, he calmed a crowd of angry blacks protesting housing discrimination.[71] His skill as a mediator validated his worth to the city and raised his stock as a black council member.

Although Robinson was no friend of the police, he was aware of his minority status on the council and chose his battles wisely. While never attacking the police, he always demanded accountability. George Strong recalled that "Robinson did not fight an aggressive civil rights agenda on council, but he let it be known in personal conversations that he loathed the police treatment of minorities."[72]

Police misconduct and repression became a lightning rod for local political activism nationwide. The lack of effective controls and checks and balances on police authority gave rise to new minority challengers, whose target was at-large voting for city and county office. This was by far the most effective means of white control of local politics. Political reapportionment was the smoking gun of political reform efforts.[73] In the early 1960s and the 1970s, local minority leaders in Houston sued to end at-large voting and demanded that the courts force the city to implement single-member voting districts.[74] Whites, aided by a sympathetic federal court, argued that the proposed single-member system was unfair to them. However, they underestimated the role of the Justice Department, which believed that annexation, at-large elections, and single-member districts benefited the dominant political class. All the parties involved knew that blacks and Hispanics could carry only their specific districts or wards, creating a new triracial political equation for Houston.

In the 1970s, new legal arguments were raised regarding the city council's representation patterns and territorial annexation. Robert Thomas and Richard Murray write that "two federal system principles" lay at the heart of the Houston council reforms: "community determination versus larger political system determination."[75] The combination of territorial annexation and city council reforms served as a one-two punch for old-time establishment politics in the city, though federal judge Allan G. Hannay supported the pro-Houston establishment and, dismissing the claim of racism, let stand the city's at-large voting districts. According to Hannay, "The present method of selecting councilmen in Houston's city government is not rooted in racial discrimination."[76]

Despite Judge Hannay's position, changes were on the way. The U.S. Department of Justice sought a political compromise by ruling that territorial annexation in Houston could be voided if a compromise on reapportionment was not reached.[77] The local political establishment hoped to avoid any changes in the existing political structure, but, sensing the inevitability of change, officials became advocates of nine single-member districts and five at-large districts. Under this system, some city council members would be elected from districts while others would be elected through the current citywide at-large voting system.[78]

A favorable court ruling on the creation of nine single-member districts changed local politics.[79] Ernest McGowen Sr. recalled that "blacks went to Mayor McConn and convinced him to support the court's action." In turn, city officials realized that the court might impose sanctions that could substantially alter city government if a compromise were not reached. Moreover, the Department of Justice's intervention in local affairs opened the city up for major political changes.[80] Arnoldo de León concludes that "in the end the Justice Department of the United States ordered the city of Houston to implement a fairer method of representation."[81] Local authorities were actually forced into compromise by the Justice Department, which threatened them with other litigation over annexation.[82]

In August, 1979, the city voted on a 9-5-1 plan, which would create nine single-member-district seats and five at-large seats and which provided that the mayor be elected citywide.[83] The new city council equation spelled doom for traditional policing. The presence of minority representatives on the Houston city council from newly created districts quickly made alleged police improprieties reviewable for error.[84] They asked for a citizen review board or some kind of police oversight. Although the old-line council coalition led by Homer Ford and Larry MacKasle tabled the issue, the pressure applied by minority representatives led to closer scrutiny of police conduct.[85]

Chief Harry Caldwell fell victim to this more intense scrutiny. He had been a member of the force for over twenty-six years, and his primary loyalty was to his officers. It was this steadfast defense of the department that placed him in harm's way. On March 3, 1979, he complained that the "police are the last minority that it is fashionable to stereotype and all 3,000 officers suffered over the Torres case."[86] By June, 1979, his brilliant career was in shambles and he was engaging in what amounted to damage control. The police were embroiled in controversy and political chaos. State Rep. Ben Reyes, the chair of the Public Interest Advocacy Center, put the chief on his heels in a critical report, which, according to Caldwell, "gives the implication, that Houston officers are killing disproportionate numbers of people. This is one that's simply not true."[87]

After Caldwell's failure to clean up the HPD, it became evident to many of the city's leaders that the police department was in need of new management. Mayor McConn took on the onerous task of trying to fix the police while trying to maintain the political control of the "good old boys" in the coming city elections.[88] Mayor McConn's administration suffered a dramatic blow, however, when Chief Caldwell, feeling that he had failed to achieve his goals, resigned on February 12, 1980. He accepted responsibility for the chaos in the force but argued that he had done the best he could to restore decency and respect for the force.[89]

The new city council forced conservative Mayor McConn to change some of his policies. He tried in vain to fend off attacks on all fronts by hostile state officials, angry minority constituents, and the nervous ruling elite. In short, he found himself in the middle of a political firestorm with federal authorities looking into police improprieties. McConn had become, in effect, a lame duck mayor but would not concede defeat.

In 1979, the police department had embarked on a new chapter that would ultimately place its fate in the hands of outside forces. In his last days in office, McConn appointed a committee to choose a police chief. This committee, according to Ernest McGowen Sr., knew it was trying to find a chief who was a professional and who came from outside the existing HPD structure. Longtime political leaders agreed, because they wanted to keep control of city politics and because they saw that the police department, with its reputation for brutality, had become a target for those who favored even more sweeping reforms in Houston.[90]

The police thus became victims of their own racist aggression. The HPD had made many enemies and now found itself without allies who would risk their career by expressing public support for the department. Controversy negatively affected the department's public image, and the police had hurt Houston's image. The Supreme Court's guaranteeing the rights of the accused placed the police in a defensive posture. In fact, by late 1979, the HPD had become the national poster child for aberrant police behavior.

The mayoral election of 1980 provided a litmus test for good old boy politics in Houston. Houston's inner city had become almost exclusively minority. Historically, the at-large system had allowed white voters to elect the majority of the city council, but now they had to share the power. When former outsiders entered the chambers of city government, the traditional structure and practice of the police department became casualties. Reform of the police department became the best campaign issue in the city's history. Change in the racial composition of the city council caused a firestorm of politically motivated changes on the HPD. Its future would now be shaped by a reform-minded coalition.

When you are leading, people will hit you with anything that they can think of without any regard to whether it has any truth.

—Katherine J. Whitmire

CHAPTER 6 Calming the Raging Sea

Katherine J. Whitmire, Lee P. Brown, and the High Tide of Change for the Police Department, 1981–90

By the 1980s, the Houston Police Department had earned a reputation as mean, racist, and brutal because of its long history of episodic violence against the citizens of Houston. This is a harsh but accurate depiction of the forces that shaped the HPD's public image and defined its character to this point. The HPD, like other conservative institutions in the North and the South, had reacted aggressively to rising crime rates and had impeded social change for nearly three decades. Its efforts at social control and crime reduction resulted in the denial of individual rights and a failure fully to extend even basic liberties to some of Houston's ordinary citizens. This created a nearly insurmountable wall of anger and mistrust between the police and the community.

Police conservatism was in conflict with the forces of modernization and integration in Houston, which led to organized community demands for policy changes within the department. These challenges led to an ideological clash that brought on bureaucratic changes within the HPD and culminated in its politically guided transformation.

This chapter begins with a brief discussion of citizens' fear of rising crime rates in the city, then discusses the state of the department in 1980. It establishes a backdrop for the political collapse of the good old boy network and chronicles the rise of Mayor Katherine J. Whitmire and her attempts to reform local government, especially the police.[1] It ends with the tenure of Lee Patrick Brown, the HPD's first African American police chief.[2]

Demands for police reforms in the 1980s grew out of fear of the upward spiral in the crime rate that began in the 1960s. Houston led cities of the same size in the number of violent offenses, and the HPD capitalized on the anxiety caused by growing crime and social agitation in the 1960s and the 1970s to secure increases in the size of the force and additional funding for the department. It failed miserably at curbing the crime rate, however.[3]

For most minorities, the rising crime rates were a double-edged sword. The police, on one hand, looked at all minorities as potential criminals, but on the other, they rarely tried to prevent crime in minority neighborhoods.[4] The HPD interpreted public fears caused by the rising crime rate as a willingness to accept more aggressive policing. Therefore, by 1980, police conduct was deemed out of control by many in the city. Yet despite the HPD's ineptitude, the police department experienced a dramatic growth from 1970 through 1980. This growth created new internal divisions along generational, ethnic, and gender lines.

In 1980, the Houston Police Department had approximately 3,200 officers to serve a city with a population of 1.5 million. The ratio of police to citizens in Houston was 1.9 per 1,000, well below the FBI's recommended standard ratio of 2.5.[5] The small size of the police force grew out of the city's legacy of fiscal frugality and the continued effects of aggressive annexation, which expanded the city's borders from 433.9 square miles in 1977 to approximately 565.0 square miles in 1980. The most important factor in these annexations was the increase of the suburban white population.

The HPD was overwhelmed by spatial complexities, service delivery problems caused by growing patrol areas, and increased functional limitations caused by a severe labor shortage. This led to frustration on the part of police, who increasingly complained of low pay and high work volume. In the end, growth caused heightened tensions between citizens and the patrol divisions throughout the city and magnified many police officers' sense of alienation.[6]

By January, 1980, the fallout from the Billy Keith Joyvies, Randall Webster, and José Campos Torres killings and a series of police brutality and corruption allegations had permanently altered departmental policies. Top-level managerial changes resulted, revealing even deeper internal divisions. These divisions and public controversies caused the demise of Harry Caldwell, the HPD's first police chief with an advanced degree in criminal justice. Caldwell had assumed command of the department in 1973, during one of its greatest periods of turmoil. He wanted to create a police college to improve performance and bring consistency to training. The new chief labeled his first year "a year of crisis and a most traumatic experience."[7] Despite his abilities, his twenty-six years with the force made it difficult for him to be objective during the continual string of police controversies, including questions of how adequately to address the issue of minority promotions. In a reflective mood, the gravelly voiced Caldwell, who was tired of meddling by the city council, tendered his resignation to Mayor McConn on February 12, 1980. He informed the mayor that "he was tired after a hard 26 or 27 years as a police officer," particularly the "very hectic schedule of the last three years." His resignation was effective February 29.[8]

Houston's increasing ethnic diversity compounded the HPD's problems, as the city's African American population reached 27 percent and the Hispanic population mushroomed to 17 percent of the total population between 1970 and 1981. The HPD did not reflect the demographics of the community it served, causing major problems between it and the citizenry. This inequity and the violence of the HPD's past led local activists to call for political reforms and became the primary catalysts for the shifts in the city's voting patterns (see Table 6).

Citizens placed much of the blame on the HPD's failure adequately to address contentious issues from the 1960s through the 1970s. Moreover, societal expectations of acceptable behavior for public servants also changed. These changes were demonstrated by the actions of local community activists, who demanded that city officials apply municipal civil service laws to ensure that more minorities were recruited, hired, and promoted by the police department. In response, a recalcitrant HPD management refused to consider the activists' requests and lashed out as minorities organized legally and politically to force change not only in the police department but also in city government.

Minorities' ongoing legal efforts paid off when court-ordered electoral reforms brought sweeping changes in the city elections of 1979 and 1981. In those elections, blacks and Hispanics increased their political representation, thereby changing the city's political culture.[9] Many of them used police reform as an effective campaign issue and claimed they would demand immediate changes in city government.

Minorities in Houston had increased their political leverage in the city with help from the U.S. Department of Justice when no political compromise was offered by the city council. City leaders, however, complained about federal intervention. They had to this point been able to keep federal authorities from moving local affairs in directions the local elite did not care to go.[10]

A curious combination of the city's conservative fiscal policies and poor minority/police relations finally brought federal money and investigators into the city. First, local police, who had received federal Law Enforcement Assistance Program (LEAP) dollars for equipment and training and who now had to meet TCLEOSE standards of accountability, were closely scrutinized by the Department of Justice. Second, the city's failure to address adequately the problems of police violence and corruption provided a perfect moment for the Department of Justice to demand changes in city government. The end result of federal intervention was the restructuring of the city council with nine at-large and five single-member districts and a mayor elected at large. This restructuring placed more minorities on the city council, but, most important, the nine-to-five council representation rules gave minorities direct representation and helped them determine or influence mayoral politics. After the 1979 election, the Houston city council included three blacks, one woman, and one Hispanic.[11]

Some old-timers on the council immediately lashed out at the new members, their complaints ranging from the petty to the caustic. On one occasion, longtime councilman Homer Ford engaged in a shouting match with newly elected colleague Eleanor Tinsley over what floor in city hall she could have an office on, as a new council member.[12] Tinsley had received a choice office on the floor with veteran council members.

Custom and protocol demanded that new council members understand the pecking order. They had to learn fast because old-timers were unforgiving. Mayor Pro Tem Johnny Goyen chastised the new council members for being late to their first meeting, complaining that "in 24 years on the council, bid opening had never started so late."[13] However, members quickly reconciled and by the end of the first one hundred days, the various factions were building coalitions.[14] To the dismay of many in the city, police reform was not a major agenda item during the first session, which now included the new minority members.

From 1979 through 1981, the city council placed few constraints on the HPD, giving the department unqualified support. Robert Thomas and Richard Murray suggest that "the second precursor of the 1980s was an incongruity between what the council had the authority to do and what it had propensities to try and do."[15] Thus, the council's failure to provide direction for the police department reflected both its fear of change and the absence of a consensus on how effectively to address police issues. Plus, many council members saw the police force as a formidable political entity that could influence the outcome of an election. Even activists on the council, such as Ben Reyes, defended the police, emphasizing that "we know we have some rotten apples, but a lot of officers are trying to do a good job."[16] Immediately after the election, some in the city questioned whether the liberal and conservative factions on the city council could work together on tough issues. Compromise was the dominant feature of Houston's political culture in 1979. Understanding this, activists who served on the council moderated their positions in order to win some agenda items.[17] Most council members had always accepted the police force as a politically autonomous organization that served the needs of the establishment; it was the ghost of the HPD's most recent past, not council initiatives, that made it vulnerable to reform efforts.

Another issue confounding the city council from 1979 through 1980 was its tenuous relationship with two-term mayor Jim McConn. The city council believed that he had failed to provide decisive leadership for the police department and that he did not adjust well to the new city council makeup. The council was convinced that he had "failed to use his Mayoral powers to promote the institutional development on the Council."[18]

By the middle of his second term, he had fallen from grace with the council, which challenged him for supremacy, thereby threatening the city's strong-mayor form of government. The council harshly criticized him for allegedly refusing to fight vigorously for the city's interests in

Austin before the legislature.[19] The city council's antagonism toward Mayor McConn grew beyond ambiguities between their role and his; council members saw him as a weak and lethargic leader. Moreover, they felt that he had harmed the city because he had failed to set an adequate council agenda and provide necessary information for meetings.

The growing antagonism between Mayor McConn and the city council provided city controller Katherine J. Whitmire with a window of opportunity to run for mayor. No other political event signaled that the "firestorm of political change" was upon the city and the police department more clearly than her campaign and election in 1981 as the city's first female mayor.[20] She is a small, demure, native Houstonian who attended Houston public schools. She earned a BS and an MS in accounting from the University of Houston and became a certified public accountant. Her training made her a systematic, task-oriented manager who demanded organizational and functional efficiency.[21] Her immediate goal was to make the city's bureaucracy more professional. She based her criticism of the police on her observations as city controller and personal experience as a lifelong Houston resident. She abhorred the aggressive behavior of public servants, and she considered HPD members among the worst offenders.[22]

Whitmire's campaign was a master class in political chess, as she pounced on Mayor McConn's personal limitations as well as his distaste for debating and political maneuvering. She benefited from the liberal/conservative and minority coalitions that had helped elect former mayor Fred Hofheinz.[23] Whitmire understood that she had an uphill battle in the mayoral race, so she ingratiated herself with Houston's fringe communities. This strategy worked, as she secured not only their votes but also their financial support. Her ability to reach bankers as well as the minority and gay communities gave her a firm foothold on the race without securing endorsements from large organizations.

Since she had shown herself to be a capable administrator as city controller, her election became a referendum on police reform. Her platform addressed five key issues: (1) police protection; (2) mass transportation; (3) management of city services; (4) streets and highway systems; and (5) traffic flow.[24] The police department had been a sacred cow in past mayoral elections, but it was clear that police issues were an important campaign issue in this election.

As city controller, Whitmire had distinguished herself by changing the city's budget process and improving the overall bond rating. As a manager and a politician, she insisted on accountability and professionalism as the hallmarks of public service. These two issues were merely a reflection of her business training and not of her perceived liberal social views. Her proposed administrative reforms for city government were viewed as political smoke, which would mean no immediate change in the city's political culture. Her most contentious campaign issue was that of police reform, which she claimed was nonnegotiable. This ultimately helped her get elected.

During the 1981 election, power politics in Houston was permanently altered when the good old boy candidate and incumbent mayor, Jim McConn, "finished a dismal fourth" in the general election.[25] Mayor McConn received only 13 percent of the popular vote, compared to Whitmire's 37 percent and Harris County sheriff Jack Heard's 35 percent. Interestingly, after she beat McConn, Whitmire gained the backing of his supporters, including the city's big-money advocates and business leaders.[26] Newly elected city controller Lance Lalor characterized her during the campaign as a social liberal but a fiscal conservative who would do what was best for the city if elected.

Whitmire's emergence during the campaign as the front-runner heightened the police unions' fear that she was antipolice. Her police-reform campaign rhetoric was consistent with her strategic plan for the city. This plan would bring professional bureaucratic efficiency to the city and the police department. The police unions campaigned vigorously against Whitmire but, despite their efforts, she shocked establishment politicians in the city by thrashing Jack Heard in the runoff, with 62 percent of the popular vote.[27]

Her election immediately increased the feeling of alienation and abandonment among many within the HPD, as the unions fanned the anti-Whitmire flames in the department. Whitmire had stood her ground and boldly campaigned on police reform. She even bested the conservative *Houston Chronicle*, which attacked her on all her positions while endorsing Heard in the runoff.

At her inauguration on January 2,1982, Mayor Katherine Jane Whitmire clearly stated her objectives, emphasizing that "there will be differences of opinion and unpopular decisions which must be made to move forward toward our common goals." She added, "There may be some in the city bureaucracy who will balk at the introductions of effective business and personnel practices in City Hall; but in the long run, not only the taxpayer but also the men and women of our city work force will reap the benefits of efficient city government."[28] On January 4, she informed *Houston Business Journal* writer Millie Budd that "there is also need for substantial improvement in the police department. We need to reduce response time, get more citizens involved in crime control, improve the science of the police force."[29]

These comments sent tremors through the patrol unions, which angrily denounced her as antipolice. Mayor Whitmire's comments created an antagonism between the police union and her that lasted most of her four terms as mayor.

Whitmire was a decisive mayor who believed in making decisions and delegating authority. She moved quickly to fill the chief of police vacancy. She kept her promise to look outside the HPD for a new chief, because the internal candidates were weak. Because the chief was the department's link to the city, some inside the department feared that a chief from outside might not respect the force's customs. Because the chief was a political appointee, the new mayor held all the cards. The police chief had historically occupied a nebulous position, often walking a fine line between departmental custom and the political culture of the city. The police force had, however, remained independent of most political constraints until the late 1970s, when changes in council representation and mayoral politics facilitated dramatic changes in expectations of the police. By the 1980s, most citizens felt that a chief from outside was necessary to effect change in the HPD, although some felt that the appointment of a new chief alone would not be enough.

The second hotly debated area of proposed change was the regulation of police behavior through a civilian review board (CRB).[30] The proposed CRB oversight committee was to be made up of business leaders, private citizens, and community professionals who would review police improprieties. The HPD rank and file hated the idea of civilian review. They felt that it would open them up to scrutiny by a population that did not understand their role.

Interestingly, the police force feared the loss of authority, and politicians feared the loss of the police department's support. This was evidenced by the fact that mayor after mayor before Whitmire had refused to consider civilian oversight. Even former liberal-coalition mayor Fred Hofheinz Jr. opposed this idea, emphasizing that the "civil review was not necessary in Houston, because the police department had an internal mechanism of accountability."[31] This issue was the true measure of the police unions as a political force, for it made most local politicians wary of pressing for radical police reform out of fear of angering the police and the city's conservative factions.

The HPD's internal policing had not worked well. The HPD, like police forces in general, became increasingly violent in its attempt to ameliorate the crime rates. This prompted a rise in complaints of brutality throughout the 1980s. Having witnessed this firsthand in Houston, Whitmire questioned the character of the police during her first campaign and intimated that there might be criminal elements within the police department. The white police unions reacted with hostility.[32]

Following her election, the mayor's comments regarding police conduct were thrown back in her face by the police unions, which picked a nasty public fight with her. Shortly after her inauguration, though, Mayor Whitmire pacified them when she accepted an invitation to meet with the Houston Police Patrol Union (HPPU) on March 16, during a union meeting. She offered a veiled apology for any misquoted comments reported during her campaign: "I am very sorry that some of the officers felt that I was attacking their integrity." The HPPU accepted her apology, and tensions within the organization subsided.[33]

The HPOA, the department's largest union, was far more skeptical and criticized the mayor's cautious apology to the HPPU. On March 19, Mayor Whitmire met with HPOA representatives to explain her campaign statements. Her appearance was a show of political force and personal charisma, as she invited herself to the union meeting. Her presence stunned many HPOA members, who listened to her cautiously, but intently. During her talk, she backpedaled, then won many over with an apology. During the meeting, she strongly cautioned members to remember that as public officials they must be "concerned about the way our statements can be manipulated for political ends by institutions such as the *Houston Chronicle.*" Then, in vintage Whitmire style, she beguiled them into believing that she was not antipolice and that they had a mayor they could work with in city hall.[34]

Even though tensions between the mayor and the police unions were temporarily improved, relations between the mayor and some segments of the police department remained strained. This strain was evidenced at the end of her first term, when the police unions financed an ad campaign against her.

While on the surface it appeared that her battle was with the police unions, the mayor knew that her major obstacle to reforming the city's bureaucracy lay with the Civil Service Commission. For any of Mayor Whitmire's proposed reforms to be successful, she would have to convince the state legislature and the Civil Service Commission to change the promotion rules within the police department and the city bureaucracy.[35] She knew that she would face stiff opposition from city officials who wanted to maintain the status quo, the police unions, and state officials who wanted civil service matters relating to police and fire fighters left up to them. She wanted to give the newly appointed chief the power to effect change, but the existing civil service laws would not allow her or the candidate for chief to pick command staff from outside the promotions list. Thus, her reforms depended on either civil service reform or a pliant civil service commission that would help facilitate reform efforts by liberally interpreting the existing standards for promotion.

The appointment of a chief was the primary concern of the HPOA and the HPPU.[36] Although the police department had floundered, it found temporary relief with the appointment of insider Bradley K. Johnson as chief in 1980.[37] However, Johnson immediately stepped down after Whitmire's election as mayor, emphasizing, "I couldn't see myself working for the present administration in the capacity of an appointed official."[38] The mayor showed her political grit when she did not yield to pressure from the HPOA to rehire Johnson, who was opposed by the HPPU on the grounds that he lacked both the desire and the ability to lead the force.

Mayor Whitmire used the division between the two police unions as an opportunity to find solutions to the problems plaguing the police department. She felt these were beyond the department's ability and expertise to correct. She tried to solve the problems by appointing a new chief from outside the Houston Police Department's command structure. However, the impulse for an external search for a new chief of police did not originate with Mayor Whitmire. According to former city councilman Ernest McGowen Sr., it began with "Mayor McConn [who] yielded to pressure from the community and members on council when he appointed a committee to explore finding a new chief."[39] Almost unrelenting controversy dogged the department and fueled public demands for the appointment of an external candidate as chief of police, particularly in light of Chief Johnson's handling of allegations of mistreatment of the mentally ill.[40] Thus, the city was ripe for changes that might improve police conduct and service delivery.

Mayor Whitmire exerted her power as mayor and shook up the police department in January, 1982, when she circumvented the HPD's hierarchical structure to appoint John Bales as interim chief. In disgust, former interim chief Johnson, though he felt that he was next in line, remained as an assistant chief. While Bales was well liked within the HPD, internal gossip suggested that many officers felt that he was weak and indecisive.

Bales wanted the job; however, he knew that he would not be automatically appointed. The mayor used the ambivalence within the department over Bales's appointment as an opportunity to examine her options, which included considering appointing an external candidate for the position of chief of police. In recent HPD history, no outsider had been appointed chief. Moreover, the rank and file felt that promotion from within was the only way to choose a new police chief.

The mayor's ability to choose the chief was crucial to her plans to reform the police. This would be no easy task, given that she let it be known that she would look outside the force. Her first obstacle was the parochial attitudes of local politicians, who did not want an outsider and did not trust her understanding of police issues. On February 16, the mayor released the names of thirteen men she and her staff recommended for the job. When pressed by reporters, she reminded them that there was no timetable for selecting a chief. The list included writer Joseph Wambaugh; Harris County constable Walter Rankin; Robert Franck, a former special agent in charge of the FBI in Houston; and eleven other applicants, including two HPD officers.[41] Most of the candidates were from outside the force and the city, yet none of the applications caused as much of a ruckus in Houston as that of Lee Patrick Brown, Atlanta's public safety commissioner. Brown's name was not on the original list and he did not submit a formal application, as the others had. Moreover, Whitmire kept her conversations with him strictly confidential.

The two white patrol unions were outraged that Whitmire was considering appointing an outsider.[42] When rumors surfaced that Lee P. Brown was a candidate, tempers within the department flared. As Brown emerged as the front-runner for the job, the HPPU and the HPOA united in opposition to him. The HPOA's president, Bill Elkins, said that he was "shocked and surprised" and suggested that the mayor put Brown on the list because he was black and not because of his qualifications.[43] The union sent three officers to Atlanta to do background checks on Brown. The delegation reported that it had "facts surrounding Mr. Brown's record of mismanagement." According to its report, "Brown did not delegate authority; he was strictly hands on." Whitmire smirked and said that "it seems to me their investigation was as effort to develop some sort of data to support their already established position but they did not seem to have developed very much [negative] data."[44]

The union's smear campaign failed as Mayor Whitmire stayed one step ahead of them. She subverted criticism and public disclosure of Brown's résumé by accepting only an oral application, which did not violate the Texas Open Records Act.[45] Plus, she understood that the council's and the HPD's opposition was limited in that they could do little to stop the hiring of an outside chief, particularly now that minorities on the council supported the mayor.[46]

Brown's outsider status was a formidable obstacle in the minds of many members of the Houston Police Department.[47] Police factions argued that, as an outsider, he did not know the city's political history or the laws of the state of Texas. This was not a very logically thought out argument, because Brown was not the only person on the list from outside the city. He was, however, the only one on the list with a PhD in criminal justice. Moreover, his qualifications fit the mayor's ideal for an experienced, professional manager for the police department.[48] Ironically, Brown had more in common with most officers than they could imagine. For example, he was from a working-class background, like that of most HPD officers, and, like many of them, had pulled himself up by his bootstraps and through the ranks to become a competent administrator.

Brown was the son of sharecroppers from Wewoka, Oklahoma, who had migrated to San Jose, California, during the Great Depression. He received his bachelor's degree from Fresno State University (1960), a master's in sociology from San Jose State University (1964), and a doctorate in criminal justice from the University of California at Berkeley (1970). He was characterized by Larry Craig, a former assistant director of criminal justice in Portland, Oregon, where Brown had served as director of the Criminal Justice Department, as "the smartest criminal justice person I know."[49] Craig, who succeeded Brown in Portland, stated that Brown "was the most intellectual Criminal Justice person I ever met. He understands what those numbers mean." In regards to Brown's style as an administrator, Craig added that "he [Brown] won't say much to you. He just gets the job done."[50] James Baldwin characterizes Brown as an "indisputably honorable, even gallant man, confronting an enormity with dignity."[51]

Race was obviously one factor in the opposition to Brown. Many whites feared that a black chief would lower standards by promoting what they felt would be unqualified blacks. They feared displacement, because they had systematically denied minorities promotions and advancement. Moreover, the system in place within the HPD had perpetuated itself by passing promotions from white officers to other white officers. Increased minority presence in any form meant altering this system.

Conservatives on the city council tried to stall Brown's confirmation. Frank Mancuso, Christiana Hartung, and Larry MacKasle all opposed his appointment.[52] Minorities and activists, however, heralded the appointment as a move in the right direction for the city.[53] Council members Ben Reyes, Ernest McGowen Sr., Anthony Hall, and Judson Robinson Jr. gave the mayor their unqualified support.[54]

The debate in the city council centered around Brown's status as an outsider rather than his qualifications. Believing that Brown would bring professional leadership, capable administrative direction, and goal-oriented management to the police department, the mayor forged a coalition of supporters for him on the city council. On March 23, 1982, he was confirmed as chief of the Houston Police Department by an eleven to three vote.[55]

Whitmire's decision to appoint him as the city's first African American chief of police showed tremendous courage and a sense of the new social and cultural realities in Houston. It also illustrated the growing political clout that enabled her to challenge and defeat the two most conservative factions in city government: the police, and conservatives on the city council. His appointment began one of the greatest period of transformation in the city and the HPD. His appointment also created a great degree of uncertainty and animosity among whites within the department. Former interim chief B. K. Johnson suggested that the difficulty for Brown was that he was an outsider who had to win over city officials.[56]

On Monday, April 19, Lee Patrick Brown was sworn in during a private ceremony in the mayor's office. In his stoic and professional way, Chief Brown immediately went to work by taking a guided tour of the station with Assistant Chief John P. Bales.[57]

Brown's swearing-in represented a first for the city in many ways: he was the first black to serve as chief, and the first chief to be sworn in in a private ceremony. District E Councilman Frank Mancuso, one of the three council members who voted against Brown's appointment, was livid. He grumbled that Brown should have been sworn in inside the city council chambers like everyone else before him. Mayor Whitmire sidestepped him and then defended her decision saying, "As you know I am not a person who stands on ceremony a great deal."[58]

Chief Brown's media debut at HPD headquarters revealed what would become his trademark style of either providing straightforward answers that gave very little information regarding strategy or deferring comments until later. When asked what his first order of business would be, he informed the *Houston Chronicle* that he did not have any immediate changes in mind. Given the tension in the department, Chief Brown wisely employed caution as he assembled his staff.

From the beginning, it was clear that Brown was his own man. He divided and conquered within the HPD by refusing to meet with the command staff collectively; instead, he personally interviewed each member. This frightened many older officers, who felt that it was their time for promotion. They complained that Brown was upsetting long-established departmental promotion customs. The patrol unions publicly suggested that Brown was guilty of discrimination. Mayor Whitmire quieted them when she and Brown promised to adhere to the established internal promotion procedures. Yet the unions became even more suspicious of Brown when he informed reporters in an interview on March 14, 1982, that he supported racial quotas, because "the ethnic makeup [of a police department] should correspond to the ethnic makeup of the whole city. The same should be true of promotions."[59] Although weary, white unions and longtime HPD insiders pinned their ears back for a nasty fight over this issue. However, Brown did not immediately attempt to change the department's makeup; instead, he employed subtlety in outlining his proposed reforms.

Although Brown introduced major reform items in increments, any changes that he suggested were opposed by varying segments of the force. Undaunted, Brown articulated his goals for the department during a citizen forum, when, according to the *Houston Chronicle,* the "Police Chief Sets Priorities: Top Problems Must Be Identified Quickly": (1) improve working conditions for officers; (2) increase the size of the force to correspond with the growth of the city; (3) procure new equipment; (4) improve internal communications; and (5) improve HPD response time.[60] His strong political position and the support of the mayor allowed him to move forward with cautious regard for his opposition. His wariness was warranted, as his most contentious plan, community policing, was yet to be unveiled.

Brown, a pioneer in neighborhood policing, was determined to make the HPD responsive to the needs to the communities it served. Many within the department hated the concept, because it placed them in what they felt was hostile territory. He outlined his plan in an article entitled "Bridges over Troubled Waters," emphasizing that "within the black community, police harassment, police brutality, and police corruption do exist. The abuses do not accidentally occur and they are not acts of malice on the part of the individual. The abuses are built into the police system by virtue of its composition and organization structure, and maintained by the articulation of the police mission. Void of power, the black community remains the unfortunate recipient of misuse by police."[61] The consensus of most police in the city was that getting to know the community had little merit; moreover, they were not social workers.[62]

Community policing was not a new idea. It grew out of the neighborhood watch system of the 1960s, and had been used with a degree of success since then. In theory, community policing forged a relationship between the police and the communities they served by forcing personal interaction. Robert C. Trojanowinz suggests that the key to community policing is service delivery, not law enforcement.[63] Most police agencies approached community policing in the 1980s with a great degree of skepticism. The problem reformers faced was that of trying to get the decentralized and physically estranged police to reintegrate into service-delivery areas in a more personal manner. Many within the HPD resented the idea of personalizing police/community relations.

Brown also caught flak from minorities, who believed that he should have immediately corrected the historically biased promotion practices. The two minority unions quickly took offense as he reshaped his command staff with whites. Brown insisted that qualifications and not race would serve as the criteria for promotion. Members of the Afro-American Patrolmen's Union felt that the new chief had let them down.[64] Former HPD Chief C. O. Bradford, then an executive officer in the Afro-American Patrolmen's Union, said that "Brown really made you mad. He would just listen to you, then say he would take it under advisement."[65] But Brown did hear them and, more important, he understood their concerns. Bradford and Mae Walker recalled that "the chief asked us [African American] officers what we wanted most, an assistant chief or more minorities promoted to the rank of sergeant? We said, we wanted sergeants."[66] Brown did increase the number of minority sergeants on the police force.

Training was a high priority for the chief, and he set out to make important changes in the police academy. He, perceptively, understood that police misconduct often stemmed from improper training and failure to adhere to department policy and procedures. Therefore, he set reform of the training academy as a battle that he could not lose. African Americans on the force felt that he was not doing enough to change things and publicly criticized him. C. O. Bradford recalled a meeting with Brown when "the Chief [Brown] told me that I could be part of the solution or part of the problem. It is better to change things from inside than trying to change things from outside."[67] The conservative nature of police forces in general and the HPD's customs therefore complicated Brown's reform efforts.

On May 18, when Chief Brown addressed problems with HPD's Field Training Officers Program (FTO), "12 white training officers resigned, saying that the chief discriminated by reinstating 2 black probationary officers recommended for dismissal from the force." The FTO officers believed that the chief was guilty of a "blatant case of discrimination." They felt that the standards of the previously all-white FTO program were fair and just and that it was their birthright to be standard-bearers for the police department.[68] The officers did not understand that their group affiliation had made them the privileged class within the police department for more than one hundred years or that they had created an exclusive brotherhood that had made advancement possible for whites only. Thus, the reform measures by Chief Brown, an outsider, impugned the integrity of this traditional, self-perpetuating system.

While Brown's actions cut against the grain, he felt that racial bias was present in the FTO program where the two black rookie officers were stationed.[69] A vocal majority of white officers was incensed that he ignored their recommendations to fire the two officers. He reinstated them, one a black male and the other a black female, and then he ordered that they be retrained in a new police academy class in the fall of 1982.

On August 9, the chief created a triethnic review panel for the FTO program. The panel consisted of one African American officer, one Hispanic officer, and one white patrol sergeant. The review panel was instituted to hear grievances and make recommendations on the cases of suspended or harshly graded rookie patrol officers who felt that senior field officers rating their field performance unfairly. The HPPU's president was angered, emphasizing that Chief Brown's "decision reflected that racism does exist in the training program."[70]

In spite of their protest, however, training at the police academy took on a new face in the fall of 1982. A new training staff that included minorities brought a fresh perspective to the academy. This created an atmosphere that allowed for diverse opinions. Brown had quietly given minority officers opportunity and access to compete for training jobs. He felt that part of being a police officer meant conforming to the existing rules, so he did not violate civil service law when he moved minorities into spots previously denied them by HPD's structure.

Cheers were still a long way off, though, because paramilitary-style training made radical change too difficult. Many of the changes instituted under Brown were made to ameliorate the effects of pending lawsuits against the city by minorities.

The Comeaux and Kelly cases inadvertently provided the perfect segue for the mayor's civil service reforms. These lawsuits were filed in 1975 and 1976, respectively, and challenged the city of Houston's promotion and hiring practices. The suits alleged that testing and promotions in the Houston Police Department were racially biased. When the Fifth Circuit Court remanded the cases back to the trial courts, the cases were reborn via *Edwards v. City of Houston.* The case was decided in 1992; however, as a result of this and other pending litigation, the police and the fire departments began to increase the numbers of blacks in supervisory roles.

On Thursday, June 3,1982, less than six months after taking office, Mayor Whitmire formed a "special citizens' committee to collect petition signatures calling for an August 14 referendum aimed at getting local control of the civil service system as it "affects police officers and firefighters." Fire and police unions were livid. HPOA president Bill Elkins informed the *Houston Post* that "I think now we are seeing the mayor's true colors," and that "her pure intent is to be dictator of the city of Houston."[71] This time the mayor had a coalition of black and white business leaders behind her.[72] This coalition proved to be invaluable, as she had their unqualified support when she held open forums regarding a referendum to amend state civil service law 1269M, passed in 1947 to protect fire fighters and police officers from the effects of political patronage.

Across the state, police agencies saw 1269M as a savior and a sign that they were free of political control. In truth, however, the legislature's intent had been to outlaw collective bargaining and subvert any efforts at radical unionization of the state's police and fire departments.[73] The union mounted an aggressive campaign against the referendum, but it failed to take responsibility for its predicament, instead blaming the decline in both public respect for the department and officer morale on the previous two mayoral administrations.

Community leaders showed little sympathy when the unions proselytized against the referendum. Moreover, the lack of action left them vulnerable to Mayor Whitmire and open to even more public scrutiny. The unions' public protest also failed because most major companies and local business leaders supported the mayor's efforts to reform civil service.

The August, 1982, referendum passed, and the police and fire unions could only angrily protest the outcome, because most in the city felt that the referendum was a major step toward substantive changes in the police department. However, police officers viewed the issue as a challenge to their integrity. They let the issue further estrange them from the community they served.

Fixing the HPD's image was one of Chief Brown's goals, but it would be a harder job than he imagined. In a speech on May 20, 1982, to the Downtown Rotary Club, Brown said that he would consult "professionals" about repairing the negative image of the Houston Police Department. He added that his "major goal is to advance the professionalism and efficiency of the Police Department so that it becomes a showcase for policing in America."[74]

Then he went to work on the most important detail, the department's public image. He required that officers wear ties and hats with their uniforms effective November 1. In a formal notice, he stressed that "the purpose of this change is to project a uniform appearance which should have a positive effect on the department's public image and enhance officer self-esteem and pride in the department."[75] The unions again attacked Brown by implying that he had lost his mind. They claimed that uniforms would do little good when morale was so low.

The unions had shown nothing but contempt for the mayor, and their hatred of her increased after her reelection in 1983. During the campaign, they financed a negative ad campaign in which they called the mayor "Tootsie" after a character in a popular movie. In June, 1983, Houston's economy was stalled because of a national recession, and the mayor announced that there would be an decrease in dependent health care benefits. HPD officers blamed her for the economy, and feelings reached the boiling point when three hundred angry police officers stormed city council chambers on June 15, 1983, and interrupted the council session. Their aggressiveness frightened Mayor Whitmire, who got no help from the city council when she asked to adjourn the meeting. As the television cameras rolled, some of the officers shouted obscenities at the mayor. Most of the officers who came to council chambers were on vacation, but others came during regular work hours and thus violated city rules.[76] Chief Brown disciplined the officers he could identify who had orally assaulted the mayor.

Chief Brown was serious about improving the image of the HPD, and his actions showed that he could handle the disgruntled unions. How he chose the members of his command staff was a sensitive morale issue. Thus, he moved cautiously, as he recommended three white males for assistant chiefs of police.

In 1984, however, Brown suggested changes in promotion procedures and questioned the validity of the testing method used for choosing high-ranking officers. He continued to be attacked by elements of the HPPU, which was now publishing a monthly diatribe called the *Sentinel*. On October 20, 1985, Tommy Britt, president of the HPPU, which now had two thousand members, and *Sentinel* editor, Don Cook, declared war on Whitmire and Brown. They urged their members to seek revenge on Brown by embarrassing him during the meeting in Houston of the International Association of Chiefs of Police in October.[77] Brown ignored them and pressed forward with his agenda.

Even Chief Brown could not change some things, because the police were so entrenched in traditional attitudes that they had fought him and the mayor on almost every issue. However, he pointed the HPD in the right direction, and its command staff and reputation had improved dramatically by 1986. Between 1985 and 1987, he faced more serious internal incidents caused by the continued presence of criminal elements within the department. A massive drug-related corruption case in 1986 and the fact that Whitmire's popularity was fading led many to believe that Brown had done all he could do. New opportunities were calling, as he was highly sought after as a lecturer and expert in the field of policing. On January 18, 1990, Brown moved on, accepting a position as the superintendent of the nation's largest police force, in New York City. It was clear that Brown had supporters in the national Democratic Party interested in him as a possible political appointee.

Brown's tenure was the beginning of the bureaucratic transformation of the Houston Police Department. It suggested that the department's racist past had reached a turning point and that the department must now go in another direction. Moreover, overt acts of racism would no longer be tolerated under the guise of policing and within the spirit of the law. Brown had entered his position with confidence, caution, and a proven record as a capable administrator. The city would never be the same. Neither would the HPD.

Conclusion

Urbanization and modernization engulfed twentieth-century Houston. From 1900 to 1990, the city's population increased fiftyfold, but the police department never grew large enough to protect the city adequately. The HPD's steadfast desire to maintain tradition, including racial segregation and exclusion, became a most formidable barrier to change. The department's professional growth was impeded by poor management, a limited budget, and racist attitudes that often prevented officers from extending even basic civility to large segments of the population in the discharge of their duties. The failure to provide adequate, efficient, and professional service hurt minority communities especially, and the department's resistance to reform limited its growth and hampered its professional and bureaucratic development.

This book shows that change within the Houston Police Department was not monolithic, but dynamic and multifaceted. It evolved slowly and painfully into a modern police force. The hiring of Lee Patrick Brown symbolized the washing away of the HPD's long history of maintaining the status quo, traditionalism, and racism. White and black officers alike were fearful of the changes to come. Moreover, they were, for a time, all locked in a self-perpetuating cycle of violence and unprofessional conduct caused by improper and outmoded training. During Brown's tenure, the white beneficiaries of HPD's managerial apartheid fretted and worried about payback from an outsider chief, whom they viewed as the new black knight of justice. The fears and hopes of minorities in the police department, anticipating more benefit than harm from the impending changes, were high.

The department had much to fear because it had been extremely effective at moderating or controlling the effects of internal change. Change within the police department had historically originated as a pragmatic rank-and-file action, which was later implemented throughout the department. Therefore, racism was a convenient tool of social control and unfettered power. By accepting and internalizing the ethos of racial segregation, the HPD developed internal policies, procedures, and attitudes that led it to try to control, rather than to protect, society. With race as both an impediment to change and a shield against bureaucratic innovation, the police department stumbled forward, insisting on maintaining Jim Crow in a city that had modernized and undergone tremendous changes in its racial and ethnic composition.

The breakdown of Jim Crow was not the result of genuine changes in attitude within. For example, promotion of minorities in the 1970s was quieted by aggressive activism and allayed the department's fear of losing the support of Houston's business community. The latter, because of the HPD's reputation for violence and corruption, believed that societal change was inevitable and increasingly viewed the department as a political liability.

By 1982, the HPD's unsavory past had led to the ultimate symbol of impending institutional change and increased professionalism: the hiring of outsider Lee Patrick Brown. He became the new model of a professional police manager, which the city followed in hiring each successive chief. After some painful mistakes, the HPD had finally had to accept the inevitability of change.

In 1990, Mayor Whitmire used her prerogative to reach way down the police promotional ladder to appoint Capt. Elizabeth Watson as the first woman chief of the Houston Police Department.[1] Watson's appointment was the result of the civil service referendum that allowed the mayor to appoint anyone who met the qualifications for police chief. Chief Watson was a seventeen-year HPD veteran who had risen through the ranks to become the first female captain and deputy chief. Both unions on the force welcomed her appointment, but some segments of the HPD expressed anger at the appointment of a woman and a captain, which they regarded as a gross violation of department promotion customs.

Chief Watson continued Brown's legacy by supporting neighborhood policing. Her appointments of qualified women and minorities in key management positions, such as assistant chief and department head, exponentially changed the face of the police department.

In 1992, Bob Lanier defeated Whitmire in a nasty mayoral race that marked the return, in mentality, at least, of good-old-boy politics. Lanier, a wealthy attorney who is a member of Houston's establishment, wanted the return of elite political traditions and customs in the city. Mayor Lanier waited forty-two days, then appointed former veteran HPD police officer and federal prosecutor Sam Nuchia as chief of police. He removed Watson as chief and returned her to deputy chief. Watson showed no bitterness at her dismissal, telling reporters at a press conference that "I didn't ask to be chief, and I didn't ask to be fired." Chief Nuchia continued to appoint qualified police officers to supervisory positions, including talented and well-educated African Americans. However, he did dramatically reduce neighborhood policing.

On November 8, 1996, Nuchia retired to pursue elective office as a probate judge, and Mayor Lanier replaced him with central command assistant chief Clarence O. Bradford. Bradford was the second African American police chief of the HPD. Unlike Brown, however, Bradford was an HPD insider, who, at the time of his appointment was a seventeen-year veteran of the police department. There was no angry outburst by police unions or allegation of violation of internal customs. Hans Marticiuc, president of the HPOU, said, "We are happy to see him." Bradford's appointment immediately opened the lines of communication between the officers, the chief, and the mayor. An elated Bradford stated, "It is a good time to be chief, employees are doing a fine job, the community is very supportive, the police-community relationship is no longer vacillating, HPD's role is firm and it is proper."[2]

On November 17, 1996, nine days after Bradford's appointment, the *Houston Chronicle* ran an article entitled "A Different World: Asian Female Officers Melt Old Distrust." It discusses the recruitment, trials, and triumphs that faced the first female Asian officers in Houston.

The Houston Police Department has evolved from a Jim Crow police force in the 1930s, corrupted by racism and political cronyism. The force is now a professionally managed and trained police force. In 1999, the HPD could claim that it had had a second minority police chief, one woman as chief, and one judge as chief. Although there are miles to go, a change did come in the Bayou City. The police are now part of the city's vanguard rather than a feared shepherd of the old guard.

Notes

Introduction

1. "Jim Crow" is the term used to define the system of racial subordination that separated the races in the United States on the basis of color. It originates from a popular minstrel tune in the 1840s. White minstrels put on blackface and danced like stereotypical "happy Negroes." The term "Negro" was used in the official documents of the HPD, and, when necessary, I shall use it as a literary device to convey status and racist sentiment which changed through time.
2. Litwack, *Trouble in Mind,* 263. Litwack sees the courts and the police as a conjoined unit that ensured white supremacy through the control of southern blacks.
3. Muse, *Don't Buy a Car,* 59. In this anecdotal piece, Muse ascribes the Houston police force's reputation as the worst cops in the nation to department self-rule.
4. Lane, *Policing the City,* 1.
5. Monkennen, *Police in Urban America,* xiii, both quotations.
6. Rousey, *Policing the Southern City,* 8, 9.
7. Rubinstein, *City Police,* ix, xi.
8. Radelet, *Police and the Community,* 29.
9. *Report of the National Advisory Commission on Civil Disorders,* 51.
10. Wilson, *Thinking about Crime,* 137.
11. Wilson, *Bureaucracy,* 170.
12. S. Walker, *Critical History of Police Reform,* ix.
13. Rudwick, *Negro Police in the South,* 4.
14. Dulaney, *Black Police in America,* xiv.

Chapter 1

1. Marchiafava, *Houston Police,* 63–64, adds that Houston's Civil Service Commission, which was designed to limit the effects of political patronage, was ineffective in protecting employees in its early days.
2. Houston Police Department, Annual Report, 1931. This is an unpublished report prepared by the department and submitted to the mayor. Photostat copies were provided me by the Houston Police Department Museum. See also Denny Hair, "An Outline of Police History," 16, for Prohibition-related statistics in the 1930s. Police museum curator, Denny Hair, gave me a copy of this document.

3. "Percy Heard Named City's Police Chief."
4. See ibid. and "Police Shake-up Effected" for a detailed account of Chief Heard's personnel changes.
5. Marchiafava, *Houston Police,* 51–54, also n35, p.91; Griffenhagen and Associates, Consultants in Public Administration. "City of Houston: The Police Department." Survey, December 28, 1939. Report no. 3, vol. 1, 57.
6. Marchiafava, *Houston Police,* 62–73, shows that patronage won out over the legal challenges and civil service reform efforts.
7. These data are compiled from the U.S. Census, 1900, 1910, 1920, 1930, and 1940.
8. Feagin, *Free Enterprise City*, 47.
9. Various newspaper accounts and general histories of Houston reflect that city officials were always more concerned about fire and floods than about police protection during the late nineteenth and the early twentieth centuries.
10. The use of special officers in the HPD developed out of both political patronage and economic necessity. These officers had all the rights of regular police officers, but they were paid less and they were subject to the right of the council and the mayor to hire and fire them at will. They were often hired as a result of patronage, which created management problems for the department.
11. Platt, *City Building,* 90. Platt does not address the establishment of police services, which supports my argument that HPD officers were municipal enforcers who were important as protectors of the property of the city's elite and only reacted to crime rather than trying to prevent it.
12. Marchiafava, *Houston Police*, 12.
13. Ibid., 54.
14. Radelet, *Police and the Community*, 8, 14.
15. For a discussions of the third degree as a national problem, see Chafee, Pollak, and Stern, *Third Degree*. The third degree was used by police nationally from 1930 to 1960 as a coercive method of interrogation. In 1930, President Hoover, reacting to complaints about the abuse of police power, convened the national Commission on Law Observance and Enforcement, or the Wickersham Commission, to address police reform. The commission was one of the last great progressive-era reform efforts.
16. Griffenhagen and Associates, *Griffenhagen Survey*, 58.
17. "Officer Pares Dies of Wounds Received in Fight with Bandit," *Houston Post-Dispatch,* September 21 and 29, 1930.
18. "Percy Heard Is Candidate for Sheriff." The article was a glowing political advertisement for Heard, who was photographed dressed in parade uniform and looking very official. Heard's political ambition would cost him his job twice.
19. Houston Police Department, Annual Report, 1930. See also "Houston Cops Fully Armed."

20. "Machine Gun Practice Set by Policemen."
21. Radelet, *Police and the Community*, 14. See also Kelling, "Community Paradigm of Policing," which discusses the impact of early police reformers such as August Vollmer, William Parker, O. W. Wilson, and J. Edgar Hoover.
22. Radelet, *Police and the Community*, 14, 36–37. See also Chafee, Pollak, and Stern, *Third Degree*, 21.
23. Bittner, "Florence Nightingale," 17; Banton, "Authority and the Mass Society," 10 (quoted in Radelet, *Police and the Community*, 2n9). Radelet argues that police authority is conservative in nature and derived from the power assumed from the people.
24. Houston Police Department, Annual Report, 1930, "Budget Increased to Purchase Weapons."
25. Ibid.
26. "Machine Gun Practice Set by Policemen."
27. Ibid.
28. Denny Hair, "History of the Houston Police." Hair gives no reason for the firings other than money woes; however, four of the firings were for corruption, incompetence, and unprofessional conduct ("New Police Chief Fires Four the First Day").
29. Marchiafava, *Houston Police*, 63–64.
30. "Houston." Chief Heard's editorial was also an attempt to garner support for the HPD for future negotiations with the city.
31. Feagin, *Free Enterprise City*, 61.
32. "Fund to Operate Plant Is Sought."
33. "Percy Heard Is Candidate for Sheriff." This race pitted Heard against Delery, incumbent sheriff T. A. Binford, and T. N. Benson.
34. Quoted in "Fund to Operate Plant Is Sought."
35. "City Buys 300 New Pistols." The city purchased 300 Colt .44-caliber revolvers at a cost of $27.00 each, for a total cost of $8,100.00. They were distributed to HPD officers at cost. HPD officers still purchase their own side arms. The minimum allowed is a .38-caliber.
36. Some of Heard's policy changes were not well planned, nor were they of much strategic significance to the department. True reform did not begin within the department until 1938. The national impulse for reforming police departments began in 1931 with the National Commission on Law Observance and Enforcement. One key recommendation was the creation of schools for all police training. Ironically, societal changes brought on by World War II served as the impetus for systematic police education. See Radelet, *Police and the Community*, 14, 36–37, 52, for a more thorough discussion of the commission's efforts.
37. "Mayor Monteith Enthusiastic over Police Radio after Test." For a general discussion of the impact of radio technology, see S. Walker, *Popular Justice*, 190.
38. "Police Radio Is Given Its First Test."

39. Ibid., September 3, 1932.
40. "Police Radio is Given Its First Tests," *Houston Press*, November 1, 1932.
41. Davidson, *Biracial Politics*, 20–21.
42. *Smith v. Allwright*, 321 U.S. 657 (1944). For a discussion of the origins and impact of the *Smith* decision and the Terrell election law, see Hine, *Black Victory*, 4–5, 23–45.
43. Radelet, *Police and the Community*, 109–27.
44. SoRelle, "Darker Side of Heaven," 1–20.
45. Denny Hair interview, June 18, 1998.
46. Bullard, *Invisible Houston*, 11.
47. Hine, *Black Victory*, 4–5, 23–45; SoRelle, "Darker Side of Heaven," 283–309.
48. "Shake-up in City Police Department Due Today," *Houston Post*, April 29, 1933.
49. Ibid.
50. "Detective Lieutenant Dismissed," *Houston Press*, May 5, 1933; "Shake-up in City Police Department Due Today," *Houston Post*, April 29,1933.
51. "Outline of a History of the Houston Police Department," 18.
52. Houston Police Department, Annual Report, 1935. The report to the mayor and city council details a rise in HPD expenditures.
53. Sibley, *Port of Houston*, 175; McComb, *Houston*, 127; Feagin, *Free Enterprise City*, 61–69. Feagin documents how the diversified economy lessened the effects of the Depression on the city. Also see Thomas and Murray, *Progrowth Politics*, 43–46. They suggest that Houston's development was fueled by manufacturing growth, which they divide into three distinct phases.
54. Feagin, *Free Enterprise City*, 54–55, 64–66.
55. Ibid., 62–63.
56. Sibley, *Port of Houston*, 190; see also Feagin, *Free Enterprise City*, 65–66.
57. Sibley, *Port of Houston*, 189.
58. "26 Demoted, 7 Are Retired, 3 Fired in Police Shakeup."
59. Biles, *The South and the New Deal*, 14.
60. Gillette, "Rise of the NAACP in Texas."
61. SoRelle, "Darker Side of Heaven," 251.
62. Wesley, "Clean Your Yards and Neighborhoods."
63. Davidson, *Biracial Politics*, 19–20; Bullard, *Invisible Houston*, 22–31.
64. Vermel Cook interview, June 30, 1997. She graduated from Phyllis Wheatley High School in the Fifth Ward in 1939, and has lived in the Third Ward since 1943.
65. Bullard, *Invisible Houston*, 11–12.
66. Teaford, *Twentieth-Century American City*, 109.
67. Kellar, "Make Haste Slowly," 81–84. Decisions on school funding were representative of the attitudes of most of Houston's public officials that something was better than nothing. The failure of national poli-

cies that address educational needs in the poor rural areas followed migrants to the city, where the same racist attitudes trapped them in poverty and a marginal existence. But even urban Jim Crow was an improvement over anything they could have hoped for in some rural areas at the time.

68. Weiss, *Farewell to the Party of Lincoln*, 36–37.
69. Houston police officer Lee Sparks, quoted in Haynes, "Houston Mutiny and Riot of 1917," 438.
70. S. Walker, *Critical History of Police Reform*, 125.
71. Woodward, *Strange Career of Jim Crow*, 129–42. Woodward offers an excellent appraisal of the clash of traditional white culture and the changes that occurred in the post–World War II years. He suggests that southerners felt that they had no choice but to defend their Jim Crow way of life.
72. Nash, *Crucial Era*, 157.
73. Michael Botson interview, Houston, November 12, 1997.
74. Letter to Walter White, NAACP field secretary, from Carter Wesley, editor of the *Houston Informer*, December, 1943, NAACP Papers, Box 2, Manuscript Division, Library of Congress.
75. Ibid.
76. Letter from Carter Wesley to NAACP chief legal counsel Thurgood Marshall, December, 1943, Thurgood Marshall Papers, Record Group C, Manuscript Division, Library of Congress. This letter admonishes Marshall and the NAACP for not being more aggressive in the *Smith* case. Challenges to police and the demand for respect were actually present throughout the South. Alexander Pierre (A. P.) Toureau, a noted black civil rights attorney in New Orleans, petitioned the state and federal courts to address the issue of police brutality. Beginning in 1931, he filed brief after brief requesting relief from police brutality on behalf of blacks in Louisiana. This summary is gathered from his legal files relating to police brutality.
77. "Rehearing on Negro Voting Will Be Asked." Governor Coke Stevenson declared it within the legislature's power to increase the poll tax or specify a literacy test as a voting prerequisite ("South's Devices Run Thin"). Also see Green, *The Establishment in Texas Politics*, 46–47, for a thorough discussion of political attitudes in Texas regarding the *Smith* decision.
78. "Negroes May Vote in Texas Democratic Primaries, Court Rules."
79. Pollenberg, *War and Society*, 126–29. For an account of the Beaumont riot, see Olson and Phair, "Anatomy of a Race Riot"; Burran, "Violence in an Arsenal of Democracy"; Shabazz, "Desegregation of Lamar State College of Technology," 57–60.
80. Pollenberg, *War and Society*, 127.
81. Hine, *Black Victory*, 210–29. Also see idem, "Elusive Ballot," or the case file for *Smith v. Allwright*, 321 U.S. 657, Supreme Court 757 (1944).
82. Hine, *Black Victory*, 210–20.

83. Payne, *I've Got the Light of Freedom*, 93. Davidson, *Biracial Politics*, 36–60, downplays the significance of the victory, saying it merely opened Negroes in the city up to victimization by the Democratic Party.
84. S. Walker, *Popular Justice*, 195.
85. Hair, "History of the Houston Police Department."

Chapter 2

1. Wilson, *Bureaucracy*, ix–xii.
2. Davidson, *Biracial Politics*, 11–22. See also Thomas and Murray, *Progrowth Politics*, 74.
3. Ernest McGowen Sr. interview, August 5, 1998. The Rev. McGowen is the first black associate pastor assigned to a white United Methodist congregation in Texas (in 1973).
4. Davidson, *Biracial Politics*, 5.
5. Green, *The Establishment in Texas Politics*, 155. He suggests that black labor was used to galvanize white support for conservative Democrat Allan Shivers in the 1954 governor's race against liberal Ralph Yarborough. Elites throughout the state overwhelmingly voted for Shivers, fearing Yarborough's support of integration.
6. Key, *Southern Politics*, 5.
7. Houston Police Department, Annual Report, 1945. This was the average number of officers listed in the department's annual report.
8. Houston Police Department, Annual Reports, 1940–45. This average figure includes only those who were classified as police officers. Some blacks were listed on the report as porters, cooks, and garage men.
9. For an account of the integration of downtown stores, see Coles, *No Color Is My Kind*.
10. McComb, *Houston*, 112–13; Feagin, *Free Enterprise City*, 120, 242; Carlton, *Red Scare*, 65–71.
11. E. J. Stringfellow, quoted in M. Walker, *History of the Black Police Officers*, 14.
12. Myrdal, *An American Dilemma*, 535, quoted in R. Kennedy, *Race, Crime, and the Law*, 113.
13. Hair, "An Outline of Police History"; E. J. Stringfellow (HPD narcotics officer, 1954–80, and city marshal, 1980–93) interview, January 27, 1998; Frederick Black interview, September 12, 1997; Oliver Brown interview, September 22, 1997.
14. Older black officers recalled stories told them by retired black patrol officers from the 1930s and the 1940s. White recruiters tried to get them mad during the interviews by insulting them.
15. Dulaney, "Texas Negro Peace Officers Association," 65.
16. Stringfellow interview.
17. Dunbar, "We Wear the Mask," in *Complete Poems*, 71.
18. During this high period of social volatility and political upheaval, Black police were compared to slave drivers in the American South.

For an ideological discussion of slave drivers, see Blassingame, *Slave Community*, 258–60.

19. Stringfellow interview.
20. Green, *The Establishment in Texas Politics*. In chapters 9 and 10, Green provides a useful context for understanding the racial climate that existed in the state's politics from 1938 to 1957. He suggests that race was a pawn that conservatives and liberals used in their attempt to control the state's political future. For a masterly journey through the segregated maze of Texas' racial and political culture's effort to resist the desegregation of higher education, see Shabazz, "Opening of the Southern Mind."
21. Studies of white police actions in black communities across the country characterize police presence as it was practiced as violent and unwanted. See R. Kennedy, *Race, Crime, and the Law,* 144, for the legal issues that police presence caused in black communities. For police attitudes toward blacks, see Skolnick, *Justice without Trial.*
22. Minutes of Houston City Council, 1945. Holcombe was arguably the city's first modern political leader. He was ever the politician, and he understood the political benefit of being perceived as the mayor who made the streets safe.
23. Radelet, *Community Policing,* 109–27.
24. SoRelle, "Darker Side of Heaven," 1–20.
25. Houston Police Department Annual Reports, 1940–45.
26. Hair interview.
27. S. Walker, *Critical History of Police Reform*, 171.
28. The 8-F Group was a group of Houston business leaders, including George and Herman Brown, Gus Wortham, Judge James Elkins, and Jim Abercrombie, who met at the Lamar Hotel downtown. Police and fire fighters believed that this group controlled all of Houston's political and economic decisions. See Pratt, "8F and Many More."
29. Hair interview.
30. Mark Haller quoted in S. Walker, *Critical History of Police Reform,* 56.
31. Stringfellow interview.
32. Carleton, *Red Scare,* 12. For a discussion of black union efforts along the Gulf Coast, see Starks, "Road to Jericho."
33. Carleton, *Red Scare,* 12.
34. Green, *The Establishment in Texas Politics,* 108–20. This work offers a useful discussion of the politics of antiunionism in the state during the Jester years. Also see Marchiafava, *Houston Police,* for a discussion of local efforts to secure the passage of 1269M.
35. Brown interview.
36. Black interview.
37. Stringfellow interview.
38. Green, *The Establishment in Texas Politics,* 1–19.
39. *Houston Chronicle,* January 15, 1946, sec. 1,1.
40. Wintersmith, *Police and the Black Community,* 37.

41. A. V. Young interview quoted in M. Walker, *History of the Black Police Officers*, 32.
42. Albert Blair interview, June 11, 1995.
43. Black interview.
44. Brown interview.
45. Brown interview. Black, Stringfellow, and Blair also recalled being told to sit in the back of the class.
46. Black interview.
47. Ibid.
48. Stringfellow interview.
49. Ibid.
50. For an examination of workplace alienation and racism endured by blacks in the South, see Harris, *The Harder We Run*.
51. Brown interview.
52. Black interview.
53. Ibid.
54. Brown interview.
55. Robert Crain graduated from the police academy in 1950, class number 4. He was part of a group of five black officers who all graduated. See M. Walker, "History of the Black Police Officers," 14.
56. Ibid.
57. Stringfellow interview.
58. Brown interview.
59. Ibid. For an account of the origins of the Gamewell box, see Horton and Turner, *Lone Star Justice*, 132.
60. Brown interview.
61. Black interview.
62. Laws of the City of Houston, Ordinance No. 57-322, passed March 20, 1957. Amending Section 1: Ordinance No. 705, passed by the City Council, October 13, 1954.
63. Black interview.
64. Dulaney, *Black Police in America*, 51.
65. Black and Brown interviews. Both men told me the same story. A thorough discussion of workplace discrimination through hazardous job assignments for blacks is found in Kelly, *Hammer and Hoe*, 143.
66. Brown interview.
67. Stringfellow interview.
68. Dulaney, *Black Police in America*, 120.
69. Black interview.
70. Brown interview.
71. George McElroy, telephone conversation with the author, September 27, 1993. He is the former editor of the *Houston Informer* and was a tireless critic of the police in the 1950s and the 1960s.
72. Alex, *Black in Blue*, 17.
73. Malcolm Ashford interview, February 12, 1998.
74. Black interview.

75. Brown interview.
76. For a discussion of the feelings and pressures felt by black officers, see Alex, *Black in Blue,* 115–31.
77. Black interview.
78. Cole, "The Negro Police Officer of Texas," 13–20. Cole's study revealed that the San Antonio Police Department, which served a city racially similar to Houston, had a different attitude about the benefits of black police. He illustrates that San Antonio's police viewed blacks as essential for the gathering of intelligence in black areas. He further reveals that the HPD failed to respond to his questionnaire and seemed to view the use of black patrol officers as a necessary evil. Nonetheless, blacks in the HPD performed a similar service as intelligence gatherers.
79. Stringfellow interview. The Rev. William Lawson was a local minister who founded the Wheeler Avenue Baptist Church and was an emerging social activist in the 1950s.
80. Coles, *No Color Is My Kind,* 16.
81. Blair interview.

Chapter 3

1. Fred Hofheinz, telephone interview, March 2, 1999.
2. For a general discussion of police reaction to the changing social dynamics in America, see Farber, *Chicago '68.* See also Moody, *Coming of Age in Mississippi,* for a first-person account of police repression in Mississippi during the 1960s. Both sources establish a context for the tensions and reactions created by the movement for social change in Houston.
3. Marchiafava, *The Houston Police,* 98. Marchiafava offers an accurate assessment of the impetus for change in the department through the 1960s.
4. The members of the HPD bureaucracy had all matured together on the force following World War II. They were a part of what has been called "the greatest generation." In postwar Houston, they tended to resist social differences and block racial change.
5. Skolnick, *Politics of Protest,* 85. See also Radelet, *Police and the Community,* 40–45; and Cray, *Enemy in the Streets,* 299–305.
6. Trice and Beyers, *Cultures of Work Organizations,* 234.
7. Thomas and Murray, *Progrowth Politics,* 43–48.
8. McComb, *Houston,* 143.
9. City of Houston, Annual Budget, 1960, 144.
10. Houston Police Department, Annual Report, 1960.
11. Ibid.
12. Cooper, *Police and the Ghetto,* 3.
13. DuVall, "Policeman Must be Wise."
14. Houston Police Department, Annual Reports,1960–64.

15. Interview conducted by the author with a local historian who asked not to be identified.
16. Cray, "Politics of Blue Power," quoted in Radelet, *Police and the Community,* 392n29.
17. Wilson was superintendent of the Chicago Police Department from 1956 to 1967. He became a professor of law at the University of Wisconsin after his retirement and was a leading proponent of the professionalization of urban police departments.
18. "Police Must Be Wise, Noble, and Firm in Duties," *Houston Post,* June 7, 1963.
19. Wilson, *Bureaucracy,* 132
20. Skolnick, *Politics of Protest,* 259–60.
21. "Police Ranks Slim."
22. "Police Department Makes while Cutrer Mayor."
23. Biography from Houston Public Library, Texas Room, clippings file on Herman Short and a Sons of the American Revolution press release dated 1970.
24. "How Much Crime Houston Has."
25. For a discussion of the discontent and conditions that preceded the Watts riot, see Bullock, ed., *Watts*; Branch, *Pillar of Fire;* and Horne, *Fire This Time.*
26. Liu, "Presidential Message," 46–47.
27. Schrotel, "Crowd Control in a Period of Social Change," 162–63.
28. Skolnick, *Politics of Protest,* 251.
29. For the best account of the motivations and impact of the antiwar movement, see Buzzanco, *Masters of War.*
30. Source information on Quentin Meese was taken from an interview conducted as part of a PBS special, "The Strange Demise of Jim Crow," shown on June 25, 1998. See also Coles, *No Color Is My Kind,* 94–95.
31. Young, "Welch Hopes to Resolve Police-Negro Relations."
32. Ibid.
33. Ibid.
34. Bullard, *Invisible Houston,* 33–35.
35. Davidson, *Biracial Politics,* 27.
36. Banks, "Discretionary Justice," 40.
37. U.S. Senate, *Hearing before the Permanent Sub-Committee on Investigations,* 14–21; National Advisory Commission on Civil Disorders, *Report,* 3–33.
38. Matusow, *Unraveling of America,* 345–76, argues that most African American youths never really accepted nonviolence, and by the late 1960s, many had all but rejected it as an effective strategy.
39. Coombs, *Black Experience in America,* 201. For a firsthand account of youths' reaction to strategy of the civil rights movement and related legislation, see Moody, *Coming of Age in Mississippi.*
40. See Grier and Cobbs, *Black Rage,* for a highly detailed discussion of the origins and manifestations of black anger and frustration.

41. Matusow, *Unraveling of America*, 345–76. See also Carson, *In Struggle*.
42. Baldwin, *Nobody Knows My Name*, 65–66.
43. Matusow, *Unraveling of America*, 367–74.
44. The name "TSU Riot" was created by the Houston Police Department to garner support for its actions on the campus during the incident.
45. Donald Jefferson (former TSU student and now professor of psychology) interview, November 23, 1993.
46. John Westbury (TSU registrar at the time of the riot) interview, August 30, 1992.
47. The theme of "outside agitation" as the source of local discontent during the protest years is common in the literature on civil rights. However, most of the leadership in the Houston struggle was from the city or surrounding areas. Interestingly, when whites joined local protests led by blacks, the newspapers and the police assumed that the whites were leading the blacks. See "Hippies Join TSU Courthouse Sit-In."
48. A flier entitled "Friends of the Student Non-Violent Coordinating Committee" called for new members and appeared on the Texas Southern University campus in the fall of 1966. For the origins of the Student Nonviolent Coordinating Committee from the perspectives of participants and observers, see Carson, *In Struggle*; Sellers, *River of No Return*; Branch, *Parting the Waters*.
49. Letter from James Jones, dean of students, to the Friends of SNCC, dated March 11, 1967. This letter is part of the personal archives of Mack H. Jones.
50. Letter from James B. Jones, dean of students, to the Friends of SNCC, dated January 20, 1967.
51. Mack H. Jones interview, December 21, 1992. At the time of our interview, Jones was chairman of the Social and Political Division at Prairie View A&M University.
52. Ibid.
53. Vernon Hunt interview, June 28, 1994. Hunt was a student at Texas Southern University in 1967 and vice-president of the student body.
54. Flier produced by "Friends of SNCC," dated March, 1967, Mack H. Jones archives.
55. Memorandum calling for meeting to discuss "Police Brutality Throughout the State of Texas," probably printed around March 5, 1967, Mack H. Jones archives.
56. Ibid.
57. Letter from James B. Jones, dean of men, to the Friends of SNCC, dated March 8, 1967, Mack H. Jones archives.
58. Mack Jones interview, December 21,1992.
59. Letter from Henry Bullock, chair of the Social Sciences Division, to Mack H. Jones, dated March 21, 1967, Mack H. Jones archives.
60. Mack Jones interview, December 21, 1992.
61. Letter from John Biggers, president of Faculty Council, to President Pierce, dated April 8, 1967, Mack H. Jones archives.

62. D. Smith, "TSU Demonstration Disrupts Classes."
63. "Ex-U.I.Student: Mack Jones Firing Starts TSU Lie-in."
64. "Texas Southern University."
65. Ibid.
66. "Police Arresting TSU Protest Heads."
67. For various accounts of the events leading up to the TSU incidents, see *Houston Post*, April 4–7, 1967; and *Houston Chronicle*, April 5, 1967.
68. Mack Jones interview, December, 1992. See also Schneider, "Death Stood Next to Him."
69. Bill Lawson interview, October 12, 1993.
70. "Peace Bond Hearing Today," *Houston Post*, April 6, 1967.
71. "Protestors Peace-Bonded," *Houston Post*, April 7, 1967.
72. Ibid.
73. Ibid. For legal statutes regarding peace bonds, see Vernon's Texas Penal Code Art. 7.03, General and Special Laws of the State of Texas, Fifty-ninth Legislature. This law gives broad discretionary power to magistrates in setting the parameters of peace bonds.
74. Barbara Jones interview, December 21, 1992.
75. Lawson interview.
76. Mack Jones interview, December 21, 1992.
77. Blaylock quoted in John Makeig, "Inches Away from a Major Riot."
78. Blair interview.
79. Mack Jones interview, December 21, 1992.
80. Lawson interview.
81. Ibid.
82. Beckwith, "Police Did Right Thing." Many persons involved in the TSU incident suspected that Kirkpatrick was an informant. I found no evidence to corroborate this allegation, however, although he seemed always to avoid being present at protests where the police were most aggressive.
83. "Bush Backs Police on Riot Action."
84. Lawson, "A Second Look at the 'TSU Riots.'"
85. For a detailed examination of police and institutional reaction to black student protests after 1966, see Nelson and Bass, *Orangeburg Massacre*, and Spofford, *Lynch Street.*
86. Lawson, "A Second Look at the 'TSU Riots.'"
87. *Forward Times*, June 10, 1967.
88. D. L. Lee, "The New Integrationist," in *Black Poets.*
89. Lawson interview.
90. Wilson, *Thinking about Crime*, 110.
91. Ibid., 111.
92. These cases particularly angered the police community, which felt that the court had placed unreasonable limitations on their power. *Mapp v. Ohio*, 367 U.S. 643, 1961, ruled regarding the suppression of illegally obtained evidence; *Miranda v. Arizona*, 384 U.S. 436, 1966, prohibited the police from using illegally obtained confessions and

evidence. For a look at the judicial aftermath of *Miranda,* see Lewis and Peoples, *The Supreme Court.*

93. Fogelson, *Violence as Protest,* 27. See also Wilson, *Thinking about Crime,* 109.
94. *Houston Post,* August 8, 1968. This article does not provided any details regarding the infractions or their punishment.
95. Bob Tuft, "Two Policemen to Surrender on Murder Charges," *Houston Post,* September 10, 1969. Officers J. A. McMahon and Arthur N. Hill were indicted on charges of murder with malice in the death of Bobby Conner and charges of assault for the beating of Larry Taylor. Both officers were indefinitely suspended by Chief Short, though they were later exonerated of all charges.
96. *Houston Post,* August 30, 1969.
97. Wilson, *Thinking about Crime,* 5.
98. Bob Tuft, "Welch Sees No Cause for Short's Resignation," *Houston Post,* May 20, 1969.
99. For the black press's account of the problems of recruiting and promoting minorities, see T. Wright, "Apparent Inability to Compete with White Officers." Short blamed the failure of minorities to become police on poor schools and test-taking ability.
100. Ibid.
101. Matusow, *Unraveling of America.*
102. For a discussion of the surveillance of black student activists nationally by the FBI and the police, see Branch, *Parting the Waters*; Marx, *Undercover*; Gentry, *J. Edgar Hoover,* 603–6.
103. Pleasantville is one of the original enclave communities for blacks living outside the central wards of Houston.
104. Herman Short, *Houston Post,* 1971.
105. Chandler Davidson, *Biracial Politics,* 127; see also *Houston Post,* December 4, 1971.
106. Davidson, *Biracial Politics,* 128.
107. For different accounts of the Dowling Street shootout, see George Rosenblatt and Steve Singer, "Black Militant Slain on Dowling: Police Gunmen Exchange Fire; 52 Arrested," *Houston Post,* July 27, 1970; Artice Vaughn, "Moments after Dowling Standoff," *Forward Times,* August 1, 1970; and Thomas Wright, "Diacritical View of Dowling Street Confrontation," *Forward Times,* July 25, 1970.
108. Davidson, *Biracial Politics,* 126–27.
109. Edward Walsh, "Welch Calls Ouster Demands 'Babblings'," *Houston Chronicle,* July 29, 1970.

Chapter 4

1. Jones, "Introduction," 4.
2. Radelet, *Police and the Community,* 173–88.
3. My use of the terms "liberal" or "liberalization" does not imply that

a political shift to the left occurred, but suggests that new political figures emerged in the 1970–79 period who did not fit the Texas political establishment mold. These politicians had a broader and more inclusive sense of the role of government and its function that included consideration of voters' needs.

4. Dick Gottlieb quoted in McNutt, "What the Mayor Is All About." During the campaign, Hofheinz courted and received 95 percent of the black vote, which gave him a decisive edge in the runoff with Gottlieb (because of low voter turnout).
5. Marchiafava interview, January 21, 1999.
6. Discussions with police officers who knew Short revealed that he was conducting his real estate business from his office in the last months of his tenure as chief.
7. S. Walker, *Popular Justice*, 211–12.
8. Hofheinz interview.
9. George Strong interview, March 26, 1999. Strong relocated to Houston in 1969 to become director of the Southwest Center for Urban Research at the University of Houston. He helped manage Hofheinz's campaigns and served as his ombudsman, responsible for the Fire, Police, Planning, and Health Departments, and for Government Relations.
10. Marchiafava interview, January 17, 1999.
11. Splitter, "The Controversial Career of Carroll Lynn."
12. Strong interview.
13. Northcott, "Cops as Robbers," 5–7.
14. Hofheinz interview.
15. Strong interview.
16. Houston Police Department, Annual Report, 1974.
17. City of Houston, Annual Budget, 1974 and 1975, 185–89. The police department requested additional funding to increase personnel supervision. It also proposed increases in in-service training and putting more desk officers back on the street by replacing them with clerks.
18. Treviño, "History of Hispanic Police Officers in Houston."
19. Strong interview.
20. C. O. Bradford interview, June 12, 1997. Bradford was then assistant chief of Central Command at the HPD.
21. M. Walker, *History of the Black Police Officers*, 56, 57.
22. Splitter, "The Controversial Career of Carroll Lynn."
23. For an account of the firing of Jack Heard Jr. and Wayne Jones, see Ann James, "Sheriff's Son, Jones Fired."
24. Ibid.
25. "Police Chief Announces New Posts."
26. Hair interview, June 18, 1998. Hair revealed that Chief Short felt that Caldwell was too intellectual for a cop and would hurt the department.
27. James, "Deputy Police Chief Gets 2-week Suspension."

28. Hofheinz interview.
29. For an examination of FBI and police surveillance techniques, see Blackstock, *Cointelpro*. Also see J. Davis, *Spying on America*; and "A Nation of Law?"
30. Radelet, *Police and the Community*, 312. Also see Wilson, *Thinking about Crime*, 36.
31. Scheingold, *Politics of Law and Order*, 83–86.
32. Strong interview.
33. Wilson, *Thinking about Crime*, 238.
34. For an explanation of the commission's work, see *Rules and Regulations*.
35. Houston Police Department, Annual Report, 1975.
36. "No Racism in HPD,"*Houston Chronicle*, June 5, 1976.
37. Troutt, "Bond Plans to Resign."
38. Ibid.; Strong interview.
39. Troutt, "Caldwell with Police."
40. Strong interview.
41. Brennan, "1975 Shooting."
42. Ibid.
43. Christy Drennan, "FBI Is Probing Killing of Joyvies Youth by Police," *Houston Chronicle*, April 23, 1978.
44. Drennan, "FBI Is Probing Killing of Joyvies."
45. Hair interview.
46. A recent rash of fatalities revealed that a police officer's adrenaline rush created more aggression at chase scenes. Police arriving at a scene must wait for backup before transporting a suspect to jail. Furthermore, studies suggest that officers involved in high-speed chases are twice as likely to use force as those who come as backup or to transport the perpetrator.
47. Hair interview.
48. Anonymous FBI agent interview, May 10, 1998.
49. Paulsen, "Police Conduct and the Public," 255.
50. Radelet, *Police and the Community*, 246.
51. Ibid., 246, 250.
52. General orders were the department's effort at placing some responsibility on individual officers for training lapses. This practice was controversial.

Chapter 5

1. Taylor, "Police Rookie Recounts Arrest of Joe Torres."
2. For a discussion of the impact of the Torres death on local politics, see De León, *Ethnicity in the Sunbelt*, 209–11.
3. Troutt, "Mayor Calls Police Image Illness."
4. Muse, *Don't Buy a Car Made on Monday*, quoted in Ashby, "Wrong Reason." See also Curtis, "Support Your Local Police." This article not

only discusses Torres's death, but also gives a summary history of institutionalized brutality within the HPD.

5. Taylor, "Torres Violent When Drunk, NCO Recalls." During the trial, the HPD officers' attorney put Torres's character on trial. His former first sergeant described him as a man who could not handle alcohol and was a misfit. The judge disallowed most of his testimony as hearsay.
6. Drennan, "Vance, Caldwell Says Executions Would Curb Holdup-Murders." This pro–death penalty article displays a clear anti-minority bias. It suggests that the death penalty would be a deterrent to murder. The history of Torres and the HPD emanates from a series of family disturbances or barroom brawls.
7. For accounts of the arrest, see Curtis, "Support Your Local Police," 85; Taylor, "Police Rookie Recounts Arrest of Joe Torres."
8. Skolnick quoted in Radelet, *Police and the Community,* 95.
9. Curtis, "Support Your Local Police," 85; Taylor, "Police Rookie Recounts Arrest of Joe Torres."
10. For a thorough discussion of the officers' action in the dead zone, see Drennan, "The Hole"
11. "Police Rookie Recounts Arrest of Joe Torres," *Houston Post,* September 12, 1977.
12. Ibid.
13. Taylor, "Oh, My God, They've Really Thrown Him In."
14. Associated Press, A.M. cycle, Huntsville, Texas, September 26, 1977, http:web.lexis-nexis.com/universe/doc.
15. Curtis, "Support Your Local Police," 180.
16. Torres's blood alcohol level was twice the legal limit. For the cause of death and toxicological reports, see Jachimczyk, Autopsy Report.
17. Wittenberg, "City Police Rookie Recounts Testimony in Torres Death."
18. Ibid.
19. For a discussion of the code of silence, see Skolnick and Fyfe, *Above the Law,* 108–10; Scheingold, *Politics of Law and Order,* 96–98.
20. H. G. Tucker, Coroner's Investigator's Report, #77-2272, "Jose Campos Torres," May 8, 1977, reveals that Pérez and her husband called and came to the morgue to identify the body.
21. "Jail Blotter" is the trade name of the booking sheet. All inmates arrested and processed at the jail were signed in to maintain the chain of custody. Chain of custody is established when a prisoner is signed into a jail or prison. The facility then becomes responsible for the prisoner's care, custody, and treatment.
22. For a discussion of police powers in an arrest, see Texas Code of Criminal Procedure, Art. 2.13. [37] [44] [45], Duties and Powers [of Police Officers], Law of the State of Texas:

(a) It is the duty of every peace officer to preserve the peace within the officer's jurisdiction. To effect this purpose, the officer shall use all lawful means.

(b) The officer shall:

(1) in every case authorized by the provisions of this Code, interfere without warrant to prevent or suppress crime;

(2) execute all lawful process issued to the officer by any magistrate or court;

(3) give notice to some magistrate of all offenses committed within the officer's jurisdiction, where the officer has good reason to believe there has been a violation of the penal law; and

(4) arrest offenders without warrant in every case where the officer is authorized by law, in order that they may be taken before the proper magistrate or court and be tried.

(c) It is the duty of every officer to take possession of a child under Article 62.009(g). Acts 1965, 59th Leg., vol. 2, p. 317, chap. 722. Amended by Acts 1999, 76th Leg., chap. 685, §1, eff. Sept. 1, 1999.

23. Tucker, Coroner's Investigator's Report.
24. Ibid.
25. Thomason and Escobar, Coroner's Investigator's Report. Until his family identified the clothing he was wearing on the day he died, Torres's body was assigned Morgue #105-858.
26. Jachimczyk, Autopsy Report, 1. For a graphic discussion of Torres's autopsy, see James, "Body Bruised, Autopsy Shows." The advanced stages of decomposition of the body made it impossible to tell if the injuries Torres sustained as a result of the beating contributed more to his death than being dumped, in his drunken condition, into the bayou.
27. Troutt, "Bond Will Form Internal Affairs Division."
28. Ibid.
29. Internal police department gossip suggested that Short would have considered the job had Wallace won. Short was a segregationist but a pragmatic racist who used race to control and motivate many within the department. Although he accepted federal funds in the late 1960s and the 1970s, he actively tried to minimize federal intrusion into local police affairs.
30. Hofheinz interview.
31. Troutt, "5 of 6 Officers Fired in the Torres Death Case."
32. "Reyes Asks Hofheinz to Back Police Inquiry." Also see De León, *Ethnicity in the Sunbelt,* 209–11. For an ideological discussion of the political evolution of the Chicano movement in the 1970s, see Gutiérrez, *Walls and Mirrors,* 179–205; and Acuña, *Occupied America.*
33. The Torres Justice Coalition included several middle class–oriented groups, such as the Coalition for Responsible Law Enforcement, the Political Association of Spanish-Speaking Organizations (PASO), the

American GI Forum, the Mexican American Legal Defense and Educational Fund (MALDEF), and Image of Houston. The fireworks started when Barrios Unidos and the Raza Unida Party (RUP) stated that they were speaking for the working class, or *colonia*. This fight actually became a strategy referendum for the Mexican American community. See De León, *Ethnicity in the Sunbelt*, 211–13.

34. Strong interview.
35. Bond resigned to take over as head of corporate security at Tenneco Oil in Houston. He quit despite urging by the mayor and other city leaders to remain. He actually stepped aside in June, 1977, and Mayor Hofheinz named Harry Caldwell as his successor.
36. Troutt, "5 of 6 Officers Fired in Torres Death Case."
37. Ibid.
38. Mike Ramsey and Bob Bennett were considered to be among the top trial lawyers in Harris County. Ramsey had won the acquittal of another police officer charged with killing a prisoner in 1972.
39. Troutt, "5 of 6 Officers Fired in Torres Death Case."
40. For testimony about a patrolman's fear of breaking the code of silence during the Torres trial, see Taylor, "Oh, My God They've Really Thrown Him In." Also see Skolnick and Fyfe, *Above the Law,* 108–10.
41. Elliot had actually told his father, Louis Elliot, a seventeen-year HPD patrol veteran, about the incident immediately after it happened. The senior Elliot then called Asst. Chief B. K. Johnson and informed him of the beating and that the suspect was let go after being made to swim the bayou (Hevener, "Responsibility Is Topmost to Officer"). See Taylor, "Orlando Says He Lied When First Queried."
42. Coulter, "Huntsville Selected." See Texas Code of Criminal Procedure, Art. 31.03 [562] [628] [615]: "Granted on motion of defendant (a) A change of venue may be granted in any felony or misdemeanor case punishable by confinement on the written motion of the defendant, supported by his own affidavit and the affidavit of at least two credible persons, residents of the county where the prosecution is instituted, for either of the following causes, the truth and sufficiency of which the court shall determine" (Acts 1965, 59th Leg., p. 317, chap. 722, §1, eff. Jan. 1, 1966. Amended by Acts 1979, 66th Leg., p. 266, chap. 140, §1, eff. Aug. 27, 1979).
43. Gary Taylor, "Finding of Body Recounted."
44. Foreman quoted in Curtis, "Support Your Local Police," 83. Frank Briscoe was the Harris County district attorney from 1961 to 1966.
45. Details of the trial were carried by all of the major daily newspapers. For an analysis of the court activities and personalities, see S. Wilson, "Texas Is Our Mississippi," 24–28.
46. Nelson, "Search and Kill Policy Once Used." This article is part of the clippings file labeled "H-Police-Misconduct," Texas Room, Houston Public Library.
47. Troutt, "Bond Going in the Direction of Firing 5 Officers."

48. Bert Graham interview, April 24, 2002. Mr. Graham told me that "we knew it would be hard to pick a jury in Walker County that would convict police officers of anything, let alone murder."
49. Taylor, "Orlando Says He Lied." It should be noted that in cases involving police officers, cases are usually won or lost on the issue of intent and with sympathetic juries.
50. Taylor, "Movie Like Atmosphere."
51. Taylor, "Police Rookie Recounts Arrest of Joe Torres."
52. Taylor, "Jury Set to Begin Deliberating Today."
53. Wittenberg, "Jokes of Alleged Pushing of Torres 'Hero Worship.'"
54. Original indictment as quoted in appellant brief of *United States v. Terry Wayne Denson, Stephen Orlando and Joseph James Janish,* U.S. Court of Appeals, Fifth Circuit, 603 F.2d 1143: U.S. App. Lexis 11403.
55. Boland, "Sinderson Displayed Forceful Style." This was the first criminal civil rights case for Sinderson and the first case against police officers charged with brutality in seven years. The Metropolitan Research Center of the Houston Public Library has a nearly complete newspaper clipping file of the Torres case.
56. Max B. Skelton, Associated Press, AM cycle, April 6,1978, http:web.lexis-nexis.com/universe/doc. Judge Sterling blamed the police department for Torres's death, and the light sentences were his way saying that these men did it, but the department was responsible.
57. Flynn, "McConn Warns 'Trash' on the Force."
58. Jim Barlow and Pete Brewton, "Torres Case Sentences Hit in Two Marches," *Houston Press,* April 2,1978. Also see De León, *Ethnicity in the Sunbelt,* 211–13. For a discussion of the shifting political ethos of Mexican Americans in Houston in the 1970s, see Chávez, *Lost Land,* 154.
59. For a useful account of the rise of Mexican American/Chicano activism, see Muñoz, *Youth, Identity, Power.* Also see De León, *Ethnicity in the Sunbelt,* 211–13. For a detailed discussion of the "Moody Park Disturbance," see Feagin, *Free Enterprise City,* 258–59.
60. Police continued to confront social agitation aggressively rather than back off and contain a perimeter. They acted as if they had to assert their authority and impose order. The war on crime made anyone who questioned their authority the enemy.
61. Wiessler, "Police Plan Close Scrutiny"; Chávez, *Lost Land,* 154.
62. Skolnick, *Politics of Protest,* 241–42. Skolnick suggests that prejudice and racial hostility shape the majority of police actions. For a discussion of police attitudes and problems with accountability, see Hudson, "Police Review Boards and Police Accountability"; President's Commission on Law Enforcement and Administration of Justice, *Challenge of Crime.*
63. The police advocated a zero-tolerance policy with regard to public demonstrations that led to acts of aggression when they had to enforce it.

64. James H. Rubin, Associated Press, May 17, 1978, A.M. cycle, Washington, D.C., http:web.lexis-nexis.com/universe/doc. Ramsey and Bennett suggested that the Justice Department was acting out of political motivation, because there was no legal basis for the appeal.
65. Petition for Writ of Mandamus, United States Court of Appeals for the Fifth Circuit, 78-2102, 2. J. A. "Tony" Canales, United States Attorney.
66. Rob Wood, Associated Press, October 30, 1979, A.M. cycle, Houston, Texas, http:web.lexis-nexis.com/universe/doc.
67. Davidson, *Race and Class*, 249.
68. Ibid.
69. Bullard, *Invisible Houston*, 135–36; Thomas and Murray, *Progrowth Politics*, 213.
70. Bullard, *Invisible Houston*, 136.
71. Bullard, *Invisible Houston*, 73.
72. Strong interview.
73. McGowen interview, August 8, 1998.
74. Barbara Jordan challenged the logic of at-large voting in 1962, arguing before the federal district court in Houston, Texas, that minorities could not win a citywide election.
75. Thomas and Murray, *Progrowth Politics*, 213.
76. Ibid. For Judge Hannay's opinion, see Price and Davis, "4 Councilmen Favor Vote on City Election System."
77. The Fifth Circuit Court became involved in the reapportionment case when it was apparent that local officials were using legal semantics to try to get around a federal court mandate. However, Judge Woodrow Seals was a conservative and ruled against the plaintiffs, forcing the Justice Department to circumvent him and force a compromise solution. See De León, *Ethnicity in the Sunbelt*, 214–15. Also see Thomas and Murray, *Progrowth Politics*, 213, for a fuller discussion of the Justice Department's actions.
78. In a single-member district, the candidate is elected from a geographically designated district, which is usually defined by ethnicity. In the at-large system, candidates are elected from a city pool of electors. This latter system was advantageous for whites, who made up the majority of the city's population. Initially, Mexican Americans opposed the plan, fearing a possible weakening of the minority vote. See De León, *Ethnicity in the Sunbelt*, 214–15; Murray and Thomas, *Progrowth Politics*, 206–7.
79. Murray and Thomas, *Progrowth Politics*, 206–7.
80. McGowen interview.
81. De León, *Ethnicity in the Sunbelt*, 214–15; also see Thomas and Murray, *Progrowth Politics*, 219–21.
82. Murray and Thomas, *Progrowth Politics*, 218.
83. Ibid.; De León, *Ethnicity in the Sunbelt*, 214–15.
84. McGowen interview.

85. The issue of civilian oversight of the police has been a contentious one in the United States. Police and conservative groups have been very successful at killing most referendums that would establish a civilian review board.
86. Phyllis Splittler, "Caldwell Raps Report on Police Shootings Here," *Houston Post*, March 4, 1979.
87. Ibid.
88. Ibid.
89. T. Kennedy, "Caldwell Resigns as Police Chief."
90. McGowen interview.

Chapter 6

1. Katherine J. Whitmire was elected in 1979 as the controller for the City of Houston. In the 1981 mayoral election, she defeated a strong field of male establishment politicians. She served an unprecedented four terms.
2. For a discussion of Brown's appointment, see Bullard, *Invisible Houston*; Thomas and Murray, *Progrowth Politics*, 244, 405.
3. S. Walker, *Popular Justice*, 201–2. During the 1960s, the HPD successfully lobbied for and received marginal increases in appropriations. Chief Herman Short was particularly adept at getting funds from the city council by raising the banner of rising crime and potential "Negro insurrection" in Houston.
4. For discussion of the effects of crime and policing in Houston's African American community, see Bullard, *Invisible Houston*, 100–113; Feagin, *Free Enterprise City*, 257.
5. Houston Police Department, Annual Report, 1980, 6, submitted to the mayor and city council June 29, 1981. Houston's budget in 1980 was half that of cities of comparable size. Houston spent an average of $58.13 per capita for police service and had five police officers per square mile, compared to Philadelphia's sixty-four. Statistical data also quoted in Bullard, *Invisible Houston*, Table 9.3, 104.
6. Thomas and Murray, *Progrowth Politics*, 217.
7. "Summary of Caldwell's Tenure."
8. "Caldwell Resigns as Police Chief." *Houston Post,* February 13, 1980. Mayor McConn thought perhaps low pay was one of the main reasons Caldwell was leaving. Caldwell was making approximately $56,000 dollars a year. He was reportedly offered nearly twice that to head security for Tenneco.
9. For a discussion of city council reform, see Thomas and Murray, *Progrowth Politics*, 207–22; Bullard, *Invisible Houston*, 136–37; Feagin, *Free Enterprise City*, 275; Davidson, *Race and Class*, 229.
10. Thomas and Murray, *Progrowth Politics*, 213–18.
11. De León, *Ethnicity in the Sunbelt,* 214–15; Thomas and Murray, *Progrowth Politics*, 218–22.

12. Paul Reyes, "Observers Were Wrong in Predicting Woes for an Expanded City Council," Houston Chronicle, October 19, 1981.
13. See "Goyen Lashes Out"; Mayor Pro Tem Goyen called the meeting on the day after the runoff election, which had fallen on council's regular meeting day, and most newly elected officials did not think it was a mandatory meeting. In 1981, council was a part-time low-paying post that met twice weekly. Council member would become a full-time position later in 1981. Goyen was particularly angry at newly elected controller, Lance Lalor, whose actions he felt indicated nothing but contempt for the old council.
14. For a discussion of council's compromises, see T. Kennedy, "City Council–The First 100 Days."
15. Thomas and Murray, *Progrowth Politics*, 193.
16. Harper and Reyes, "2 Councilmen Defend a Majority of Police."
17. It should be noted that a "liberal" politician in Houston was at best a moderate in any other city in the country. Most politicians labeled "liberal" were actually fiscal conservatives who viewed reforms of certain city functions to be essential to their political career. Reformers in Houston were historically considered liberal, which designation was viewed as a death knell for one's political future and caused some to back away from reform platforms.
18. Thomas and Murray, *Progrowth Politics*, 232–33.
19. Ibid., 230.
20. Juan R. Palomo, "Some Problems Surface Quickly for New Mayor," Houston Post, November 17, 1981.
21. Information from Houston mayor's binder, Whitmire résumé folder, the Texas Room, Houston Metropolitan Research Center, Houston Public Library.
22. The Whitmire coalition included businesspeople, minorities, women, and gays. Local political figures were stunned by her victory. By the time she left office, the good old boy networks was significantly weakened by the formation of minority and liberal coalitions. Whitmire maintained a firm hold on the city from 1981 to 1989. Houston's heavily petroleum-dependent economy struggled during the 1980s because of the Arab oil embargo, when the price of crude oil dropped from 35 dollars a barrel to less than 12 dollars a barrel. Thus, President Reagan's energy policies had a disastrous effect on Texas.
23. Thomas and Murray, *Progrowth Politics*, 192. Unfortunately, there is no political history of Houston that thoroughly covers the 1960–86 period. Thomas and Murray believed that the political forces set in motion during Mayor Hofheinz's administration, were responsible for Mayor McConn's narrow victory in 1979, and his horrible defeat by Whitmire in the 1981 general election. The best primary sources for the period are located in the archives at the Houston Metropolitan Research Collection, Texas Room, Houston Public Library.
24. Campaign flier, "Whitmire for Mayor," 1981, clippings file, Texas

Room, Houston Metropolitan Research Collection, Houston Public Library.

25. Sweeney, "What to Expect."
26. Barrett, "A New Breed of Woman Mayor," 178.
27. Ibid.
28. Snyder, "Whitmire Vows a More Responsive City Hall."
29. Budd, "Kathy Whitmire."
30. For a discussion of police reaction to civilian review boards, see S. Walker, *Critical History of Police Reform,* 56; Radelet, *Police and the Community,* 256–57, 265–66; Skolnick and Fyfe, *Above the Law,* 218, 220–36, 259.
31. No Houston mayor approved of the idea of civilian review. Even socially liberal mayors Hofheinz and Whitmire opposed the idea when the issue was pressed by activists.
32. Carlton and Snyder, "Police Union Hears Mayor."
33. T. Kennedy, "Whitmire's Comments Apparently Bridge Gap." Whitmire appealed to the HPPU as it sought to gain an edge on the HPOA by revealing her budget, which increased the appropriation for the department. The HPPU was far less hostile after her meeting with them. The split between the HPOA and the HPPU widened during Whitmire's tenure.
34. "Police Unions Hear Mayor, Still Cool," *Houston Chronicle,* March 19, 1982.
35. Mayor Whitmire faced stiff opposition from the police, fire fighters, and the legislature, all of which felt that she should not attempt to alter 1269M. The mayor, however, formed a strong progrowth coalition with the city's business and community leaders, who helped her win referendum reform in August, 1982. For a discussion and history of 1269M, see House Bill 34, passed May 15, 1947, General and Special Laws of the State of Texas, Passed by the Regular Session of the Fiftieth Legislature, Austin, 1947. The authors' notes on the bill during the various phases of amendment are particularly interesting as they give an indication of the legislature's intent.
36. Ibid.
37. Burke Watson, "Test Indicates That Lynn Lied on Probe Claim," *Houston Chronicle,* February 21, 1980.
38. Meckel, "Selection of 'Outsider' Upsets Some."
39. McGowen interview.
40. In 1981, HPD officers responded to a call at the police station involving an angry man with a knife. The officers on the scene shot the suspect, Eddie Lee Johnson, thirty times even though he was not threatening them and it was clear he was mentally deranged.
41. T. Kennedy, "Mayor Reveals Names of 13 Candidates for Police Chief."
42. Ibid.
43. Elkins quoted in Stevens, "Houston Mayor and Police at Odds." This article quotes Department of Justice statistics that placed Houston

second after New Orleans in the number of civil rights violations complaints filed against the police force.

44. "Mayor Downplays Report on Brown." The patrol unions did not make their findings public at the meeting regarding the mayor's choice for a new police chief. They leaked information to the press to create negative publicity.
45. Ibid.
46. Carreau, "Brown Appears to Have Necessary Votes." Council members Judson Robinson Jr., Ben Reyes, Ernest McGowen Sr., and Anthony Hall all supported the mayor and helped her form the coalition that confirmed Brown's appointment.
47. For a discussion of the historical bias against a chief from outside the ranks of the HPD, see Perry, "Last 'Out-of-Towner' to Be Chief." Ray Ashworth was the last outsider to become chief, named in February, 1921. Superintendent Ashworth lasted only fifteen months, but made some sweeping surface changes before his departure.
48. Simmon and Kennedy, "Brown Unspecific on Police Plans."
49. Moran, "Brown Would Bring Experience on the Beat." For a thorough discussion of African American police administrators, including Chief Lee P. Brown, see Dulaney, *Black Police in America*, 81–103.
50. Craig, quoted in Moran, "Brown Would Bring Experience on Beat."
51. Baldwin, *Evidence of Things Not Seen*, 95. Baldwin believes that Brown left Atlanta and came to Houston because the call came at the right time in his career and he had done a noble job for the city of Atlanta. He also views Brown as an admirable and honorable man.
52. Carreau, "Brown Appcars to Have Necessary Votes."
53. McGowen interview.
54. Carreau, "Brown Appears to Have Necessary Votes."
55. "Brown Confirmed by 11-3 Vote in Council."
56. Cinnelli, "Former Chiefs Say Brown Faces Tougher Job Being an Outsider."
57. Carlton, "First Day on the Job."
58. Ibid.
59. "Lee Brown." This article was taken from excerpts from Brown's writings and interviews.
60. Tony Fremantle, "Police Chief Sets Priorities."
61. Brown, "Bridges over Troubled Waters," 86–87. Brown quoted in Bullard, *Invisible Houston*, 106–107.
62. The two-way radio revolutionized policing. It also brought major changes in police/community relations. Officers no longer walked the beat in large cities strapped for cash. They were placed in cars and given authority to patrol the district or precinct. The two-way radio was introduced after World War II and stretched even farther the long arm of the law and patrol borders. By the 1970s, this impersonal approach was directly blamed for the rise in fear of police brutality and the depersonalization of policing.

63. Trojanowinz, "Foot Patrol," 481.
64. For a discussion of the origins of the Afro-American Patrolmen's Union in Texas, see Dulaney, "Texas Negro Peace Officers' Association."
65. Bradford interview.
66. Ibid.; Mae Walker interview, February 21, 1997.
67. Bradford interview.
68. Hanson, "12 HPD Training Officers Resign."
69. The two officers were stationed at the Park Place Substation in Southeast Houston, the substation where the officers involved in the shooting of Randy Webster and Billy Keith Joyvies were assigned. This substation was the subject of a plethora of allegations of corruption, racism, and brutality.
70. Dahl, "Brown Begins Reform of Training Program." The patrol unions criticized the creation of the panel as reverse racism.
71. T. Kennedy, "Whitmire Group to Push Civil Service Referendum."
72. By the mid-1980s, many white business leaders saw the police as a liability that was causing more political and economic polarization in the city.
73. For the text of 1269M, see the General and Special Laws of the State of Texas, Passed by the Regular Session of the Fiftieth Legislature, Austin, 1947. Also see Marchiafava, *Houston Police*, 84–90.
74. Drennan, "Chief Wants to Use Professionals." Chief Brown admitted that there was a crime problem in Houston and that he was not a magician, nor did he have a magic wand that he could wave to fix the ills of the police department.
75. "Brown Tells City Police to Dress Up Their Act."
76. T. Kennedy, "300 Officers Jam Council Meeting." This meeting of city council had two inflammatory agenda items: a proposed landfill in Fort Bend County; and increased health insurance premiums. The city workers present, although mostly police, also included public works employees.
77. Douglas and Kerr, "HPPU Seeks Revenge on Chief." The HPPU had shifted politically by 1984 and become essentially racist and reactionary. The union attracted large numbers of white males, who felt increasingly alienated and estranged under the leadership of a female mayor and a black chief.

Conclusion

1. For a discussion of the reactions to Elizabeth "Betsy" Watson's appointment as the sixty-third chief of the Houston Police Department, see Belkin, "Woman Named Police Chief of Houston"; Tedford and Williams, "Changing of the Guard at HPD."
2. Mason, "New Chief of Police Is Named."

Bibliography

Archival Collections

Houston Police Department Archives and Records, Houston, Texas

Fifth Circuit Court Records, National Regional Archives, Fort Worth, Tex.

Hoover, J. Edgar. Official and Confidential File, Manuscript Division, Library of Congress, Washington, D.C.

Houston Metropolitan Research Center, Texas Room, Houston Public Library, Houston Texas.

Manuscript Division, Library of Congress, Washington, D.C.

Marshall, Thurgood. Papers. Manuscript Division, Library of Congress, Washington, D.C.

National Association for the Advancement of Colored People (NAACP). Papers. Manuscript Division, Library of Congress, Washington, D.C.

National Negro Congress. Papers. Manuscript Division, Library of Congress, Washington, D.C.

National Regional Archives, Fort Worth, Tex.

Police Court Record, New Orleans Police Department, 1832–1970. New Orleans Public Library, New Orleans, La.

Toureau, Alexander P. Papers. Amistad Research Center, Tulane University, New Orleans, La.

University of Houston, Archives and Library, Houston, Tex.

Books and Articles

Abraham, Henry J. "A People's Watchdog against the Abuse of Power," 152–157. *Public Administration Review* 22 (1960).

Acuña, Rodolfo. *Occupied America: A History of Chicanos*. 2nd ed. New York: Harper & Row, 1981.

Ahern, James. *Police in Trouble: Our Frightening Crisis in Law Enforcement.* New York: Hawthorn Books, 1972.

Alex, Nicholas. *Black in Blue: A Study of the Negro Policeman*. New York: Appleton-Century- Crofts, 1969.

Alpert, Geoffrey P., and Roger G. Dunham. *Policing Urban America*. 2nd ed. Prospect Heights, Ill.: Waveland Press, 1992.

Ashby, Alan. "Wrong Reason." *Houston Post,* August 20, 1980.

Baehr, Melany; D. R. Saunders; E. C. Froemel; and J. E. Furcom. "The Prediction of Performance for Black and for White Patrolmen." In

The Urban Policeman in Transition, ed. John Snibbe and Homa Snibbe. Springfield, Ill.: Charles C. Thomas, 1973.
Baldwin, James. *The Evidence of Things Not Seen*. New York: Henry Holt, 1985.
———. *Nobody Knows My Name*. New York: Dial, 1961.
———. *Notes of a Native Son*. New York: Bantam Books, 1964.
Banks, Taunya. "Discretionary Justice and the Black Offender." In Charles E. Owens and Jimmy Bell, eds., *Blacks and the Criminal Justice System*. Lexington, Mass.: D. C. Heath and Co., 1977.
Banton, Michael. "Authority and the Mass Society." *Police Journal* (July 1970).
———. *The Policeman and the Community*. New York: Basic Books, 1964.
Barbour, Floyd B. *The Black Seventies*. Boston: Porter Sargent, 1970.
Barrett, Karen. "A New Breed of Woman Mayor: The Realpolitik of Kathy Whitmire." *Ms. Magazine* (July/August, 1982).
Bass, Sandra. "Negotiating Change: Community Organizations and the Politics of Policing," 148–177. *Urban Affairs Review* (November, 2000).
Bayley, David H., and Harold Mendelshon. *Minorities and the Police: Confrontation in America*. New York: Free Press, 1969.
Beckwith, David. "Police Did Right Thing, Says Leader." *Houston Chronicle*, May 17, 1968.
Belkin, Lisa. "Woman Named Police Chief of Houston." *New York Times*, January 20, 1990.
Bent, Alan E. *The Politics of Law Enforcement*. Lexington, Mass.: Lexington Books, 1974.
Berger, Monroe. *Equality by Statue: The Revolution in Civil Rights*. Rev. ed. Garden City, N.Y.: Anchor Books,1968.
Berry, Mary Frances. *Black Resistance/White Law: A History of Constitutional Racism in America*. New York: Appleton-Century-Crofts, 1971.
Biles, Roger. *The South and the New Deal*. Lexington: University Press of Kentucky, 1994.
Bittner, Egon. "Florence Nightingale in Pursuit of Willie Sutton: A Theory of the Police." In Herbert Jacob, ed., *The Potential for Reform of Criminal Justice*. Beverly Hills, Calif.: Sage Publications, 1974.
Blackstock, Nelson. *Cointelpro: The FBI's Secret War on Political Freedom*. New York: Vintage Books, 1975.
Blassingame, John. *The Slave Community: Plantation Life in the Antebellum South*. New York: Oxford University Press, 1972.
Boland, Moselle. "Sinderson displayed Forceful Style as One of the Torres Trial Prosecutors." *Houston Chronicle*, February 9, 1978.
Bopp, William J. *The Police Rebellion: A Quest for Blue Power*. Springfield, Ill.: Charles C. Thomas, 1971.
Boskin, Joseph. *Urban Racial Violence in the Twentieth Century*. Beverly Hills, Calif.: Glencoe Press, 1969.
Branch, Taylor. *Parting the Waters: America in the King Years, 1954–63*. New York: Simon & Schuster, 1989.

———. *Pillar of Fire: America in the King Years, 1963–65*. New York: Simon & Schuster, 1998.

Brennan, Christy. "FBI Is Probing Killing of Joyvies Youth by Police." *Houston Post*, April 23, 1978.

Brown, Lee P. "Bridges over Troubled Waters: A Perspective on Policing in the Black Community." In *Black Perspectives on Crime and the Criminal Justice System*, ed. Robert L. Woodson. Boston: G. K. and Co., 1977.

———. *The Death of Police-Community Relations*. Washington, D.C.: Institute for Urban Affairs and Research, Howard University, 1973.

———. "Handling Complaints against the Police." *Police* (May–June, 1968): 74–81.

"Brown Confirmed by 11–3 Vote in Council." *Houston Chronicle*, March 24, 1982.

"Brown Tells City Police to Dress Up Their Act." *Houston Post*, October 20, 1982.

Budd, Millie. "Kathy Whitmire: Introducing Madame Mayor." *Houston Business Journal*, January 4, 1982.

Bullard, Robert D. *Invisible Houston: The Black Experience in Boom and Bust*. College Station: Texas A&M University Press,1987.

Bullock, Paul, ed. *Watts; the Aftermath; an Inside View of the Ghetto, by the People of Watts*. New York: Grove Press, 1969.

Burger, Warren E. "Who Will Watch the Watchman?" *American University Law Review* 14 (1964): 1–23.

Burke, Roger Hopkins. "The Socio-Political Context of Zero Tolerance Policing Strategies." *Policing* 21, no. 4 (1998): 666–82.

Burran, James. "Violence in an Arsenal of Democracy: The Beaumont Race Riot, 1943." *East Texas Historical Journal* 14, no. 1 (1976): 39–51.

"Bush Backs Police on Riot Action." *Houston Post*, May 18,1967.

Business Directory for the City of Houston. Houston, Tex.: Mooney & Morrison, 1878.

Buzzanco, Robert. *Masters of War*. Cambridge: Cambridge University Press, 1996.

"Caldwell Resigns as Police Chief." *Houston Post*, February 13, 1980.

Carlton, Don E. *Red Scare: Right-Wing Hysteria, Fifties Fanaticism, and Their Legacy in Texas*. Austin: Texas Monthly Press, 1985.

Carlton, Jim. "First Day on the Job: Brown Sworn in as HPD Chief in Closed Ceremony." *Houston Chronicle*, April 20, 1982.

———, and Mike Snyde. "Police Unions Hear Mayor, Still Cool." *Houston Chronicle*, March 19, 1982.

Carreau, Mark. "Brown Appears to Have Necessary Votes to Become Houston Chief." *Houston Post*, March 21, 1982.

Carson, Clayborne. *In Struggle: SNCC and the Black Awakening of the 1960s*. Cambridge, Mass.: Harvard University Press, 1981.

Chafee, Zechariah, Jr.; Walter H. Pollak; and Carl S. Stern. *The Third Degree*. New York: Arno Press, 1969.

Chalmers, David. *And the Crooked Places Made Straight: The Struggle for*

Social Change in the Nineteen-Sixties. Baltimore, Md.: Johns Hopkins University Press, 1991.

Chávez, John R. *The Lost Land: The Chicano Image of the Southwest.* Albuquerque: University of New Mexico Press, 1984.

Cinnelli, M. "Former Chiefs Say Brown Faces Tougher Job Being an Outsider." *Houston Post*, March 10, 1982.

"City Buys 300 New Pistols." *Houston Press*, January 28, 1931.

Clark, Ramsey. *Crime in America: Observations on Its Nature, Causes, Prevention and Control*. New York: Pocket Books, 1970.

Coles, Thomas R. *No Color Is My Kind: The Life of Eldrewey Stearns and the Integration of Houston*. Austin: University of Texas Press, 1997.

Coombs, Norman. *The Black Experience in America*. New York: Hippocrene Books, 1972.

Cooper, John L. *The Police and the Ghetto*. Port Washington, N.Y.: Kennikat Press, 1980.

Correia, Mark E. "The Conceptual Ambiguity of Community in Community Policing—Filtering the Muddy Waters." *Policing* 23 (2000): 218–32.

Coulter, Bill. "Huntsville Selected, Trial in Torres Death Moved." *Houston Chronicle*, July 14, 1977.

Curtis, Tom. "Support Your Local Police. Or Else." *Texas Monthly* 5, no. 9 (September, 1977): 83–89, 156–63.

Cray, Ed. *The Enemy in the Streets: Police Malpractice in America*. New York: Doubleday, Anchor Books, 1972.

———. "The Politics of Blue Power." *Nation* 21 (April, 1969): 493–96.

Dahl, Jonathan. "Brown Begins Reform of Training Program." *Houston Chronicle*, August 10, 1982.

Davidson, Chandler. *Biracial Politics: Conflict and Coalition in the Metropolitan South*. Baton Rouge: Louisiana State University Press, 1972.

———. *Race and Class in Texas Politics*. Princeton, N.J.: Princeton University Press, 1990.

Davis, James Kirkpatrick. *Spying on America: The FBI's Domestic Counterintelligence Program*. New York: Praeger, 1992.

Davis, Kenneth Culp. *Discretionary Justice*. Baton Rouge: Louisiana State University Press, 1969.

Del Castillo; Richard Griswold; and Arnoldo De León. *North to Aztlan: A History of Mexican Americans in the United States*. New York: Twayne Publishers, 1997.

De León, Arnoldo. *Ethnicity in the Sunbelt: A History of the Mexican American in Houston*. Houston, Tex.: Mexican American Studies Program, 1991.

DeRoma, Nicholas J. "Justifiable Use of Deadly Force by the Police: A Statutory Survey." *William and Mary Law Review* 12 (1970): 67–85.

Doig, Jamesian W. "Police Problems, Proposals and Strategies for Change." *Public Administration Review* 28 (September/October 1968): 393402.

Douglas, Jack, and Katherine Kerr. "HPPU Seeks Revenge on Chief." *Houston Post*, July 17, 1985.

Downs, Brian T. "Social and Political Characteristics of Riot Cities: A Comparative Study." *Social Science Quarterly* 40 (1968): 504–20.

Drennan, Christy. "Chief Wants to Use Professionals to Change Negative Police Image." *Houston Chronicle,* May 21, 1982.

———. "FBI Is Probing Killing of Joyvies Youth by Police." *Houston Post,* April 23, 1978.

———. "The Hole: A Quiet Place Where Police Go for Various Reasons—Sometime to Talk with a Suspect." *Houston Chronicle,* May 14, 1977.

———. "1975 Shooting by City Police Being Probed." *Houston Chronicle,* April 7, 1978.

———. "Caldwell Says Executions Would Curb Holdup-Murders." *Houston Chronicle,* July 29, 1978.

DuBois, W. E. B. *The Souls of Black Folks: Essays and Sketches*. Chicago: A. G. McClurg, 1903.

Dulaney, W. Marvin. *Black Police in America.* Bloomington: Indiana University Press, 1996.

———. "Texas Negro Police Officers Association: The Origins of Black Police Unionism." *Houston Review* 12, no. 2 (1990): 59–78.

Dunbar, Paul Laurence. *The Complete Poems of Paul Laurence Dunbar*. New York: Dodd, Mead & Company, 1913.

Durrani, Shiraz. "Black Communities and Information Workers in Search of Social Justice." *New Library World* 100 (1999): 265–79.

DuVall, Allan. "Policeman Must be Wise, Noble and Firm in Duties." *Houston Post,* June 7, 1963.

Edsall, Thomas, and Mary Edsall. *Chain Reaction: The Impact of Race Rights and Taxes on America Politics*. New York: W. W. Norton, 1992.

Ellis, Nick. "A Discourse Inferno: The Pitfalls of Professionalism." *Marketing Intelligence & Planning* 17 (1999): 333–43.

Endleman, Shalom. *Violence in the Streets*. Chicago: Quadrangle Books, 1968.

"Ex-U.I. Student: Mack Jones Firing Starts TSU Lie-in." *Pittsburgh Courier,* April 2, 1967.

Fallis, David S., and Craig Whitlock. "Families' Pleas for Help End in Gunfire." *Washington Post,* July 3, 2001.

Farber, David. *Chicago '68*. Chicago: University of Chicago Press, 1988.

Feagin, Joe R. *Free Enterprise City: Houston in Political- Economic Perspective.* New Brunswick, N.J.: Rutgers University Press, 1988.

Fehrenbach, T. R. *Lone Star: A History of Texas and Texans*. New York: Macmillan, 1968.

Fink, Joseph, and Lloyd G. Sealy. *The Community and the Police: Conflict or Cooperation?* New York: John Wiley & Sons, 1974.

Flynn, George. "McConn Warns 'Trash' on the Force." *Houston Post,* April 12, 1978.

Fogelson, Robert M. "From Resentment to Confrontation: The Police, the Negroes, and the Outbreak of the Nineteen-Sixties Riots." *Political Science Quarterly* 83 (June, 1968): 217–47.

———. *Violence as Protest: A Study of Riots and Ghettos*. Garden City, N.Y.: Doubleday & Company, 1971.

Foley, Nick. *The White Scourge: Mexicans, Blacks, and Poor Whites in Texas Cotton Culture*. Berkeley & Los Angeles: University of California Press, 1997.

Fosdick, Raymond. *American Police Systems*. New York: Century, 1920.

Fremantle, Tony. "Police Chief Sets Priorities." *Houston Chronicle*, May 5, 1982.

"Fund to Operate Plant Is Sought." *Houston Post*, July 14, 1932.

Garrow, David J. *The FBI and Martin Luther King Jr.* New York: Penguin Books, 1981.

Gentry, Curtis. *J. Edgar Hoover: The Man and the Secrets*. New York: Plume, 1992.

Germann, A. C. "Changing the Police—The Impossible Dream?" *Journal of Criminal Law, Criminology and Police Science* 62 (1971): 416–21.

Gillette, Michael L. "The Rise of the NAACP in Texas." *Southwestern Historical Quarterly* 81 (April, 1978): 393–65.

Glenn, Norval D. "The Kerner Report, Social Scientists, and the American Public: Introduction to a Symposium." *Social Science Quarterly* (December, 1968): 443–47.

Glickman, Lawrence B. "The Strike in the Temple of Consumption: Consumer Activism and Twentieth-Century American Political Culture." *Journal of American History* 88 (June, 2001): 99–127.

Goldkamp, John S. "Minorities as Victims of Police Shooting: Interpretations of Racial Disproportionality and Police Use of Deadly Force." *Justice System Journal* 2 (1976): 169.

Goldstein, Herman. "Police Policy Formulation: A Proposal for Improving Police Performance." *Michigan Law Review* 65 (1967): 1123–46.

———. *Policing a Free Society*. Cambridge, Mass.: Ballinger, 1975.

"Goyen Lashes Out at Council Tardiness." *Houston Post*, October 21, 1981.

Greater Houston City Directory, 1943–44. Houston, Tex.: Morrison and Forumy, 1944

Greater Houston City Directory, 1959. Houston, Tex.: R. L. Polk, 1959.

Green, George Norris. *The Establishment in Texas Politics: The Primitive Years, 1938–1957*. Westport, Conn.: Greenwood Press, 1979.

Grier, William H., and Price M. Cobbs. *Black Rage*. New York: Basic Books, 1968.

Griffenhagen and Associates, Consultants in Public Administration. "City of Houston: The Police Department." Survey, December 28, 1939. Report no. 3, vol. 1.

Griffith, Ernest, and Charles R. Adrian. *A History of American City Government: The Formation of Traditions, 1775–1870*. Washington, D.C.: University Press of America, 1983.

Gutiérrez, David G. *Walls and Mirrors: Mexican Americans, Mexican Immigrants, and the Politics of Ethnicity*. Berkeley: University of California Press, 1995.

Haarr, Robin N. "'They're Making a Bad Name for the Department': Exploring the Link between Organizational Commitment and Police Occupational Deviance in a Police Patrol Bureau." *Policing* 20 (1997): 786–812.

Hahn, Harlan, and Joe R. Feagin. "Riot-Precipitating Police Practices: Attitudes in Urban Ghettos." *Phylon* 31 (Summer, 1970): 183–93.

Haller, Mark. "Historical Roots of Police Behavior: Chicago, 1890–1925." *Law and Society Review* 10 (1976): 303–24.

Hanson, Eric. "12 HPD Training Officers Resign: Group Says Chief Discriminated by Reinstating 2 Blacks." *Houston Chronicle,* May 18, 1982.

Harper, Fred, and Raúl Reyes. "2 Councilmen Defend a Majority of Police." *Houston Chronicle*, April 8, 1980.

Harris, William H. *The Harder We Run: Black Workers since the Civil War.* New York: Oxford University Press, 1982.

Haynes, Robert V. "The Houston Mutiny and Riot of 1917."*Southwest Historical Quarterly* 76, no. 4 (April, 1973): 418–39.

Hendrickson, Kenneth E., Jr. "Texas Politics since the New Deal." In *Texas through Time: Evolving Interpretations*, ed. Walter L. Buenger and Robert A. Calvert. College Station: Texas A&M University Press, 1991.

Hevener, Phil. "Responsibility Is Topmost to Officer." *Houston Post*, May 6, 1977.

Hine, Darlene Clark. *Black Victory: The Rise and Fall of the White Primary in Texas*. Millwood, N.Y.: KTO Press, 1979.

"Hippies Join TSU Courthouse Sit-In." *Houston Post*, March 17, 1967.

Hirsch, Herbert, and Lewis Donohew. "A Note on Negro-White Differences in Attitudes toward the Supreme Court." *Social Science Quarterly* 49: 557–62.

Horne, Gerald. *Fire This Time: The Watts Uprising and the 1960s*. Charlottesville : University Press of Virginia, 1995.

Horton, David M., and Ryan Kellus Turner. *Lone Star Justice: The Texas Criminal Justice System*. Austin, Tex.: Eakin Press, 1999.

"Houston." *Houston Post,* February 19, 1932.

Houston, City of. *City Business Directory*. Houston, Tex.: Morrison & Fourmy's, 1898.

"Houston Cops Fully Armed." *Houston Post-Dispatch,* December 2, 1930.

"How Much Crime Houston Has, and Where." *Houston Chronicle*, November 1, 1964.

Hudson, James R. "Police Review Boards and Police Accountability." *Law and Contemporary Problems* 36 (1971): 515–38.

"Inches Away from a Major Riot; Former Mayor and Others Recall Clash, Violence at TSU 30 Years Ago." *Houston Chronicle,* May 19, 1997.

Inciardi, James A. *Criminal Justice*. 6th ed. Orlando, Fla.: Harcourt Brace, 1999.

The Iron Fist and the Velvet Glove: An Analysis of the U.S. Police. 2nd ed. Berkeley: Center for Research on Criminal Justice, 1971.

James, Ann. "Body Bruised, Autopsy Shows." *Houston Post*, May 15, 1977.

———. "Deputy Police Chief Gets 2-week Suspension for Insubordination." *Houston Post*, August 17,1974.

———. "Sheriff's Son, Jones Fired by Police Chief." *Houston Post*, February 15, 1974.

Jenkins, Herbert T. *Forty Years on the Force, 1932–1972*. Atlanta, Ga.: Center for Research in Social Change, Emory University, 1973.

Johannsen, Robert W. "The Sixty-third Annual Meeting of the Organization of American Historians." *Journal of American History* 57 (September, 1970): 367–92.

Jones, Mack H. "Introduction: 1984 Minus 9 Equals Police Terror in U.S. 1975 or the Early Arrival of Big Brother." *Journal of Political Repression* 1 (June, 1975): 4–11.

Joyner, Irv. "Police Repression in America." *Journal of Political Repression* 1 (June, 1975): 41–47.

Juris, Hervey A. "The Implications of Police Unionism." *Law and Society Review* 6 (1971): 231–45.

Justice, Blair. *Violence in the City*. Dallas: Texas Christian University Press, 1969.

Kappler, Victor E., and Peter B. Kraska. "A Textual Critique of Community Policing: Police Adaptation to High Modernity." *Policing* 21 (1998): 293–313.

Kelly, Robin D. G. *Hammer and Hoe: Alabama Communists during the Great Depression*. Chapel Hill: University of North Carolina Press, 1990.

Kennedy, Randall. *Race, Crime, and the Law*. New York: Pantheon Books, 1997.

Kennedy, Tom. "Caldwell Resigns as Police Chief." *Houston Post*, February 13, 1980.

———. "City Council–The First 100 Days: Expanded Body Shedding 'Old' vs. 'New' Factions in Voting." *Houston Post*, April 7, 1980.

———."Mayor Reveals Names of 13 Candidates for Police Chief." *Houston Post*, March 21, 1982.

———. "300 Officers Jam Council Meeting." *Houston Post*, June 16, 1983.

———. "Whitmire Group to Push Civil Service Referendum." *Houston Post*, June 3, 1982.

———. "Whitmire's Comments Apparently Bridge Gap with City Police Group." *Houston Post*, March 16, 1982.

Kersten, Astrid. "Diversity Management Dialogue, Dialectics and Diversion." *Journal of Organizational Change Management* 13 (2000): 1-8. http://www.emarald-library.com/brev/02313cc1.htm.

Key, V. O. *Southern Politics: In State and Nation*. New York: Alfred A. Knopf, 1949.

Knowles, Louis L., and Kenneth Prewitt. *Institutional Racism in America*. Englewood Cliffs, N.J.: Prentice-Hall, 1969.

Kobler, Arthur L. "Figures (and Perhaps Some Facts) on Police Killing of Civilians in the United States, 1965–1969." *Journal of Social Issues* 31 (1975): 184–91.

———. "Police Homicide in a Democracy." *Journal of Social Issues* 31 (1975): 163–84.

Kohlan, Richard G. "Police Promotional Procedures in Fifteen Jurisdictions." *Public Personnel Management* (May/June, 1973): 167–70.

Kruszewski, Anthony Z.; Richard L. Hough; and Jacob Ornstein-Galicia, eds. *Politics and Society in the Southwest: Ethnicity and Chicano Pluralism.* Boulder, Colo.: Westview Press, 1982.

LaFave, Wayne R., and F. J. Remington. "Controlling the Police: The Judge's Role in Making and Reviewing Law Enforcement Decisions." *Michigan Law Review* 63 (1965): 987–1012.

Lane, Roger. *Policing the City: Boston, 1822–1885.* Cambridge, Mass.: Harvard University Press, 1967.

Lawson, Bill. "A Second Look at the "TSU Riots." *Forward Times,* May 27, 1967.

Lawson, Steven F. *Running for Freedom: Civil Rights and Black Politics in America since 1941.* Austin: University of Texas Press, 1991.

Lee, Don L. *The Black Poets.* New York: Dell, 1976.

Lee, W. L. Melville. *A History of Police in England.* London: Methuen, 1901.

"Lee Brown." *Houston Post,* March 14, 1982.

Lemann, Nicholas. *The Promised Land: The Great Black Migration and How It Changed America.* New York: Alfred A. Knopf, 1991.

Lersch, Kim Michelle. "Police Misconduct and Malpractice: a Critical Analysis of Citizens' Complaints." *Policing* 21 (1998): 1–12. http://www.emerald-library.com/brev/18121ah1.htm.

Lersch, Kim Michelle, and Tom Mieczkowski. "An Examination of the Convergence and Divergence of Internal and External Allegations of Misconduct Filed against Police Officers." *Policing* 23 (2000): 1–9. http://www.emerald-library.com/brev/18123ad1.htm.

———. "Who Are the Problem Prone Officers? An Analysis of Citizen Complaints." *American Journal of Police* 15 (1996): 23–43.

Lewis, Peter W., and Kenneth D. Peoples. *The Supreme Court and the Criminal Process.* New York: W. B. Sanders, 1978.

Lieberson, Stanley, and Arnold Silverman. "The Precipitant and Underlying Conditions of Race Riots." *American Sociological Review* 30 (December, 1965): 887–98.

Lipartito, Kenneth J., and Joseph A. Pratt. *Baker and Botts in the Development of Modern Houston.* Austin: University of Texas Press, 1991.

Litwack, Leon F. *Been in the Storm So Long: The Aftermath of Slavery.* New York: Vintage Books, 1979.

———. *Trouble in Mind: Black Southerners in the Age of Jim Crow.* New York: Alfred A. Knopf, 1998.

Liu, Daniel S. C. "The Presidential Message." In *The Police Chief.* Washington: International Association of Chiefs of Police, 1965.

"Machine Gun Practice Set by Policemen." *Houston Press,* December 12, 1930.

Marable, Manning. *Race Reform and Rebellion: The Second Reconstruction in Black America, 1945–1990.* Jackson: University Press of Mississippi, 1991.

Marchiafava, Louis. *The Houston Police: 1878–1948.* Houston, Tex.: Rice University Press, 1977.

Marenin, Otwin, ed. *Policing Change, Changing Police: International Perspectives.* New York: Garland Publishing, 1996.

Martin, Susan Ehrlich. *Breaking and Entering: Policewomen on Patrol.* Berkeley & Los Angeles: University of California Press, 1980.

Marx, Gary T. *Undercover: Police Surveillance in America.* Berkeley & Los Angeles: University of California Press, 1988.

Mason, Julie. "New Chief of Police Is Named: Mayor Picks Bradford, 17-year HPD Veteran." *Houston Chronicle,* November 8, 1996.

Masotti, Louis H., and Don R. Bowen. *Riots and Rebellion: Civil Violence in the Urban Community.* Beverly Hills, Calif.: Sage, 1968.

Mathias, William, and Stuart Anderson. *Horse to Helicopter: First Century of the Atlanta Police Department.* Atlanta: Georgia State University, 1973.

Matusow, Allen J. *The Unraveling of America: A History of Liberalism in the 1960s.* New York: Harper & Row, 1984.

"Mayor Downplays Report on Brown" *Houston Post,* March 20, 1982.

"Mayor Monteith Enthusiastic over Police Radio after Test." *Houston Press,* September 1, 1932.

McComb, David. *Houston: A History.* Austin: University of Texas Press, 1969.

McCreedy, Kenneth R., and James L. Hague. "Administrative and Legal Aspects of a Policy to Limit the Use of Firearms by Police Officers." *Police Chief* (January, 1975): 48 51.

McMillen, Neil R. *Dark Journey: Black Mississippi in the Age of Jim Crow.* Chicago: University of Illinois Press, 1990.

McMullen, John L. "Policing Reform and Moral Discourse: The Genesis of a Modern Institution." *Policing* 21 (1998): 1–12. http://www.emara.d-library.com/brev/1821ah1.htm.

McNutt, Gayle. "What the Mayor Is All About." *Houston Chronicle,* December 2, 1973.

Meckel, Bob. "Selection of 'Outsider' Upsets Some." *Houston Post,* March 10, 1982.

Metz, Allan. "Right-Wing Opposition to Bill Clinton and His Presidency: An Annotated Bibliography." *Reference Services Review* 27 (1999): 1–38. http://www.emerald-library.com/brev/24027ab1.htm.

Milton, Catherine H.; J. W. Lardner; and G. L. Abrecht. *Police Use of Deadly Force.* Washington, D.C.: Police Foundation, 1977.

Mitchell, George T.; Taunya L. Banks; and Leslie B. McLemore. "Police Conduct and the Black Community: The Case of Jackson, Mississippi." *Journal of Political Repression* 1 (June, 1975): 97–110.

Monkennen, Eric. *Police in Urban America, 1860–1920.* Cambridge: Cambridge University Press, 1981.

Moody, Anne. *Coming of Age in Mississippi.* New York: Dell, 1968.

Moran, Tom. "Brown Would Bring Experience on the Beat, in Classroom to HPD." *Houston Chronicle,* March 10, 1982.

Morris, Aldon D. *The Origins of the Civil Rights Movement: Black Community Organizing for Change*. New York: Collier Macmillan Publishers, 1984.

Morris, Charles R. *A Time of Passion: America 1960–1980.* New York: Penguin, 1984.

Moss, Larry. *Black Political Ascendancy in Urban Centers and Black Control of the Local Police Function: An Exploratory Analysis*. San Francisco: R&E Research Associates, 1977.

———. "Police-Community Relations in a Black-Controlled City: The Case of Atlanta." *Journal of Political Repression* 1 (June, 1975): 48–70.

Muñoz, Carlos. *Youth, Identity, Power: The Chicano Movement.* New York: Verso, 1989.

Muse, Vance. *Don't Buy a Car Made on Monday: An Arbitrary Encyclopedia of Things to Be Afraid Of.* New York: New York Times Books, 1979.

Myrdal, Gunnar. *An American Dilemma: The Negro Problem and Modern Democracy*. Vol. 2. New York: Harper and Brothers, 1944.

Narrow, Harvey G., and E. E. Levitt. "Formal Assessment Procedures in Police Selection." *Psychological Reports* 12 (1963): 691–93.

Nash, Gerald D. *The Crucial Era : The Great Depression and World War II, 1929–1945*. 2nd ed. New York: St. Martin's Press, 1992.

National Advisory Commission on Civil Disorders. *Report of the National Advisory Commission on Civil Disorders*. New York: Bantam Books, 1968.

National Institute of Law Enforcement and Criminal Justice. *Police Training and Performance Study*. Washington, D.C.: U.S. Government Printing Office, 1970.

"Negroes May Vote in Texas Democratic Primaries, Court Rules." *Washington Post,* April 3, 1944.

Nelson, Rick. "Search and Kill Policy Once Used, Canales Says." *Houston Post,* March 4, 1979.

Nelson, Jack, and Jack Bass. *The Orangeburg Massacre*. New York: Ballantine Press, 1972.

Newby, I. A. *The South: A History*. New York: Holt, Rinehart and Winston, 1978.

———. *The Development of Segregationist Thought*. Homewood, Ill.: Dorsey Press, 1968.

———. *Jim Crow's Defense: Anti-Negro Thought in America, 1900–1930.* Baton Rouge: Louisiana State University Press, 1965.

"New Police Chief Fires Four the First Day." *Houston Press,* September 1, 1930.

Niederhoffer, Arthur. *Behind the Shield: The Police in Urban Society*. Garden City, N.Y.: Doubleday, 1967.

———, and Abraham S. Blumberg, eds. *The Ambivalent Force: Perspectives on the Police*. 2nd ed. New York: Dryden Press, 1976.

Niederhoffer, Arthur, and Elaine Niederhoffer. *The Police Family*. Lexington, Mass.: D. C. Heath and Company, 1978.

Northcott, Kaye. "Cops as Robbers." *Texas Observer,* March 29, 1974, pp. 5–7.

Oden, Roger K., and Linda Faye Williams. "Repression and Power in City Politics: The Police Department and the Black Community in Chicago." *Journal of Political Repression* 1 (June, 1975): 13–40.

Olson, James, and Sharon Phair. "The Anatomy of a Race Riot, Beaumont, Texas, 1943." *Texana* 2: 64–72.

"An Outline of a History of the Houston Police Department." *Houston Police Department.*

Palmer, Edward. "Black Police in America." *Black Scholar* 5 (October, 1973): 19–27.

Palmiotto, Michael J.; Michael L. Birzer; and N. Prabha Unnithan. "Training in Community Policing: A Suggested Curriculum." *Policing* 23 (2000): 8–21.

Paulsen, Monrad G. "Police Conduct and the Public." In Louis A Radelet, *The Police and the Community,* 4th ed. New York: Macmillan, 1986.

Payne, Charles. *I've Got the Light of Freedom: The Mississippi Organizing Tradition.* Berkeley & Los Angeles: University of California Press, 1995.

"Percy Heard Is Candidate for Sheriff." *Houston Press,* May 2, 1932. "Percy Heard Is Candidate for Sheriff." *Houston Press,* May 2, 1932.

"Percy Heard Named City's Police Chief." *Houston Press,* August 19,1930.

Perry, Ira. "Last 'Out-of-Towner' to Be Chief Met Tough Resistance to Changes." *Houston Post,* March 12, 1982.

Pitre, Merline. *In Struggle against Jim Crow: Lulu B. White and the NAACP, 1900–1957.* College Station: Texas A&M University Press, 1999.

Platt, Harold L. *City Building in the New South: The Growth of Public Services in Houston, Texas, 1830–1910.* Philadelphia: Temple University Press, 1983.

"Police Arresting TSU Protest Heads." *Houston Post,* April 4,1967.

"Police Chief Announces New Posts." *Houston Post,* February 2, 1974.

"Police Department Makes while Cutrer Mayor." *Houston Post,* November 8, 1963.

"Police Radio Is Given Its First Test." *Houston Press,* September 12, 1932.

"Police Ranks Slim, under National Rate." *Houston Post,* June 3, 1963.

"Police Shake-up Effected; Tatum is Senior Chief." *Houston Chronicle,* September 1,1930.

Pollenberg, Richard. *War and Society: The United States, 1941–1945.* New York: J. B. Lippincott, 1972.

Pratt, Joseph A. "8F and Many More: Business and Civic Leadership in Modern Houston." *Houston Review of History and Culture* 1, no. 2: 2–7, 31–44.

Pratt, Joseph A., and Christopher J. Castañeda. *Builders: Herman and George R. Brown.* College Station: Texas A&M University Press, 1999.

President's Commission on Law Enforcement and Administration of Justice. *The Challenge of Crime in a Free Society.* Washington, D.C.: U.S. Government Printing Office, 1967.

Price, Jorjanna, and Frank Davis. "4 Councilmen Favor Vote on City Election System." *Houston Post,* March 9, 1977.

Radelet, Louis A. *The Police and the Community.* 4th ed. New York: Macmillan, 1986.

Recheck, Milton. "The Value Gap Between Police and Policed." *Journal of Social Issues* 27 (1971).

"Rehearing on Negro Voting Will Be Asked." *Houston Chronicle,* April 4, 1944.

Reiss, Albert J., Jr. "Police Brutality: Answers to Key Questions." *Trans-Action* (July/August, 1968): 10–19.

Report of the National Advisory Commission on Civil Disorders. New York: Bantam Books, 1968.

Report on a Pilot Study in the District of Columbia on Victimization and Attitudes toward Law Enforcement and Administration of Justice, Field Survey I. Washington, D.C.: U.S. Government Printing Office, 1967.

"Reyes Asks Hofheinz to Back Police Inquiry." *Houston Chronicle,* May 18, 1977.

Richardson, James F. *The New York Police: Colonial Times to 1901.* New York: Oxford University Press, 1970.

Riley, David. "Should Communities Control Their Police?" *Civil Rights Digest* (Fall, 1969): 3–7, 57.

Rokeach, Milton Miller, and J. A. Snyder. "The Value Gap between the Police and the Policed. *Journal of Social Issues* (1971): 27, 155–71.

Rousey, Dennis. *Policing the Southern City: New Orleans 1836-1885.* Baton Rouge: Louisiana State University Press, 1997.

Rubinstein, Jonathan. *City Police.* New York: Farrar, Straus and Giroux, 1986.

Ruchelman, Leonard. *Police Politics: A Comparative Study of Three Cities.* Cambridge, Mass.: Ballinger, 1974.

Rudwick, Elliot. *Negro Police in the South: 1954–1961.* Atlanta, Ga.: Southern Regional Council Annual Report, 1962.

———. *The Unequal Badge: Negro Policemen in the South.* Atlanta, Ga.: Southern Regional Council, 1962.

Ruiz, Vicki L. *From Out of the Shadows: Mexican Women in Twentieth-Century America.* New York: Oxford University Press, 1998.

Rules and Regulations: The State of Texas Commission on Law Enforcement Officer Standards and Education. Austin: State of Texas, 1976.

Scheingold, Stuart A. *The Politics of Law and Order: Street Crime and Public Policy.* New York: Longman, 1984.

Schneider, Charley. "Death Stood Next to Him." *Houston Post,* May 18, 1967.

Schrotel, Stanley R. "Crowd Control in a Period of Social Change." *The Police Yearbook, 1965,* 162–63. Also published in Proceedings of the 71st Annual Conference of the International Association of Chiefs of Police, Inc.

Schwartz, Barry N., and Robert Disch. *White Racism: Its History, Pathology and Practice.* New York: Dell, 1970.

Scott, James F. "Racial Group Membership, Role Orientation, and Police Conduct among Urban Policemen." *Phylon* 31, no. 1 (1970): 5–15.

Sellers Cleveland, with Robert Terrel. *The River of No Return: The Autobiography of a Black Militant and the Life and Death of SNCC*. New York: Morrow, 1973.

Shockley, John S. *Chicano Revolt in a Texas Town*. Notre Dame, Ind.: University of Notre Dame Press, 1974.

Sibley, Marilyn McAdams. *The Port of Houston: A History*. Austin: University of Texas Press, 1968.

Silver, Isidore. *The Challenge of Crime in a Free Society*. New York: Avon Books, 1969.

———. *The Police and the Urban Ghetto*. Chicago: American Bar Foundation, 1968.

Simmon, J., and T. Kennedy. "Brown Unspecific on Police Plans." *Houston Post*, March 11, 1982.

Skolnick, Jerome. *The Politics of Protest*. New York: Ballantine Books, 1969.

———, and James J. Fyfe. *Above the Law: Police and the Excessive Use of Force*. New York: Free Press, 1993.

———. *Justice without Trial: Law Enforcement in a Democratic Society*. 2nd ed. New York: John Wiley & Sons, 1975.

Smith, Bruce. *Police Systems in the United States*. 2nd ed. New York: Harper & Row, 1960.

Smith, Donnie. "TSU Demonstration Disrupts Classes." *Houston Post*, March 28, 1967.

Snyder, Mike. "Whitmire Vows a More Responsive City Hall." *Houston Chronicle*, January 3, 1982.

"South's Devices Run Thin." *New York Times*, April 5, 1944, secs. 1, 2.

Splitter, Phyllis. "Caldwell Raps Report on Police Shootings Here." *Houston Chronicle*, June 9,1979.

Splinter, Phyllis. "The Controversial Career of Carroll Lynn." *Houston Chronicle*, April 4, 1978.

Spofford, Tim. *Lynch Street: The May 1970 Slayings at Jackson State College*. Kent, Oh.: Kent State University Press, 1988.

Stevens, William K. "Houston Mayor and Police at Odds." *New York Times*, March 15, 1982.

Stone, Donald. "On the Question of Repression: An Analysis of Repression and the Response of the Black Community." *Journal on Political Repression* 1 (June, 1975): 71–96.

Sugarman, Tracy. *Stranger at the Gates: A Summer in Mississippi*. New York: Hill and Wang, 1996.

"Summary of Caldwell's Tenure." *Houston Post*, February 13, 1980.

A Survey of the Police Department, Atlanta, Georgia. Washington, D.C.: International Association of Chiefs of Police, 1971.

Sweeney, Paul. "What to Expect." *Texas Observer*, December 4, 1981.

Task Force Report: The Police. Washington, D.C.: U.S. Government Printing Office, 1967.

Taylor, Gary. "Finding of Body Recounted." *Houston Post,* September 14, 1977.

———. "Jury Set to Begin Deliberating Today in Trial of Officer." *Houston Post,* October 4, 1977.

———. "Movie Like Atmosphere Surrounds Torres Case." *Houston Post,* October 2, 1977.

——— "Oh, My God They've Really Thrown Him In." *Houston Post,* September 16, 1978.

———. "Orlando Says He Lied When First Queried." *Houston Post,* September 29, 1977.

———. "Police Rookie Recounts Arrest of Joe Torres." *Houston Post,* September 15, 1977.

———. "Torres Violent When Drunk, NCO Recalls." *Houston Post,* April 5, 1978.

Teaford, Jon C. *The Twentieth-century American City: Problem, Promise, and Reality.* Baltimore, Md.: Johns Hopkins University Press, 1986.

Tedford, Deborah, and John Williams. "Changing of the Guard at HPD." *Houston Chronicle,* January 20, 1990.

"Texas Southern University." *Houston Post,* April 2, 1967.

Thomas, Robert D., and Richard W. Murray. *Progrowth Politics: Change and Governance in Houston.* Berkeley, Calif.: Institute of Governmental Studies Press, 1991.

Toch, Hans. "Cops and Blacks: Warring Minorities." *Nation* (April, 1969): 491–93.

———. *Peacekeeping: Police Prisons and Violence.* Lexington, Mass.: Lexington Books, 1976.

———. "Research and Reform in Community Policing." *American Journal of Police* 24(1995): 1–10.

Treviño, Victor. "History of Hispanic Police Officers in Houston." In Dorothy F. Caram, ed., *Hispanics in Houston and Harris County, 1519–1986.* Houston, Tex.: Houston Hispanic Forum, 1989.

Trice, Harrison M., and Janice M. Beyer. *The Cultures of Work Organizations.* Englewood Cliffs, N.J.: Prentice Hall, 1993.

Trice, Leo. "The Black Community and Law Enforcement in St. Louis." *Journal of Political Repression* 1 (June, 1975): 79–96.

Trojanowinz, Robert C. "Foot Patrol: Improving Police-Citizen Contact." In Louis A. Radelet, *The Police and the Community,* 4th ed. New York: Macmillan, 1986.

Troutt, Larry. "Bond Going in the Direction of Firing 5 Officers Involved in Torres Case." *Houston Post,* May 12, 1977.

———. "Bond Plans to Resign before Elections." *Houston Post,* May 7, 1977.

———. "Bond Will Form Internal Affairs Division." *Houston Post,* May 7, 1977.

———."Caldwell with Police for 24 Years." *Houston Post,* June 11, 1977.

———. "5 of 6 Officers Fired in the Torres Death Case." *Houston Post,* June 28, 1977.

———. "Mayor Calls Police Image Illness." *Houston Post,* April 4, 1978.

Turner, William W. *The Police Establishment.* New York: Tower Publications, 1968.

"26 Demoted, 7 Are Retired, 3 Fired in Police Shakeup." *Houston Post,* January 17, 22, 1939.

U.S. Senate. *Hearing before the Permanent Sub-Committee on Investigations, Part I.* Washington, D.C.: U.S. Government Printing Office, 1967.

United States v. Denson, 603 F.2d 1143.

Vila, Bryan. "Tired Cops: Probable Connections between Fatigue and the Performance , Health and Safety of Patrol Officers." *American Journal of Police* 15 (1996): 51–92.

Vollmer, August. *The Police and Modern Society.* College Park, Md.: McGrath Publishing, 1966.

Walker, Mae. *The History of the Black Police Officers in the Houston Police Department, 1878–1988.* Dallas, Tex.: Taylor Publishing Company, 1988.

Walker, Samuel. *Popular Justice: A History of American Criminal Justice.* New York: Oxford University Press, 1980.

———. *A Critical History of Police Reform: The Emergence of Professionalism.* Lexington, Mass.: Lexington Books, 1977.

———. *Popular Justice: A History of American Criminal Justice.* 2nd ed. New York: Oxford University Press, 1998.

Walker, Samuel, and Charles M. Katz. *The Police in America: An Introduction.* 4th ed. Boston: McGraw Hill, 2002.

Waskow, Arthur I. *From Race Riot to Sit-In: 1919 and the 1960s.* Garden City, N.Y.: Doubleday, 1962.

Weiss, Nancy. *Farewell to the Party of Lincoln: Black Politics in the Age of FDR.* Princeton, N.J.: Princeton University Press, 1983.

Wesley, Carter. "Clean Your Yards and Neighborhoods." *Houston Informer,* October 12, 1939.

White, G. Edward. "The Constitution and The New Deal." *Law and Politics Book Review* 11 (March, 2001): 128–30.

Whitlock, Craig. "Officers Killed with Impunity." *Washington Post,* July 1, 2001.

———. "Police Routinely Clear Their Own." *Washington Post,* July 2, 2002.

Wiebe, Robert H. *The Search for Order 1877–1920.* New York: Hill and Wang, 1987.

Wiessler, Judy. "Police Plan Close Scrutiny of Those at Torres Rallies." *Houston Chronicle,* March 31,1978.

Williamson, Joel. *A Rage for Order: Black-White Relations in the American South since Emancipation.* New York: Oxford University Press, 1986.

Wilson, James Q. *Bureaucracy: What Government Agencies Do and Why They Do It.* New York: Basic Books, 1989.

———. "The Closing of the American City." *New Republic* 218 (May, 1998):30–38.

———. *Thinking about Crime.* New York: Vintage Books, 1975.

———. *Varieties of Police Behavior: The Management of Law and Order in Eight Communities*. Cambridge, Mass.: Harvard University Press, 1968.

Wintersmith, Robert. *Police and the Black Community*. Lexington, Mass.: Lexington Books, 1974.

Wintz, Cary D. *Blacks in Houston*. Houston, Tex.: Houston Center of the Humanities, 1982.

Wittenberg, Pete. "City Police Rookie Recounts Testimony in Torres Death." *Houston Press*, January 27, 1978.

———. "Jokes of Alleged Pushing of Torres 'Hero Worship,' Denson Maintains." *Houston Post*, February 2, 1978.

Woodward, C. Vann. *The Strange Career of Jim Crow*. 3rd ed. New York: Oxford University Press, 1975.

———. *The Origins of the New South: 1877–1913*. Baton Rouge: Louisiana State University Press, 1951.

Wright, Richard A., and J. Mitchell Miller. "The Most-Cited Scholars and Works in Police Studies." *Policing* 21 (1998): 240–54.

Wright, Thomas. "Apparent Inability to Compete with White Officers." *Forward Times*, February 28, 1970.

Young, Mel. "Welch Hopes to Resolve Police-Negro Relations." *Houston Chronicle*, March 4, 1966.

Zinn, Howard. *Disobedience and Democracy: Nine Fallacies on Law and Order*. New York: Vintage Books, 1968.

Theses, Dissertations, and Unpublished Manuscripts

Cole, Donald. "The Negro Police Officer of Texas." M.A. thesis, Sam Houston State Teachers College, 1968.

Hair, Denny. "An Outline of Police History." Unpublished paper, 1995. In possession of the author.

Hine, Darlene Clark. "The Elusive Ballot: The Black Struggle against the Texas Democratic White Primary, 1932–1945." *Southwestern Historical Quarterly* 81, no. 4 (April, 1978): 371–92.

House Bill 34, Fiftieth Legislature, Regular Session, Records of the Legislature (Box-4-19/40). Archives Division, Texas State Library, Austin.

Houston, City of. Annual Budget, 1960, 1974–75.

Houston City Council. Minutes, 1945.

Houston Police Department. Annual Reports, 1900–80. Unpublished reports prepared by the department and submitted to the mayor. Houston Police Department Museum.

Jachimczyk, Joseph A., M.D., J.D., chief medical examiner. Autopsy Report, Case #77-2272. Pathological Diagnoses on the Body of Jose Campos Torres. Harris County Medical Examiner's Office, Houston, Texas.

Kellar, William Henry. "Make Haste Slowly: A History of School Desegregation in Houston, Texas." Ph.D. dissertation, University of Houston, 1994.

"A Nation of Law? 1968–1971." *Eyes on the Prize II: America at the Crossroads,* episode 6.

"An Outline of the History of Houston Police." Houston Police Museum, Houston, Tex.

Starks, Ernest O. "The Road to Jericho: Black Workers, the Fair Employment Practices Commission and the Struggle for Racial Equality on the Upper Texas Gulf Coast, 1941–1947." Ph.D. dissertation, University of Houston, 1995.

Shabazz, Amilcar. "The Desegregation of Lamar State College of Technology: An Analysis of Race and Education in South Texas." M.A. thesis, Lamar University, 1990.

———. "The Opening of the Southern Mind: The Desegregation of Higher Education in Texas, 1865–1965." Ph.D. dissertation, University of Houston, 1996.

SoRelle, James. "The Darker Side of Heaven: The Black Community in Houston, Texas." Ph.D. dissertation, Kent State University, 1976.

"34 Days: A Police Officer: TSU Riot Houston, Texas, May 16 and 17, 1967." Houston, Tex.: Planning and Research Division of the Houston Police Department, 1967.

Thomason, J. C., and M. C. Escobar. Coroner's Investigator's Report, Case #77-2272, Body of Jose Campos Torres. May 8, 1977. Harris County Medical Examiner's Office, Houston Texas.

Tucker, H. G. Coroner's Investigator's Report, #77-2272, "Jose Campos Torres," May 8, 1977.

Wilson, Steve. "Texas Is Our Mississippi." Unpublished.

Interviews by Author

Aaron, Donald, March 20, 1999, Houston, Tex.
Ashford, Malcolm 'Chili Mac,' February 12, 1998, Fort Worth, Tex.
Black, Frederick, September 12, 1997, Houston, Tex.
Blair, Albert, June 11, 1995, Houston, Tex.
Botson, Michael, November 12, 1997, Houston, Tex.
Bradford, C. O., June 12, 1997, Houston, Tex.
Brown, Oliver, September 22, 1997, Houston, Tex.
Cook, Vermel, June 30, 1997, Houston, Tex.
Dotson, Jimmie, June 10, 1995, Houston, Tex.
FBI agent, anonymous, May 10,1998.
Graham, Bert, telephone interview, April 24, 2002.
Hair, Denny, June 18, 1998, Houston, Tex.
Hofheinz, Fred, telephone interview, March 2, 1999, Houston, Tex.
Hunt, Vernon, June 28, 1994, Houston, Tex.
Jefferson, Donald, November 21, 1993, Deer Park, Tex.
Jones, Barbara A. P., December 21, 1992, Houston, Tex.
Jones, Mack H., December 21, 1992 and March 21, 1999, Houston, Tex.

Lawson, the Rev. Bill, October 12, 1993, Houston, Tex.
Marchiafava, Louis, January 17 and 21, 1999, Houston, Tex.
McElroy, George, February 12, 1993, Houston, Tex.
McGowen Sr., the Rev. Ernest, August 8, 1998, Houston, Tex.
Nuchia, Sam, February 22, 1995, Houston, Tex.
Stringfellow, E. J., January 27, 1998, Houston, Tex.
Strong, George, March 26, 1999, Houston, Tex.
Walker, Mae, interview, February 21, 1997, Houston, Tex.
Westbury, John, August 30, 1992, Houston, Tex.
Woodward, Margaret, February 22, 1993, Houston, Tex.

Index

ISBN 1-58544-437-5

54400

9 781585 444373